STUDIES IN ISLAMIC SCIENCE AND POLITY

Also by Masudul Alam Choudhury

ALTERNATIVE PERSPECTIVES IN THIRD-WORLD
DEVELOPMENT (*editor with U. A. Malik and M. A. Adnan*)

THE EPISTEMOLOGICAL FOUNDATIONS OF ISLAMIC
ECONOMIC, SOCIAL AND SCIENTIFIC ORDER (6 volumes)

Studies in Islamic Science and Polity

Masudul Alam Choudhury
Professor of Economics
University College of Cape Breton
Sydney
Nova Scotia, Canada

Foreword by M. Umer Chapra
Senior Economic Adviser
Saudi Arabian Monetary Agency
Riyadh, Saudi Arabia

First published in Great Britain 1998 by
MACMILLAN PRESS LTD
Houndmills, Basingstoke, Hampshire RG21 6XS and London
Companies and representatives throughout the world

A catalogue record for this book is available from the British Library.

ISBN 0-333-69773-1

First published in the United States of America 1998 by
ST. MARTIN'S PRESS, INC.,
Scholarly and Reference Division,
175 Fifth Avenue, New York, N.Y. 10010

ISBN 0-312-17740-2

Library of Congress Cataloging-in-Publication Data
Choudhury, Masudul Alam, 1948–
Studies in Islamic science and polity / Masudul Alam Choudhury.
p.   cm.
Includes bibliographical references and index.
ISBN 0-312-17740-2 (cloth)
1. Economics—Islamic countries.   2. Islam—Economic aspects.
I. Title.
HB126.4.C493 1998
330'.0917'671—dc21   97–22307
                                                        CIP

This book is printed on paper suitable for recycling and made from fully managed and sustained forest sources.

10   9   8   7   6   5   4   3   - 2   1
07   06   05   04   03   02   01   00   99   98

Printed and bound in Great Britain by
Antony Rowe Ltd, Chippenham, Wiltshire

This book is dedicated to all those who have surrendered their lives in the cause of Islam

And say not of those
Who are slain in the way
Of Allah: 'They are dead.'
Nay, they are living,
Though ye perceive (it) not.

(*Al-Qur'an*, Chapter II, Verse 154)

Contents

List of Figures and Tables

Figures

Tables

Glossary of Arabic Terms

A glossary of principal Arabic terms used in this book is provided below. Others are defined at their appropriate places in the text.

A'dl	justice
Ahkam	rules derived from the sources of *Qur'an* and *Sunnah* (see below)
Akhira	Hereafter, treated in this book as the Event of manifestation of the full Stock of Divine Knowledge
Al-Hisbah (fil Islam)	social regulation of market functions in Islamic law
Bait-al-Mal	Islamic public treasury
Ba'y Muajjal	leasing according to Islamic law
Ehsan	kindness
Fard Ayn	obligatory knowledge acquired through learning and education
Fard Kifaya	recommended knowledge acquired through learning and education
Fuqaha	the interpreters of *Ahkam* derived from Islamic law
Hablum Minallah	inner relations with God
Hablum Minannas	external relations with the world through inner relations with God
Haqq	entitlement
Huquq-al-Allah	duties of God
Huquq-al-Ibadah	duties to the world through one's belief in God
Ijara	rental
Ijma	social consensus
Ijtihad	discourse on Islamic issues for developing *Ahkam* (see above) for reaching consensus
Israf	wasteful consumption, production, resources – waste of all types
Istihsan	preferences
Khalq	natural order, creation
Muamalat	socio-economic order

Mudarabah	profit-sharing under Islamic economic co-operation
Murabaha	mark-up pricing
Musharakah	equity participation under Islamic economic cooperation
Mujtahid	the most learned in Islamic law
Qard-e-hasanah	interest-free loan
Qur'an	the principal Islamic text revealed to the Prophet Muhammad
Qiyas	Islamic analogy for developing social consensus by the most learned in Islamic jurisprudence
Riba	excess over due worth of a thing, usually used for financial interest
Sharees	experts in *Shari'ah* (Islamic law)
Shari'ah	Islamic Law, literaly meaning the way
Shura (hence *Shuratic*)	the Islamic consultative institution but extended to the meaning of pervasive and embryonic interactions that occur among agents, agencies and scientific relations at every stage and system of creation
Sidrathul Muntaha	Prophet Muhammad's mystic flight to the realm of Complete Knowledge
Sunnah (hence *Sunnatic*)	Traditions and guidance of the Prophet Muhammad
Tawhid (hence *Tawhidi*)	Oneness of God as the Absolute in Knowledge, Creator and Cherisher of the worlds
Usul	epistemology, foundation
Waqf	endowment
Zakah	wealth tax (2.5 per cent) in Islam with a specified structure of collectibles and disbursement as explained in the *Qur'an*

Foreword: Why Islamic Political Economy?

Since the independence of Muslim countries from Western domination, there has been increasing public demand for the economies of these countries to be brought into line with the Islamic vision of a just society. This has brought Islamic economics into the limelight after a hiatus of several hundred years. There has been a phenomenal growth in the literature on the subject and a number of universities, including some in the West, have started to teach the subject. In addition several research institutions have been established. Nevertheless a great deal more needs to be done. Professor Choudhury, who has made several contributions in the past, has added another plume to his hat with *Studies in Islamic Science and Polity*. This new book is aimed at bringing about 'a direction of conceptualisation of Islamic socio-economic thinking that has been derived from the Qur'anic *ahkam*' (rules of behaviour).

The purpose of this foreword is not to review this book's merits and pitfalls. It is rather to provide a simple introduction to Islamic political economy to enable reader to obtain a clearer grasp of the subject. This is perhaps necessary because the book is mathematically oriented and difficult to understand, in spite of the author's attempt in the text, as well as in several summaries, to make the reader's task somewhat less difficult.

Since the subject matter of economics is the allocation and distribution of scarce resources that have alternative uses, the question that may crop up in the reader's mind is: what is the need for Islamic economics when well-developed conventional economics is available to perform this task?[1] It may be difficult to answer this question satisfactorily without first answering the five epistemological questions that Choudhury has pertinently raised.

The first of these is about the purpose of knowledge. This question is particularly important for Muslims because time and all the other resources at the disposal of human beings are considered a trust from God, and Muslims are accountable to Him to use them in the most useful manner. It is perhaps because of this that one of the frequent prayers of the Prophet (may the peace and blessings of God be on him) was: 'Oh God! I seek Your refuge from knowledge that is of no use.'[2] The question, however, is: what is meant by 'usefulness' in the case of a social science such as economics? Should usefulness be measured primarily in terms of the generally recognised goals of analysis and prediction, or should there also be some other criterion? Within the framework of Islamic values, usefulness may have to be measured in terms of the contribution made to human well-being (*falah*), which is the ultimate goal of all Islamic teachings. Even analysis and prediction may have to be viewed with well-being as the point of reference.

This may not take us very far because we are immediately faced with the question of what constitutes human well-being and how it can be realised. The answer that Islam provides, like most other religions, is that well-being does not lie merely in maximising material possessions and satisfying wants. There must also be peace of mind (*al-nafs al-mutma'innah* – tranquil soul – in the words of the *Qur'an*), which may not necessarily be a function merely of the individual's material possessions and want satisfaction. While peace of mind requires the satisfaction of all the basic physiological needs of the human body and the provision of necessary comforts, it also requires inner peace and absence of tension. Tensions, however, tend to arise when there is socio-economic injustice – when resources become concentrated in a few hands, people do not fulfil their obligations towards others, the basic needs of all individuals in society are not fulfilled and there is misery alongside affluence. The *Qur'an* therefore states categorically that 'those who believe and do not mix their faith with injustice, for them there is peace, for they are the ones who are on the right path' (*Qur'an*, 6: 82).

It is the just use of resources and the caring and brotherly attitude of human beings towards each other in conformity with moral values that helps minimise tensions in human society. In the absence of justice, brotherhood and moral strength, material possessions become the sole end of life. 'Satisfaction' is not then just a function of what one has, but also of what others have. Conspicuous consumption becomes the highest measure of human achievement. The self-display of pace setters, along with unjust income distribution, keeps a person perpetually griping and unhappy, and constantly running hard to acquire material possessions. Very little time or energy is left for spiritual pursuits, for the upbringing of children, and for social solidarity (*'aṣabiyyah*, in the terminology of Ibn Khaldun). Children suffer, social solidarity weakens, tensions rise and society degenerates. There is an increased manifestation of all the symptoms of anomie, such as frustration, crime, alcoholism, divorce, alienation between parents and children, mental illness and suicide.

Choudhury is thus right to argue that dualism (separation of the material and the spiritual) does not lead to the kind of well-being that Islam stands for. It is necessary to integrate the spiritual and the material in such a way that they serve as a source of mutual strength and together build a solid foundation for true human well-being.

This brings into focus the second epistemological question raised by Choudhury – about the source of knowledge. One of the most crucial aspects of knowledge are the values, or rules of behaviour, that enable individuals to fulfil their social obligations, to help bring about harmony between individual preferences and social priorities in resource use, and thereby lead to a just socio-economic order. However, while an increasing number of people accept the role of values in the creation of a just order, some tend to argue in favour of human beings formulating their own values. This leads us to two interrelated issues. The first is related to the place of reason and revelation in human affairs – can reliance on reason alone enable human beings to formulate values that will be accepted by all members of society as absolute and beyond dispute? The second issue is about motivation – can the single-minded pursuit of this-worldly self-interest motivate human beings to serve the social interest even when this tends to contradict their self-interest?

Reason has its limitations and may not by itself be able to lead to values that are beyond dispute. Revelation can play an indispensable role here. The Supreme Being who created human beings is alone capable of understanding their nature, their needs, their strengths and their limitations, and of serving as the sole guide and the only source of all values. One could present a number of logical arguments to support this contention, but two are of particular significance here. Firstly, rules of behaviour prepared by human beings may tend to be influenced by the personal judgement of those who formulate them. It may not be possible for them to remain impartial, particularly if they are committed to serving their own self-interest. If wealth and power are not distributed equitably, it may be possible for the rich and the powerful to tilt these rules in favour of their own vested interests. Even the slightest doubt about impartiality may negate the chances of consensus. Secondly, human beings may not necessarily have the information necessary to assess the effect of their own actions on others, especially those more remotely affected by them. Therefore they may need an impartial, well-meaning and knowledgeable outsider who knows human beings very well and has all the information needed to visualise such effects. Who could that outsider be other than the Creator of human beings?

The question of motivation still remains. The serving of self-interest undoubtedly plays a strong motivating role in human development, and any system that does not allow individuals to serve their self-interest may not work. Moral values do not, however, prevent a person from serving his or her self-interest. Rather they give self-interest a longer-term perspective by stretching it beyond the span of this world to the hereafter. While the pursuit of this-worldly self-interest by individuals does serve the social interest, as Adam Smith argued, it tends to do so primarily where self-interest and social interest are in harmony. However if there is a conflict, it may be necessary to have some other motivation, if controls and coercion, which are not effective anyway, are to be ruled out. The inner goodness of human nature, which is one of the teaching of the *Qur'an* about human nature, is undoubtedly one of the factors that induces individuals to serve the social interest. However, the concept of individuals' accountability before God in the hereafter is also necessary to provide an added boost. While individuals' self-interest may be served in this world by being selfish in the use of resources, their interest in the hereafter cannot be served except by fulfilling their social obligations. It is this longer-term perspective of self-interest, along with individuals' inner goodness and accountability before the Supreme Being, that may motivate them to restrict their claims on resources to within the limits of general well-being. The effective operation of moral values may thus be able to complement the price mechanisms in promoting greater efficiency and equity, and thereby reducing the need for excessive government intervention in the economy to promote general well-being.

Toynbee and Durant concluded after their extensive study of history that moral uplift and social solidarity may not be possible without the moral sanction that religions provide. Toynbee asserts that 'religions tend to quicken rather than destroy the sense of social obligation in their votaries', and that 'the brotherhood of Man presupposes the fatherhood of God – a truth which involves the converse proposition that, if the divine father of the human family is left out of the reckoning, there is no possibility of forging any alternative bond of purely human texture, which will avail itself to hold mankind together.'[3] Will and Ariel Durant also observed that 'there is no significant example in history, before out time, of a society successfully maintaining moral life without the aid of religion.'[4]

This analysis implies that market forces, relying primarily on the serving of self-interest, may be able to bring about efficiency in the allocation of scarce resources. They may not, however, be able to ensure equitable distribution and a just social order unless moral values and a proper motivating mechanism for serving the social interest are injected into the market system. Conventional economics, however, insists on value neutrality and argues that self-interest and market forces can by themselves bring about a just economic order. So far they have been unable to do so in spite of the welfare role played by the state. Now that the welfare state is facing a crisis everywhere because of the macroeconomic imbalances it has led to, should the world abandon the dream of building a just society? Not necessarily. What the welfare state did was to assign a greater role to the government, leaving everything else unchanged. This led to increased spending and budgetary and balance of payments deficits, which could not be sustained for long. The welfare state therefore had to be rolled back.

What is needed is the injection of a moral dimension into the political, social and economic spheres of human life to minimise inequities and create a just and caring society. The market by itself is not able to ensure justice, and shifting the entire responsibility for the well-being of the poor on to the government leads to the breakdown of fiscal policy. It is important to reform human beings as well as the families, societies and polities in which they live, so that they may all contribute to human well-being. This may necessitate taking into account specific political, social and historical factors, instead of just economic factors, in the allocation and distribution of resources. It is perhaps because of this that Choudhury prefers to use the term 'Islamic political economy' rather than 'Islamic economics', and feels that efficiency and equity may not be possible if Islamic political economy is pursued within the methodologies and axiomatic bounds of mainstream economics. A number of other writers are attempting to contribute to the development of such a discipline.[5] If they succeed it may help create a new world order where the well-being of everyone is made possible without undoing the market system or assigning an excessive role to the state.

M. Umer Chapra
Senior Economic Adviser
Saudi Arabian Monetary Agency
Riyadh, Saudi Arabia

Preface

The Muslim world in general and truly Islamic movements throughout the globe in particular, have been under attack from the West and its protagonists in the Muslim world. Armed conflict, intellectual and political suppression, have left the mark of bondage on these peoples. Yet like the Phoenix they have risen up from the ashes of their temporary setbacks.

There are those who have yielded to *Taqlid* or blind following of the West by imitating the cultural pluralism of the latter and using it for some kind of Islamic meaning. This intellectual oddity marks a repetition of the age of the rationalists that started about a century after the death of the Prophet Muhammad. It was an age of temporary darkness regarding the true understanding of the Islamic world view of unity in the life and thought of the *Ummah*, the conscious world nation of Islam. It saw the rise of Hellenic cultural integration in the body framework of Muslim thought. Rationalist philosophers such as Ibn Sina, Ibn Rushd, Al-Farabi, the Ikhwan as-Safa, to an extent Ibn Khaldun and others, excelled in rationalist inquiry, borrowing from Greek traditions and adapting *Qur'anic* knowledge to these rationalist roots. The onslaught of *Taqlid* was so widespread that Imam Ghazzali opposed the speculative pursuits of Muslim mathematicians of the time, who started to use mathematics as a tool for abstruse conceptualisations of God and creation. Thus the true Islamic foundations of knowledge in all spheres of thought cannot be rooted in the rationalist legacy.

Today we are witnessing a new and even more harmful *Taqlid* by many of the Muslim intelligentsia. It is a more dangerous development than the early one, because the gap between the West and Islam has widened since the Muslim countries became subject to Western economic bondage. However, true devotees of the *Qur'an* and authentic *Sunnah* are endeavouring, against many odds, to promote the Islamic world view.

The manifestation of this world view is seen through the legacy of universalisation that was presented to humanity through the Prophet Muhammad's mystic flight into the realm of perfect knowledge, called the *Sidratul Muntaha*. Its essence, not sheer form, was embodied in the Madinah Charter. This epistemology has always been at the root of the Islamic world view, contrary to all other cultural paradigms, except where some similarity arises because the divine message pervades across reality and is universal in all.

This is the goal to which the truly devoted exponents of the *Qur'an* and *Sunnah* must today raise the banner for establishing that world view, which was blessed upon the Prophet Muhammad. Through his example, and subsequently, through *Shari'ah* (Islamic Law), has been established the permanent mark of mercy and truth. It is a realisation of truth in all spheres of life and thought, with the *Shari'ah* in its dynamic development through *Ahkams* (rules of life and thought), grounding the natural and social sciences, politics and institutions, money, trade, development and international affairs, and so on.

In a small way this book aims to nourish that rising Islamic spirit, free of *Taqlid* and directed at understanding and applying the *Qur'anic* and *Sunnatic* roots of the Islamic world view to life and thought. The discursive spirit manifested through the *Shuratic* process as an embryonic and pervasive process of investigation in all systems of life and thought by means of the divine law, invokes a progressive understanding of the *Qur'an* and *Sunnah*. This is also the process of *Ahkam* formation. It opens all categories of knowledge seeking – except the axiomatic premises of the *Qur'an* and *Sunnah* – to critical investigation, acceptance, rejection or revision. The process of change in Islamic history is thus to be studied by critical investigation in this light, subject to the premises of the *Qur'anic Ahkam*. Such rules (*Ahkam*) can only be defended by the authentic *Sunnah* (Prophetic traditions) while affirming the permanence of *Shari'ah* in all disciplines of thought.

The international Islamic movement, as long as it upholds this true banner of the *Qur'anic* world view supported by the authentic *Sunnah*, is the greatest mercy and light in this confused age of modernist paradigms. These movements are thus to fortify the arguments in terms of the *Qur'anic* intellectual, scientific, economic, socio-political and organisational capabilities toward realising the true spirit of *Ummah*. Development cooperation, markets, politics and institutions, international relations and globalisation of the *Ummah* must be taken up in this *Qur'anic* perspective. This is the only way towards a true Islamic identity; for Muslims to live self-reliantly; and for humanity to uphold truth in the way the Prophet has taught us. There is no other way!

MASUDUL ALAM CHOUDHURY

Acknowledgements

My deepest thanks go to the Faculty of Economics of the National University of Malaysia. In 1994, during my time there as Visiting Professor, the lectures that form the basis of this book were presented to the faculty.

I also wish to thank the Statistical, Economic and Social Research and Training Centre for Islamic Countries, Ankara, Turkey, for inviting me to participate in research assignments and providing me with the opportunity to collect information for parts of my lecture project.

I am indebted to the University College of Cape Breton, which provided financial backing when I was researching and writing the lectures.

Finally, my list of gratitude would not be complete without sincere thanks to Mr Keith Povey, editorial consultant to Macmillan. His expert editing of this and all my earlier books published jointly by Macmillan Press Ltd and St Martin's Press, has greatly improved their quality.

MASUDUL ALAM CHOUDHURY

Introduction

This book is based on a series of lectures given at the Faculty of Economics of the National University of Malaysia during April–August 1994. Theoretical and some empirical details are provided of the knowledge-based world view of the Islamic socio-scientific order. The model is then shown to apply to problems of political economy, social choice, development, scientific epistemology and financial and developmental institutions in the context of grassroots dynamics. The knowledge-based world view is developed here as a uniquely universal interactive–integrative system guided by the premise of unification epistemology founded on *Tawhidi* (Unity of God) epistemology. This essence of reality is shown to be pervasive in all socio-scientific systems where unification rather then differentiation, cardinal laws rather then perceptions of reason, and emanation and convergence to such laws rather than individuation and speculative randomness, characterise the order of reality. Thus a history of political economy and scientific thinking as it has evolved in the West, and to a degree in the Muslim world in imitation of Western or Greek thought, is critically examined in the light of the knowledge-based unifying world view. Some of the works of early Islamic thinkers that premise the philosophy of science in the unification epistemology of *Tawhid*, are also contrasted with the Western thought and cultural process of methodological individualism and perceptual, speculative differentiation.

In Chapter 1, fundamental questions of knowledge-based model building are addressed. These are explained in terms of the substantive nature of the precept of world view against the speculative and perceptual concepts of the various reason–materialism based models of occidental culture. The world-view model is thus formalised.

In Chapter 2 the same knowledge-based world view is shown to contrast deeply with some of the mainstream thoughts in occidental political economy. The chapter brings out the fact that epistemological roots are not logically possible in occidental and oriental thought. Thus such pursuits of the human mind become sheer cultural and random persuasions reflecting an egocentricity that has influenced the entire development of Western institutions and approaches to social change.

In Chapter 3 the knowledge-based model is applied in its interactive framework to the important analytical area of social choice formation. The development of a social welfare function and the foundation of welfare economics in the light of the knowledge-based world view is shown to be distinct from and polar to the neoclassical theory of social choice and social welfare function.

In Chapter 4 the knowledge-based model is given a logical foundation in the philosophy of science from the Islamic perspective. Thus the epistemic–ontic circular causation and continuity model of unified reality (another term for the interactive–integrative model) is carried into the realm of natural sciences. The end result is to bring out the uniformity, uniqueness and universality of the world view precept in all systems, with due cognisance being given to specific problems.

In Chapter 5 the model, now developed as the *Shuratic* process (yet another term for the epistemic–ontic or interactive–integrative model of unification, renewal and continuity), is applied to the structure of Islamic political economy. Islamic economics as a terminology in the literature is critically questioned in favour of Islamic political economy, in the light of the embryonic and pervasive nature of the Islamic consultative and decision-making process termed here the *Shuratic* process. A comparative study of the history of economic thought and recent studies of Islamic economics is undertaken.

Chapter 6 substantiates what has been invoked so far in terms of the inapplicability of neoclassicism to Islamic socio-scientific behaviour. The same argument has been shown to negate much of classical and all of neoclassical perceptions in economic theory and institutionalism. A methodological orientation is maintained. The folly of market capitalism and privatisation in the framework of the Bretton Woods prescriptions of change is pointed out. The case of the Central Asian Republics is used to bring out this point.

Chapter 7 applies the knowledge-based world view to grassroots development. The case of Malaysia is taken up in the light of its concerted effort to alleviate poverty and bring about equity and efficiency in the socio-economic transformation process. Various institutional uses of development financing as prescribed by Islamic political economy, are incorporated into the knowledge-based world-view model.

Chapter 8 once again uses this model, this time to bring out the conceptual meaning of money as a financial aggregate in Islamic political economy. This concept is contrasted with the one given to money in received economic theory. It is shown that the definitions and treatment of money in received economic theory cannot free the allocation of resources from interest based transactions. In contrast, the concept of endogenous money and its institutional meaning are presented in analytical ways for an Islamic thinking.

THE GENERAL AIM

This work is aimed at bringing about a new direction of conceptualisation in Islamic socio-scientific thinking. Such re-thinking is derived from the *Qur'anic Ahkams* (rules of thought and life arising from an analytical study of the *Qur'an*). The presence of *Sunnah* in these derivation of *Qur'anic Ahkams*, also to be found in the formalisation of the *Shuratic* process, as substantively developed in this book, is taken up along with the focus on the *Qur'an* and *Sunnah*. Thus the normative premise of the *Qur'an* is fused with the positive premise of *Sunnah* in the methodology of deriving *Ahkam* in what is seen here as the essential independence of the Islamic philosophy of science. It is amply shown with the help of analytical and critical analysis that the knowledge-based world-view model developed here points to a serious examination of Islamic socio-scientific investigation in the postmodernist age, an age that needs newer roots of knowledge than occidentalism and orientalism have been able to provide.

This writing merely touches upon the vast knowledge dimension opened up by the *Qur'anic Ahqams* in socio-scientific philosophy. (For further developments in this area the reader may refer to the author's six volumes entitled *The Epistemological Foundations of Islamic Economic, Social and Scientific Order*.) Nonetheless a fairly broad discussion of the uniquely universal knowledge-based world view has been undertaken. This book is somewhat mathematical and analytical, although non-mathematical readers should be able to follow the text. This approach was adopted not merely because of the methodological preferences of the author, but also for invoking analytical discourse on this new dimension of thought in ways that remain distinct from Western approaches to epistemology, ontology and their whole gamut of social, economic and scientific consequences. Such an approach was also desired in order to keep the continuity of the subject matter of knowledge-based world view intact across various topics taken up here.

This book is aimed at graduate students, teachers and researchers in economics, political economy, philosophy of science and comparative development studies. It offers grounds for critical thinking in the comparative Islamic field of systems analysis. To the best of my knowledge, the concept of a knowledge-based world view and its formalisation have not been addressed by contemporary Islamic economic, social and scientific research or Western academics. However there has been some groping for epistemological roots by the latter in recent times.

1 Dualism, Perception and World View

Our objectives in this chapter are first, to point out that dualism, perception and world view have substantive meanings of their own. These in turn are instrumental in the development of theory constructs and institutional in frameworks. We will show that dualism and perception are the basis of occidentalism and are opposed to the precept of world view. Second, the world view construct is substantively defined by what will be termed unification epistemology. This premise will be shown to have a critical place in the understanding, development and perpetuation of the Islamic world view. Thus, once formalised and institutionalised in such an order, unification epistemology plays the key role in the realisation of the world view. The all-pervasive institution of *Shura*, the Islamic consultative agency, is then shown to assume meaning and to govern a uniquely universal process in the domain of knowledge. This process will be described here as the *Shuratic* process.

DUALISM

Let us start with the concept of dualism. The separation of the otherwise unified domain of knowledge between matter and spirit, essence and material cognition, soul and body, God and world occurred during the Age of Enlightenment as a scientific revolt against the waning Catholic Church, as the metaphysics of the latter was seen to oppose the free exercise of reason within the rationality of the 'divine domain'. The separation of matter as a cognitive substance – the *res cogitans* of Descartes – from the spiritual essence was the product of the separation of religion from science, reducing all realism to materialism. That is, materialism became a functional relationship of cognition and analysis to inference, description and realism.[1] Thus the consequence of dualism was a materialistic configuration of the idealistic state of reason that unified all relations in Greek philosophy. Reason in its abstract form, imparting content to rational analysis and continuity in the real world, became the weapon of final resort for dualism. For without it

1

the spiritual and material could not be divided into independent entities, and non-interactivity between them could not be generated.

Formal Idea of Dualism

Dualism is thus the product of separating reason based on material realism and the spiritual essence based on divinity. Rationalism is the philosophy emanating from the primordial premise of reason alone. Thereby, methodology and analysis are carried out on the basis of reason as the primal and most reduced root of knowledge.

The interconnection between reason, materialism and reality, generating dualism, is illustrated in Figure 1.1. In this figure reason (R) is surrounded by an open field of random phenomena (F) of the mind caused by materialistic preferences and inferences (M). M is in turn generated by functional relations and signals received from actions between R and F. Likewise R and F are generated by functional relations existing between the other two. Finally, in the functional relations between R, F and M there are recursive interrelationships among all these categories over different contingencies of nature. The product of this is a materialistic relation of reality, R^*.

The feedback that occurs between R, F, M and R^* in continuity, now describe reality in the structure of intensifying relationships so established. Consequently as led by R among R, F, M and R^*, scientific reality is established by intensification and universalisation of the primacy and independence of R from spiritual phenomena, S.

The intensification and universalisation process of $(R, F, M)[R^*]_i$ is shown by the loop, $a_1, a_2, \ldots a_6$ etc., as $i = 1, 2, \ldots$ Throughout this work variables or vectors such as $(R, F, M)[R]^*$ mean that all the elements are influenced by $[R^*]$. The same notation is used to explain functions such as $f(X)(R^*)$. Here i is a continuum index. As this process proceeds, dualism is shown by the intensity of the various elements, for example, R, as i assumes higher values. Note that in Figure 1.1 the region between R and F must expand continuously through the progress of $A = (a_1, a_2, \ldots, a_6)$. This is due to the intrinsically unbounded nature of the rationalistic space in the occidental order.

In the lower part of Figure 1.1 the reason domain is enclosed by the outer cover of the spiritual field, S'. Consequently, although F, M and R^* all exist in this case too, as defined above, the difference now is due to the interdependence between S and R within S' and F. The evolving outer covers of such spirit–reason interdependence or complementarity negates the fundamental premise of universal independence between the two as dualistic. It is important to note that the principle of interdependence between cause and effect in the R and S' domains requires the S' field to encompass the F field, as shown. Thus S' envelopes R and F, while evolution from S to R proceeds. However the domain of uncertainty diminishes, as the interaction between S and R shrinks the region of randomness denoted by the area between R and F. All interrelationships in this latter case are thus perpetuated and continuity is established, generating reality by means of universal complementarity. This principle negates matter–spirit independence, which is dualism.

The evolution of spirit–matter to higher levels of spiritual order in S' is shown by b_1, b_2, ..., b_7 and so on. The system in this spirit–matter interrelationship is given by $(S, S', R, F)(R*)_j$. Intensification of the process is shown by the progress towards S' through interactions between infinite sequences of S, S', R and F. This evolution is shown in the direction of S to R to F to S'.

The output of dualism as a way of life and thought occurs by means of $R*$. Thus if the entire system, $(R, F, M)(R*)$, is recursively reproduced, then the result is the philosophy of dualism. It is the deepening nature of the recursively enforcing relations of dualism that makes the latter so pervasive and empowering a feature of the occidentalist way of life and thought. Dualism thus becomes an endogenous process of movement in the framework of its own system that in turn governs human behaviour and its influence upon society and institutions. Continuity of the occidental order and civilisation must thus be perpetuated by the cause and effect of $R*$, generating dualism.

In summary, Figure 1.1 points out that the rationalistic domain of occidental epistemology, by leaving out the endogenous nature of moral law, replaces into a confined domain of complete knowledge. Such a process intensifies dualism in this order. On the other hand, in the interactive spirit–matter order of the knowledge-centred world view, the spirit domain opens up the possibility that the randomness of rationalism may disappear, as the spiritual domain generates reason, which in turn creates higher levels of belief (spirit), and so on by a circular causation and continuity process established between spirit and matter.

The question remains – can the spirit–matter complementarity of Figure 1.1 result into dualism through recursion? This is possible when (1) S does not transcend into the domain of R, as was the case of Catholic metaphysics during the advent of the Age of Enlightenment, and (2) when F does not functionally relate with outer covers of the type S', then reason perpetuates itself in its own independent domain.

Only when interrelationships are pervasive and ceaseless in all of the reason-induced or spirit–matter-induced domains can these systems continue.

One can define dualism as independence between the parts of Figure 1.1. This implies that the systems formulated by these two approaches must remain perpetually independent of each other. The social effect of this differentiating process is felt in the development of the institutions pertaining to this order. Consequently all material events comprising theoretical construct and institutionalism are determined by differentiated reason in the field F of such differentiated reason categories. Examples of differentiated institutional orders formed by random categories of reason are cultural pluralism as the premise of institutionalism,[2] the dialectical disequilibrium of Marxism and Hegelianism,[3] and the concept of the end of history as the ultimate triumph of reason in Western capitalism and democracy.[4]

The Concept of Dualism and Economic Theory

The materialistic concept of dualism is also found to be the basis of the methodological individualism that pervades the economic theory of markets and polity. It enunciates an exogenous, preference-driven model of rational choice, as individual agents become empowered to form utilitarian perspectives of self-interest. Markets and institutions are treated as similarly utilitarian agents, a fact well established by ideas such as the economic theory of democracy and public choice theory.[5] Neoclassicism champions this perspective of methodological individualism, and across the domain of economic theorising, this expression has found subtle expression in all economic theories. National institutions and world development organisations, under the influence and control of powerful agents, have perpetuated this expression of methodological individualism as a self-acclaimed truth arising from the material world. Capitalism thus survives in the midst of the deequalising consequences of a dualistic order based on individualism and alienation.

Likewise socialism and communism translated these economic principles into state action instead of markets. Consumer preferences in these latter systems remain methodologically neoclassical in nature. They are determined by authority and regimentation in the absence of markets.[6] Dialectical materialism and capitalism are governed by the ultimate supremacy of material ends, within which happiness is narrowly defined by the concept of material abundance and acquisition.

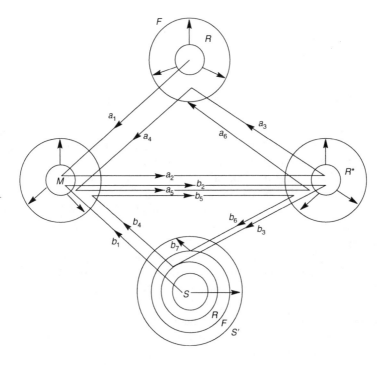

Figure 1.1   Interconnection between reason, materialism and reality, causing dualism

Markets or state institutions governed by individuated preferences thus become the domain of materialism, flourishing upon and reinforcing the relations that intensify dualism of enormous proportions.

Yet in the midst of the dualism in these systems, the intrinsically random nature of reason, making all other parts of the R^* relationship random, generates uncertainty. Uncertainty is a necessary consequence of dualism via randomness of the inherent system. With increasing uncertainty in the determination of economic results, institutional directions and formation of precise human values for unification rather than individualism, comes instability and disequilibrium. Economic models of the occidental order, together with their institutions, are thus inherently unstable and indeterminate. Such uncertainties arise not by the sheer evolutionary nature of capitalism and the dialectics of socialism/communism,[7] rather they appear as perceptions that cannot survive in the market order or under command, although these are the very institutions that neoclassicism promotes for orderly business. Economic optimality is thus assumed to support the methodological nicety involving economic rationality. The postulate of economic rationality is derived from assumptions of individualism and independence of relations.

In this neoclassical framework the most destructive consequence is thus imparted by the marginal rate of substitution between all competing economic categories, resources and goods. This is the direct result of dualism, which negates the possibility of coexistence among goods in the presence of universal substitution in the neoclassical order. What then is the effect of this marginal substitution? There is methodological error as well as moral depravity in this.

The methodological error arises from the forced nature of smooth production possibility curves and consumer indifference curves that determine allocative mechanisms with stable relative prices – such equilibrium conditions can never exist in the first place,[8] so a methodological distortion of profound magnitude is created. The absence of a smooth utility function, either in deterministic or in expected form, a consumer indifference curve and a production possibility curve makes it impossible to define the demand curve, supply curve, market equilibrium, price level and quantities of resources and goods. Hence the economic exchanges upon which neoclassical economics and its subsequent developments are premised have no meaning. If the resulting market signals on price and quantity are pursued in perfectly or imperfectly competitive situations, this generates substantial gaps between prediction and allocation. Consequently there is a perpetual conflict between the goals of economic efficiency, economic growth and stability on the one hand, and distributive justice, social welfare and quality of life on the other hand. The end result is one of utter unrealism of the concept of economic rationality, both by cause and effect, in such a manifestation of optimal conditions either in the first, second or nth best sense. After all, the latter distortions are simply the result of imperfect competition while keeping intact the marginalist principle of resource allocation.[9]

Next we turn to the problem of social deprivation in the neoclassical framework and address the social welfare and social choice functions. The neoclassical version of these functions states that an 'optimal trade-off' exists between the goals of social equity and economic efficiency. The idea of optimality is once again the assumed possibility of predictive behaviour, stability and equilibrium. All the arguments on the impossibility of such optimisation techniques hold in this case too. Furthermore a 'trade-off' in the state of social optimum is not feasible in neoclassical resource allocation.

The conflict arises between the social goals of institutions and the efficiency goals of markets. If markets of the classical and neoclassical order are disrupted by policy measures, then distortion occurs, and optimal points on the production possibility curve, utility function, consumer indifference curve and so on cannot exist. Over time, as technological induction moves the production frontier outwards, the uncertainty of the optimal points increases by the compound effects of *ex ante* investment, which remains unpredictable, and the continuing market-distorting effects of policy (institutional) measures. Thus in neither the atemporal nor the intertemporal sense can a so-called 'optimal trade-off' be realised.

On the other hand, if there are no policy (institutional) measures to affect resource allocation, then market consequentialism will wipe out all spirit of goodness and shift the price-income line or the expansion path towards economic efficiency. This defeats the meaning of the 'trade-off' because of the bias toward economic efficiency.

There is no incentive in the neoclassical resource allocation model (now taken up in the wider sense of social equity–economic efficiency allocation) to pursue distributive equity.[10] Social expenditure is a costly business and has to be financed from general tax revenues; or it can be reduced by a change in consumption, production and distribution in favour of the grassroots of society.

Increased taxes reduce real incomes and profits. These in turn adversely affect productivity and profitability. Consumption and production then contract, causing lower economic growth. The free market order will oppose social spending on such grounds. Thus, methodologically, the same kind of shift occurs in the income–price trajectory and the expansion path for socially induced resource allocation, as is the case with economic efficiency in a free market order.

A change in consumption, production and distribution can come about through an extensively interactive economy. This is the foundation of socio-economic cooperation at all levels, wherein social preferences are formed not by the aggregation of exogenous individual preferences, as in the neoclassical case, but endogenously through individual interactions within a social contract. Preference functions cannot arise from unreal ideas such as utility and social welfare functions. Consequently the neoclassical paradigm and its subsequent developments – for example, social and public choice theories, rational expectations hypothesis and new classical economics – are inadequate to treat the endogenously interactive preference-formation theory of resource allocation.[11]

Methodological individualism, independence, conflict and alienation are the natural results of the marginalist principle. This is the core of dualism in the occidental theory of political economy. Hayek stood for complete independence of markets and considered that institutions should be subservient to markets. This is his idea of 'market catallaxy', which rejects the relevance of social justice in the market order.[12] It is also the epistemological foundation of the theory forwarded by von Mises, as he held that reason alone should rule economics.[13] Marx's reductionism in political economy went as far as history could explain economic functions alone. Thus economism founded his materialistic interpretation of history.[14] Hence within the reason–materialism relation invoked earlier, Marxism too became steeped in dualism. In more recent times, Friedman on the side of monetarism, Buchanan on the side of neoclassical political behaviour, Nozick as a philosopher zealously upholding neoclassical ideas of individual freedom and entitlement, and Rawls as a philosopher signifying a second best theory of liberal institutionalism have all perpetuated the principle of neoclassical dualism.[15]

Occidental mental constructs, polity and institutionalism are thus thoroughly bathed in the system of dualism, whose instrumental features are independence, individualism and materialism. All of these are perpetuated through entrenchment of the marginalist substitution philosophy.

Formalism in the Dualistic Methodology Between Matter and Spiritual

To end this section we will show now how the abovementioned features of a dualistic system were represented in Figure 1.1. Let $S'(S)$ denote the evolving spiritual domain and $F(R)$ the evolving reason domain. A relation f in the spiritual–reason domain is defined by $f(S'[S], F[R])(R*)_j$. Clearly

$$f(S'[S], F[R])(R*)_j = f_1(S'[S])[R*]_j \cup f_2(F[R])(R*)_j; \ j \in \mathbb{R};$$

or

$$f(S'[S], F[R])(R*) = \{g_1(S'[S]) \cap g_2(F[R])\}(R**)_j; \ j \in \mathbb{R}$$

These expressions point out that if S' and F and independent they will be in conflict with each other, so it is possible for either to be zero. This is the manifestation of the dualism discussed above. If there is interaction between S' and F, then only the latter expression is possible.

Now the relation R^{**} must be different from the dualism of R^* and g must be different from f, otherwise there can be no particular reason for choosing the spiritual–reason alternative rather than the reason–materialism one. It can be seen that if either of the gs is zero the total relation f must be zero too. Furthermore increasing the value of f would necessitate increasing the value of each of the gs. Otherwise, over repeated iterations of j, constancy or decreasing values of f will be experienced. This will revert the system to the pure dualistic type. Such was the case with Catholic metaphysics during the Age of Enlightenment; it is also the case with the currently sorry state of Muslim imitations of the occidental order masquerading as Islamicisation. It is the result of ineptly addressing social questions through neoclassical models of methodological individualism.

Hence just as g remains different from f and must therefore belong to a disjoint domain, so must R^{**} remain independent from R^*, with either of these belonging to a disjoint domain. Consequently dualism is characterised by a reason domain that is independent from a non-dualistic one. Finally, because several combinations of any two of F, R and M can determine the other, generalisation of the above case of dualism as a system of reason–materialism methodological individualism is straightforward.

PERCEPTION

Dualism is a system based on and perpetuated by pure reason–materialism relations. The material world alone or the spiritual realm alone are treated as the springs of reality. Yet as we have shown in Figure 1.1, differentiation between different levels of reason in the ongoing individuation process can cause different feelings of reality. The conditioning of the mind under such sequences of feelings and responses via iterative reason–materialism relations generates mental cognitions called perceptions. Thus scientific questions are totally explained by deductionism based on matter.

We know that, historically, Catholic scholasticism confused unity and pluralism in the attribute of divine unity. Aquinas wrote, 'I answer that, the name of trinity in God signifies the determinate number of persons. And so the plurality of persons in God requires that we should use the word trinity; because what is indeterminately signified by plurality, is signified by trinity in a determinate manner.'[16] The consequence of such confusion is that, although unification is intended, methodological plurality first differentiates the realm of divinity from that of the world by inaction, and then relegates one of the emergent systemic iterations to matter and another to spirit due to the presence of inherent plurality. Consequently real unification cannot be attained. The result of plurality and its effect on materiality as the substance of reality, is that feelings and comprehension become perceptions, distanced from essential unification.

The truth is that God cannot be sensed as form or matter. Only His divine functions as signs in the universe speak of the unification and extension of His laws. Cognition as perception is then simply the product of interactions between entities in accordance with the divine laws. This is the only manifestation of God as the unifying force. Perception cannot act as a primordial premise to lead towards comprehension of truth as reality.

Perception was characterised by Bergson as the lower capacity of the mind restricted by random uncertainty and differentiated determinations of the thought process. According to Bergson, 'Pure perception, which is the lowest degree of mind – mind without memory – is really part of matter, as we understand matter.'[17] This loss of memory due to perception is yet another example of the randomness of the evolution of the reason–materialism dualistic system, which attains no convergence (that is, no unification).

According to Russell, perception arises from sensation and experience relating to matter, as they impact upon the mind to convey cognition of things sensed and experienced. Perceptions are thus local and instantaneous reflections in the mind, conveyed by cognitive sensations such as colour, sound, smell, touch and so on. Yet when localised phenomena extend to become global ones, they do not retain their original percepts. This is the case with the disparate nature of systems such as microeconomics and macroeconomics; quantum physics and relativity physics; and the utilitarian aggregation of individual preferences and social interactions.

Perception in Relation to Dualism and Plurality

In the terminology of Figure 1.1, the efficacy of local versus global systems generated by $F(R)$ and $S'(S)$, respectively, are determined by extension of the domain of explanation and the intensity of the field of reality, that is, R^{**} versus R^*. To understand this concept we proceed as follows:

R^* is a function of the series of relations described by $A = (a_1,$

$a_2, \ldots$). Likewise R^{**} is described by $B = (b_1, b_2, \ldots)$. Clearly, because of the spiritual–reason extension of $f(S'[S], F[R])$, B is more intense than A. This is also shown by the path of the B relations across the domain of $F(R)$ and $S'(S)$ in Figure 1.1. Thus R^{**} is more intense than R^*. This implies the deeper understanding of reality in R^{**} over R^*.

Next we need to prove that R^{**} also yields instantaneity in the global sense as opposed to R^*, which yields instantaneity in the local sense. This is clearly the case, because the globality of R^{**} is proven by its interactions across the spiritual–reason domain. This instantaneity of R^{**} makes it more powerful than R^* with respect to comprehension, and hence to the understanding of reality. This is seen from the fact that if $S'(S) \cup F(R)$ is treated as an 'open topological cover' for R^*, then it includes certain transformation of A, and hence includes the instantaneity of R^*. Thus the instantaneity of R^{**} explains globally much more than that of R^*.

To formalise further, let

$$R^* = f_1(a_1, a_2, \ldots)(F[R]),$$

and

$$R^{**} = f_2(b_1, b_2, \ldots)(S'[S] \cap F[R]).$$

Now $R^{**} \to R^*$ if and only if $S'(S) \cap F(R) = \phi$. Otherwise $R^{**} \neq \phi$. Therefore, in the knowledge plane, activation of the interactive–integrative process means that R^{**} becomes increasingly more intense than R^* as the cardinality of $(S'[S] \cap F[R])$ increases, while due to dualism and individualism in the F, R, M plane, $F(R)$ tends towards ϕ. Here $(S'[S] \cap F[R])$ increases in cardinality under the force of knowledge generation.

These are the substantive differences between perception, which is founded upon R^*, and essential reality, which is founded upon R^{**}. Perception is thus defined here as the localised reason–materialism relation responding to senses and experience. Such a relation loses its power by global extension. It is also differentiated by the perpetual presence of dualism in all such comprehension of sense and experience.

Hence, in conjunction with dualism as a system, we define perception, P, as follows. In the infinitely small domain of $R(\varepsilon)$ within the systems process in $R^*(A)$,

$$P = f(S'[S] \cup F[R])(R^*[A]) = f(S'[S]) \text{ with } f(F[R]) = \phi, \text{ or}$$
$$= f(F[R]) \text{ with } f(S'[S]) = \phi.$$

Here $A = (a_1, a_2, \ldots)$ is as defined in Figure 1.1. $R^*(A)$ is the reason function or topological function defined over A.

Each of the functions on the right-hand side are non-analytical, as they cannot be extended in the narrow domains of their 'open topological covers'. Hence they cannot be described continuously over the entire realm of $R^*(A)$. The cognitive creation $f(.)$ is only momentarily within an infinitesimally small and localised subset, $R(\varepsilon)$ of $R^*(A)$. As topological covers open up, carrying $R(\varepsilon)$ with them, the phenomenon is repeated over the entire $R^*(A)$ in differentiated forms. This conveys the individualistic nature of perception.

If dualism as the system $R^*(A)$ is to be perpetuated by the infinite number of differentiated individual perceptions defined by $R(\varepsilon_k)$, with $k\varepsilon\mathbb{R}$ according to evolving open covers of either $S'(S)$ or $F(R)$, then dualism is formed by a lateral aggregation of such perceptions; there is no interactive relationship between these perceptions:

$$D(R^*[A]) = \Sigma_k f(S'(S), F[R])(R[\varepsilon_k]) = \Sigma_k f(S'[S])(R[\varepsilon_k]),$$
$$\text{if } f(F[R]) = \phi, \text{ or}$$
$$= \Sigma_k f(F[R])(R[\varepsilon_k]),$$
$$\text{if } f(S'[S]) = \phi.$$

It is clear that $R^*(A) = \cup_k R(\varepsilon_k)$, and this holds for the case of dualism as a system defined by $R^*(A)$. The problem of dualism indeed now extends to plurality. It then encompasses perceptions pertaining to a plurality of gods, and their pantheistic forms are made to configurate in matter. Here one finds the logical problem posed by the concept of 'one–many'.[18] That is, it is impossible to unify percepts to form concept. It is impossible to unify materiality of sense and experience to explain universal unification. It is impossible to leave the matter of unification solely to the divine realm, which has no relevance to the material world through functional divine laws (as analytical and extendable functions depicted above).

THE EFFECT OF PERCEPTION AND DUALISM ON SCIENTIFIC METHODOLOGY

The above formalisation of perception takes account of both the temporary and non-substantive (in the sense of their non-extendability and non-analyticity) nature of pure metaphysical notions of reality (as in the case of Aquinas given above) and pure reason–materialism notions of reality. The postmodern experimental approach to scientific phenomena requires independence of treatment in random statistical experiments. Testing the statistical significance of 'treatments' in analysis of variance table is a purely inductive exercise arising from the assumption of statistical independence of treatments for estimating their optimal effects. Any presence of impurities in such treatments is seen to bias the coefficients of the underlying regression models. Thus the inductive method of statistical analysis is based on the precondition of independence between treatments of statistical variables. The end result of such an inductive method of statistical estimation is to generalise and provide policy statements based on perception.

On the other hand, deductionism is not the method of statistical inference, unless we introduce the idea of a probabilistic universe and the limitations of physical measurements as provided by Heisenberg's uncertainty principle, Keynes' theory of probability and Mach's notion of the impossibility of predicting events deterministically. Deductionism is thus a Kantian-type *a priorism* and is based on logical relations prior to experimentation. Here perception is due to reason alone, and materiality is subsequent to reason. Deductionism remains opposed to inductionism in the inferential models, as conditions of the former may not always be experimentally viable, although they may be logically sound in the context of reason.

This problem of irreconcilability when inference is sought can be seen, for example, in the problem of price determination. Market prices arise from the aggregation of consumer demand and producer supply prices. Whereas consumer and producer prices are determined by basic utility functions (consumer indifference curves) and production isoquants (iso-cost functions), market prices are inductive, as they are assumed to be observable. But consumer indifference curves are ordinal in nature, and not observed. Their rationalisation is based on deductive reasoning. How then is it possible to aggregate unobservable consumer demand functions and prices in order to come up with market demand and prices? Such is the problem posed by the disparity between the inductive and deductive routes of scientific explanation, as they independently represent perceptions belonging to these non-overlapping domains.

A similar contradiction between inductive reasoning in the economic measurement of wages and the deductive reasoning of marginal physical product is found in both micro- and macroeconomics. The inductive approach to studying the marginal product of labour enforces the measurement of wages in terms of this relation. On the other hand the deductive derivation of marginal product from optimality and the formulation of optimal objective criteria of production do not render the marginal product directly observable. The consequence of this is that exploitation of labour in capitalist labour markets and the non-existence of labour markets in socialist/communist economies allows wages to be determined as measures of labour value.[19]

The problem of disparateness between the inductive and deductive methodologies emerges in other probabilistic models of nature. It is for this reason that prices are different entities in the microeconomic and the macroeconomic levels of analysis. Events in the macro-universe of relativity physics are differently interpreted from events in the microcosmic universe of quantum physics. The disparateness of entities within and across disciplines has resulted in immense methodological inconsistencies in the social and natural sciences. In the social sciences there has been a dissociation of disciplines, and hence there is no recognisable cross-fertilisation. In the natural sciences the same type of disparateness has led to the failure to come up with a unified theory. Therefore the epistemological foundation of all sciences in the postmodern era remains ununified. The principal cause of this debility is the pervasiveness of perceptions in the systems governed by plurality and dualism of percepts.

DEDUCTIVE AND INDUCTIVE DISJUNCTION IN METHODOLOGY

Dissociation of the deductive from the inductive methodologies of scientific reasoning was brought out in our previous formalisation by denoting deductionism with $S'(S)$ and inductivism with $F(R)$. The relation of dualism (plurality) is denoted by $f(.)$. Either of these two planes is seen to result into independence between the two methodologies. The multitude of ununified disciplines in the sciences is the result of individuation caused by these subsystemic perceptions. They are further accentuated by disparity between the deductive and inductive approaches applied to these subsystems. The academic consequence from continuation of this process is bound to generate increasing individuation of the disciplines in the name of scientific rigour; but this will be at the expense of unification of knowledge for the purpose of discovering truth.

What is true of the conflict arising from the perceptual disparateness of inductivism and deductionism is equally true of the positive and the normative, and of positive law and natural law. The transition from the Age of Moral Philosophy to the Age of Enlightenment marked a vehement conflict between these two percepts of an otherwise unified reality.[20] This conflict has persisted in economic science to the present day. Friedman and Robbins promoted the positive goal as predictive accuracy for economics. Walras, von Mises and lately Boulding pursued the normative perspective of economic epistemology.[21] These perceptual differences over the goals of economics have led to economic science being unable accurately to predict the future of common social welfare, while accepting simply material goals. What has resulted is neither precision in prediction, equilibrium and optimality concepts, nor uniformity in economic reasoning on epistemological grounds to establish what Walras, Keynes and Boulding wanted to see as a moral social science.[22]

PERCEPTION, DUALISM AND POSTMODERNISM

The perpetuation and spread of the academic demise arising from the failure of the social and natural sciences to unite their knowledge due to their different perceptions is seen as inevitable in postmodernism. Modernism is the process of reducing all social and scientific phenomena to the philosophy of materiality. Out of this are assumed to emerge prescriptions that define the material pursuits of life. Thus a modernising society is argued to pass through well-defined stages of change before it comes to a state of liberal democracy, which itself is seen as evolutionary in its enhancement of material progress.[23] This is a Western view of modernism. Its dissociative and individuated process establishes methods for the sake of a system based on reason and materialism (that is, plurality of perceptions). In this framework, Schumpeterian-type technological evolution, Fukuyama's institutional development and Drucker's knowledge generation are all cause and effect of the postmodern society.[24] Thus postmodernism will witness extreme intellectual individuation among the disciplines. Every set of perceptions defining relationship with plurality (dualism) will be instrumental in this. Indeed such dissociation and the increasing departure from unified knowledge was lamented by Husserl in his *Crisis of European Sciences*.[25]

The destructive consequences of postmodernism in the intellectual field can be explained by our earlier formalisation. We refer to the process denoted by $R^*(A) = \cup_k R(\epsilon_k)$. This notation means that $A = (a_1, a_2, \ldots)$

is reduced in the limiting value to the sequence (ε_k). This limiting case of (ε_k) denotes the points of individualism in the occidental order. Postmodernism is characterised by the refinement and individuation of (ϵ_k), with each ϵ_k, $k \in \mathbb{N}$ denoting the intensification of the individuation process. This would yield, $\lim(k \to \infty)(\cap \varepsilon_k) = \phi$, for the sequence of increasingly individuating reason-set denoted by the transformation of A into (ε_k), under the force of individualism governed by their respective random fields. Consequently $\lim(k \to \infty)(\epsilon_k) = \epsilon_\infty$ and $\lim (k \to \infty)(R^*[A] = \cup_k R[\epsilon_k]) = R(\epsilon_\infty)$, which denote the reason field governed by the limiting case of (ε_k). This denotes the limiting case of perfect individualism, wherein the entire reason-set of the occidentalist order causes this order to degenerate into the corresponding point-sets. This signals complete atomism of the methodological process, inter- and intra-discipline, as the sure product of perception configuring plurality (dualism) over the evolutionary stages of the postmodernist movement signified by (ϵ_k), $k \in \mathbb{N}$. The memory of the system and its localised instantaneity are thus infinitely marginalised by the process of systemic atomism.

Does the above formalisation mean that the systems coalesce into topologically dense forms of their representation? No, because the limiting process is worked out within a given subsystem. Just as a subsystem has its own atomistic limiting point, so also do each of the infinite number of subsystems arising from the parent systems. The intellection process thus becomes extensively differentiated. Even as these atomistic systems intensify within their parent systems, so also differentiated perceptions abound increasingly with plurality. This point is easy to see in the formalisation: limiting values, such as ϵ_∞, together with the non-extendability of $R(\epsilon_\infty)$ in its limiting domain, means that the instantaneous process in R now coincides with ϵ_∞: that is, in the atomistic limiting sense of the process $R(\epsilon_\infty) = \epsilon_\infty$. Hence a perception is mapped into 'itself' by the 'open topological cover' R of localised relations. This is the same as saying that the relations attain their equilibrium in terms of perception.[26]

PERCEPTION IN ECONOMETRIC AND POLITICAL ECONOMY METHODOLOGY

A vivid example of the perceptual transformation of an idea in economics is econometrics, which is an inductive exercise in economic estimation and forecasting. What variables must be added to an econometric equation in order to specify the relationships appropriately? Both under- and overspecification of an econometric model are known to lead to biased estimates of the regressors. Consequently forecasting by means of such inappropriately specified models is fallacious. The question is whether such specification problems can be eliminated, and if not, whether there exists a concept of a reasonably admissible degree of clarity? The answers to these questions are, first, that the inductive reasoning being limited to incremental knowledge of the material world to configurate in the econometric model would be capable of specifying the model through a trial and error method. That is, falsificationism and inference go together to bring about incremental changes in the selection of values and revisions in the econometric model.[27] Second, as the model continues to be specified incrementally, there remains no limit to which it can be refined, including the choice of more robust model structures. At best we are treating a model as a partial subsystem of a greater general equilibrium system. This is not to overlook the assertion that a model is a bounded rationality of events and information under given conditions. But if this is so, then prediction will always be erroneous, for variable factors will change in the projected time. The random error term is not equipped to handle these variations, being subject to the law of large numbers and specified probability distributions. Consequently neither the bounded rationality argument in favour of model specification, nor the adequacy of such a constrained specification for reliable forecasts, can hold in favour of the perceptual nature of econometric models.[28]

In recent years the cointegration technique has been devised to preserve the predictive property of linear economic models. Cointegration is a technique for preserving the long-run stationary property of linear models. Stationary here means that the joint probability distribution of any subset of independent stochastic variables remains identical to that of other sets of independent variables drawn from the class of variables over time. When linear models are not linearly preserved they have to be in the difference form to yield the linear invariance of the resulting difference-equations model over the long run.[29]

The problem arising from cointegration with respect to the perceptual element of econometric models is that the assumption of linear invariance for prediction must be instrumental in the cointegration technique. However, both because of the time-variance of model structures and the incremental introduction of presently unknown future variables, linear models are more a matter of convenience than a general rule of reality. Consider long-run, disequilibrium, demand-driven models of economic variables such as interest rates, hyperinflation and commodity tradables. In such cases one can think of the equilibrium linear property of econometric models only in a localised sense. Application of the same model to a long-run case would yield incorrect predictions. Furthermore it is impossible to predict long-run equilibrium and stable conditions from localised, short-run cases, so new variables become necessary for specification of the econometric model over time. Basing global predictions on localised stochastic variables is as impossible as predicting reality by means of perception.

The above problems are characteristic not only of time-series models, but also of cross-sectional ones. The problem of perception in econometric estimation arises from the individuation of independent entities (variables). It is neither realistic nor efficient for the estimation to lump these entities together. When estimating a production function across nation states, neoclassicism makes the unreal assumption that the long-run movement of technological knowledge will homogenise the production functions of nation states. This is an occidental equilibrium precept of economic and political hegemony based on its localised historical experience of market capitalism. In the international factor pricing model involving trade and the production function, this hegemonic assumption is made to apply to all countries and peoples. The global result of such neoclassical impositions has been disorder in the capital and factor markets, in the external balances of developing countries, and in the debt/deficit situation of industrial countries. The same disequilibrium result arising from the prescriptive equilibrium conception in neoclassicism is illustrated by the disorder that privatisation has caused in the Central Asian countries.

In the area of political economy, a similar kind of perception-induced model can be found in Marxism. Marx's materialistic interpretation of history and his rejection of the divine foundation of scientific epistemology was a response to the intellectual bankruptcy of the Church during the Enlightenment. Marx did not search for alternative categories of historical truths, such as those based on Islam, to come up with his philosophy of economism embodying dialectical materialism. Thus history in this limited sense was seen as inferring the fall of the divine order. The result was false politico-economic prediction and entire generations of misguided scientific arguments and inferences based on them.[30]

PERCEPTION IN THE METHODOLOGY OF THE NATURAL SCIENCES

In the natural sciences, one example of a perception-based model is that of biological evolution. Did human life arise through the same process of evolution as other forms of life? The claim of evolutionists is that all life emanated from the same primordial source. If this premise is accepted, then elements such as water, air and light must be primordial life forms themselves, not simply elements that facilitate the emergence of life. Hence the kind of systemic differentiation that perception yielded in the foregoing formalisation reduces all life forms to individuated and independent entities. Yet this is not the inference one derives from the study of cosmogony, which shows that the forces of nature were united in the early universe.[31] In subsequent ages these elements could have interacted to initiate life. If this possibility is accepted, there are now two premises for the emergence of life forms. One is the individuation of life forms in the early universe (evolution); the other is individuation in latter-day biological interaction. The two are different perceptions of the same thing.

The consequences of explaining creation by the unified-universe theory are polar to those relating to latter-day biological interactions. First, the state of randomness of primordial elements as life forms to suddenly arise in the 'early' universe is rejected in favour of a law of relations rather than biological forms transcending the universe. Second, the same law pervades creation in the later universe, and so on. This is the unifying consequence of the law of relations. It is of the form, $f(S'[S], F[R]) = g_1(S'[S]) \cap g_2(F[R])(R^{**}[B])$. $R^*(A)$ reduces to $R^*(\varepsilon_k)$, as $A = (a_1, a_2, \ldots) \to (\varepsilon_k)$. Likewise $B = (b_1, b_2, \ldots)$. Now $R^{**}(B)$ means the 'functional' or the topology defined on B. The evolutionary theory reduces $f(.)$ to the following: $f(F[R])(R^*[A]) = \Sigma_{k=1}^{\infty} f(F[R])(R[\epsilon_k])$. Here each of $f(F[R])(R[\epsilon_k])$, with $k \in \mathbb{N}$, signifies individuated condition of primordial elements as life forms themselves in 'early' universe, according to biological evolutionary theory.

In the later universe, after the elements had interacted to form single-called organisms they were sifted and differentiated by the natural selection process. Social and biological Darwinism thus introduced an individuation process that took place after the creation.[32] This is yet another perceptual subsystem of the theory of evolution. Thus the perception of independence and individuation pervades the occidental concept of creation. In the social world the impact of this is seen in occidental hegemony, alienation and dualism rather than unification of knowledge.

In summary, the one-to-one link between plurality (dualism) and perception is seen to be the cause and effect of all of occidental thought and culture. The application of locally formed cognition to long-run global phenomena is found to yield absurdity and non-predictability, uncertainty and disparateness. None of these can yield an essential scientific epistemology.

WORLD VIEW[33]

The unification of knowledge under a unique set of universal laws that apply equally within and between systems, given the perceived differences in the specifications of the problem underlying the systems, is the essence of the world view. The precept of world view thus does away with the slightest possibility of the individuation and independence of similar entities. It recognises that, for the sake of the binary perfection of all systems, there can be only two types of reality. One of these pushes the system in the positive direction of growth. This is the power of truth. Conversely the other pushes the system in the negative direction of decay. This is falsehood. The only kind of individuation and independence acknowledged by the world view is that within these two disjoint realities. Yet the methodology of evolution (dynamics) that functions in the precept of world view is unique to either of these categories, with the difference that they work in different ways in the domains of increasing truth and increasing falsehood.

The world view is thus unification epistemology within and between systems over space and time. It has a distinct, two-part methodology of its own. First, there is theoretical conceptualisation. Second, there is the functionalist perspective. Through this cycle the mental process is actualised via the interactive medium of polity and institutions in concert with the grand ecological (human and cosmic) order. The two parts are linked vertically and horizontally. They establish polity–ecological interactions and integration. The end result is the creation of knowledge as unification epistemology. The dynamics of the system, by means of the world view concept, attain movements along these directions simultaneously and continuously. One part cannot exist without the other. Thus interactions and cause–effect are intrinsic to the dynamics of the world view system. Finally, out of these systemic interactions arises systemic integration. What we then have is a world view premised on a uniquely and universally coordinated and applicable interactive–integrative knowledge-based system. In its evolution, knowledge as a conscious realisation of the systemic unification epistemology plays the most fundamental part in unravelling reality and applying it to ever higher domains of perfection.

The transformation of systems by producing knowledge from knowledge makes this the permanently endogenous essence of the interative–integrative knowledge-based world view. Thus observation, perception, plurality and differentiation are all prevented from playing a role in the creative process. Now prices and quantities appear as the space–time-bounded cognitive output of a prior input of knowledge. In turn these knowledge-embodied cognitive forms create newer forms of knowledge production. In this way the understanding of the purposes underlying pricing, consumption and production leads to the implementation of a series of socio-scientific arrangements that bring about the cognitive reality of observation, use and felicity (welfare). Realisation of this purposeful act followed by its actualisation generates new rounds of the process of creation. This represents the renewal and continuity of the uniquely universal recreative process.

Epistemological Characterisation of the World View

We will first develop the conceptual part of the world-view model of reality. We start with the premise that polity, taken in its broadest sense as government, institutions and organisations, is guided by precise textual laws. The essence of these laws is unification epistemology. Hence such laws must be universally comprehensive and versatile, yet minimally constrained as too many encumbrances would weaken their unifying power. It is then assumed that all policies, programmes and guidance developed and delivered by polity emanate from the epistemological foundations of textual laws, and thereafter will be progressively refined, revised and extended in concert with the responses of the socio-scientific order for which the rules of polity are primarily meant. Thus logically developed and evolved rules of life and thought allow polity–ecology interactions on specific problems to proceed. The result is integration among the agents of both polity and the socio-scientific order. Such integration occurs not through coercion, but rather by agreement. The polity is thus decentralised in essence and fully participatory. In it are members of the various interest groups that span society at large, including consumers, producers, the government, minority groups, labour unions, educationalists and so on. The only requirement is that the participants have a good knowledge of the textual laws. Thus the socio-scientific order, of which the political economy is an example, is thoroughly well represented in polity through elected members versed in the textual laws.

On the other hand the socio-scientific system is populated by a multitude of individuals (we will ignore interactions in the natural world for the time being). This case too can be explained by the world-view model.[34] Individuals become the agents of interaction and integration within the global system, in spite of the presence of their agents in polity. Thus a complete non-coercive model of exchange and learning-by-doing is established between polity and the socio-scientific order at large. This feature of the world-view model does not of course negate the need for defence of the order. Matters such as military defence, retaliatory trade policies, policies for the protection of infant industries, consumers and so on are upheld in accordance with the justifiable will of the socio-scientific order in compliance with the interpretation of textual laws on these matters by the representative polity.

The nature of textual laws and their initial formulation need to be explained now. Textual laws are those that are both cause and effect of the most unifying element of knowledge; that are at once most logically appealing to the socio-scientific order; that are conceptually comprehensive to the populace; that are equipped with the functional instruments of rule-formation emanating from the epistemological premise; that hold out the promise of certainty for present and future regenerations; and are cost-effective in implementation. Finally, there must also be a proven history of success for all of these – of the unifying epistemological concept, the instruments of action and a prime civilisation – during which these were brought into fruition.

It is clear that the perceptual basis of plurality (dualism) and the thought process, the concepts, institutions and socio-scientific instruments built upon this order, must be excluded from candidature. The question remains: can the *res cogitans* claimed by Descartes lead to *res existence*, even though the differentiating process of reason–materialism can thereafter ensure continuity of the essence of unification epistemology, characteristic of the textual laws? The answer is negative if the primordial condition of knowledge for regeneration of the socio-scientific order is being sought, for otherwise it would legitimate the perceptual and pluralistic process. This is a logical impossibility for unification epistemology. However, manifestation of the contradictory nature of perceptions and plurality in the formation of unified knowledge can lead to the termination of this evolutionary chain of cause and effect. The new chain to engender is one defined by unification epistemology. Now a new sequence of cause–effect evolution arises from a different source of reality. Following this, discursions, interactions and integration that define the dynamics of the system can repeat cognitive appearances of the real world. Such experiences can then become knowledge-induced starting points for further comprehension of unification epistemology. The interrelationship between epistemic concepts and institutions thus proceeds interactively. Hence primordially all relations must emanate from unification epistemology. Even cognition must be defined by this as a knowledge-induced creation to launch new recreative processes of continuity, diversity and purpose.

When viewed in the sense of unification epistemology and its confirming premises, the initiating premise of the textual laws becomes the natural corollary for socio-scientific action. The perpetuation and defence of polity are enabled by the will of the many, so if – under extreme conditions – the populace fails to uphold it and votes it out of acceptance it cannot be enforced. The polity then becomes an actively global knowledge-inducing institution at large. The highly knowledge-based, organisational and active nature of the polity motivated by unification epistemology remains the distinct life-blood of its dynamics.

LIBERAL DEMOCRACY AS A POLITICAL PHILOSOPHY BASED ON PERCEPTION

How does democracy match up with this kind of polity and political economy? Democracy is a political philosophy of the liberal concept of individual rights and privileges. Thus reason and material gain are the determinants of voting preferences. Consequently polity is designed to match the preferences of voters, as liberal philosophy respects individualism rather than invariant, axiomatic laws, rules and conditions. Indeed the theory of political cycles has been developed with reference to the utilitarian behaviour of governments *vis-à-vis* the electorate.[35]

One wonders what change would occur in the presence of participatory democracy at the grassroots. The neoclassical form of conflict of substitution would allocate the resources to muster votes through a market venue that looks on capital as the efficient productive factor and labour as the factor receiving distribution. This goes against economic efficiency, and the consequence would be the appearance of a dominant capitalist player. On the other hand, if the grassroots were somehow promoted by non-governmental organisations and labour unions, then dominance here would reduce the supply of capital through a build-up of capitalist preferences. Production, consumption and markets would shrink as a result, carrying along with it deprivation of the masses. A grassroots democracy would then fail in this struggle for power. Democracy is thus essentially a regime of dominant power in a liberal pursuit of rights through institutions, mechanisms and preferences that do not evolve in reference to any precise axiomatic premise. Hence democracy cannot be supported by unification epistemology.

This aspect of liberalism is equivalent to saying that ethics, moral values, social justice and the divine laws remain totally outside the preferences of agents in democratic voting behaviour. If farmers demand equitable subsidies, it is because they are in conflict with manufacturers in the sharing of resources in the individuation process of the market. The sharing of resources between farmers and manufacturers is not brought about by complementarity between the two via their production plans. The unbridled market mechanism remains the supreme determiner of preference formation among competing agents.[36]

This perspective of democracy in either its parliamentary/presidential or its participatory form is equally true internationally. In this case the global preferences of competing nation states remain conflictual in a perpetual substitution game. The markets for votes and the global social welfare function with competing national welfare indices with individuated preferences are in turn linked to similar preferences at the microeconomic level. Thus the same kind of differentiating perceptions now characterise micro-level preferences. Hence a globally conflicting and differentiating field of preferences is generated by the neoclassical nature of liberal democracy.

It is for such reasons that the heads of industrialised nations did not care to oppose the Serbian aggression in Muslim Bosnia-Herzegovina. The Clinton administration paid only lip service to the option of air strikes on Serb positions. The Canadian government made the lame excuse that it was protecting its peacekeeping troops rather than upholding a just solution to the aggression by punishing the Serbs. The same democratic ideal is becoming an instrument of economic integration between Russia and the West. Democracy and privatisation are being used by the West to fuel the capitalist transformation of the world.

The same meaningless epistemological basis of the Western idea of global democracy and alliance can be attached to what has come to be called the 'new world order'. The idea is enforced in the economic scene by global privatisation by the Bretton Woods institutions under the auspices of Western financial and trading hegemony. The shadow of this globalisation move, which has entered Russia and East Europe in a significant way, is now being aimed at the Asian Pacific Rim through the US arm of Asia-Pacific Economic Cooperation. On the other hand, the Western strategic need to maintain low prices for critical commodities has brought about the belligerent policy of the West in the Middle East and a liberalised trade agenda for the Pacific Rim in concert with the European Union and North American Free Trade Agreement. The political economy of liberal democracy here means a hegemonic mustering of petty nation states through aid and military support by the dominant international power. An imposed dominant preference model thus configurates a false representation of global unity for capitalism and democracy as media for the sustenance of capitalism.

FORMALISATION OF THE POLITY–MARKET INTERACTIVE–INTEGRATIVE PREFERENCE

With the above characteristics and distinctions between polity based on textual laws emanating from unification epistemology and that based on liberal democracy emanating from reason–materialism roots, we can now formalise preference formation in unification epistemology. To do this we proceed in three steps. First we define the preference formation of polity. Second we define the preference formation of the market order. Third we define the interactive polity–market preferences.

Let the preference map of polity based on the textual laws be defined by P_{1i}:

$$P_{1i} = ([\geqslant_{1i}, p_i]; p_i \in [\theta_i]) = f(S'[S], F[R])(R^{**}[B])$$

meaning that policy choices can be continuously well-ordered in the reason–spiritual premise of reality by the dynamics of the trajectory in $R^{**}(B)$. $R^{**}(B)$ denotes a given comprehension of unification epistemology during the phase in (B). $f(.)$ denotes the mobilisation of textual laws, as signified by the simultaneity between divine laws, $S'(S)$, and the reason space, $F(R)$, both of which are influenced by unification epistemology. This means that a particular sequence of knowledge denoted by (Θ_i), underlying the policy enactment, are formed by $f(.)$. Hence we write $(\Theta_i) = f(.)$. These symbols were defined earlier. For simplicity of reference, from now on we will replace $f(.)$ with the symbol of knowledge formation, (θ_i). The subscript i points to the regeneration of knowledge through interactions and defines the number of iterations attached to the trajectory (B) in $R^{**}(B)$; $i \in \mathbb{N}$ (or $\mathbb{R}$). It is shown that the policy choices denoted by $(\geqslant_{1i}, p_i)$ are determined by each of the iterations.

The preference map of market order (generally of socio-scientific order or ecological order) based on the textual laws is defined by P_{2i}:

$$P_{2i} = ([\geqslant_{2i}, x_i]; \; x_i \in [\theta_i]) = f(S'[S], \; F[R])(R^{**}[B])$$

The formation of P_{2i} is similar to P_{1i}. Here x_i denotes the vector of socio-economic variables; it may contain the price variable. The basic elements of this vector are consumption, c_i, production, q_i, and distribution, d_i, which can then be further expanded by other variables.

It is important to note how p_i and x_i can both belong to the same set, (θ_i). This transformation means that $x_i = g_i(\theta_i)$. Hence socio-economic variables and policy variables are iteratively determined as knowledge responses in this system. In this way, both are epistemologically unified with the textual laws, their guidance on the delivery, interpretation and discursions, as signified by the trajectory $R^{**}(B)$.

Neither P_{1i} nor P_{2i} is capable of generating final preferences in the knowledge-induced interactive–integrative system that emanates from the world view. Only interactive and integrated preferences will be relevant, as unification epistemology and the discursive path $R^{**}(B)$ make knowledge generation, (θ_i), possible in this system.

We now define the interactive–integrative preference map in two steps. First there is the interactive preference map, P_i. Such interactions are implied by the mathematical intersection denoted by $\cap$. All other function were explained above.

$$P_i = P_{1i} \cap P_{2i} = \{(\geqslant_{12i}, x_i, p_i); \; y_i = (x_i, p_i) \in (\theta_i) = g_1\{S'(S)$$
$$\cap \; g_2(F[R])\}(R^{**}[B])\}$$

We also define the symbol $\geqslant_{12i} = (\geqslant_{1i}) \cap (\geqslant_{2i})$, $i \in \mathbb{N}$ (or $\mathbb{R}$). The form of $f(.)$ in g_1 and g_2 was explained earlier. All the expressions in this interactive preference map are specific to issues, s. Thus with s in place, the interactive preference map specific to s would read $P_i(s)$.

To transform the interactive preference map into an integrative one we proceed as follows in the limit of interactions, $i \to N(s)$, where $N(s)$ denotes a natural number or a real number corresponding to the number of interactions pertaining to the level of an issue under interaction in the particular interactive mode, denoted by s. But as this limiting process reaches $\theta_i \to \theta^*(s)$, denoting the limiting knowledge-based consensus on the issue *s* under discussion, interactive–integrative preference map, $P_{N(s)}$ for $N(s)$, is now well-defined. The meaning here is that as interactions continue, temporary consensus is reached, followed by new knowledge creation. The latter phase describes the concept of interaction–integration. It is preconditioned here by the subscript *s*.

$$P_{N(s)} = \lim(i \to N[s])(P_i[s]) = \lim(\theta_i \to \theta^*[s])(P_i[s])(\theta_i[s])$$

$$= \{(\geqslant_{12i}, x_i, p_i)(\theta^*[s]); \ y_i = g(x_i, p_i)(\theta^*[s])$$

$$= \{g_1(S'[S]) \cap g_2(F[R])\}\{R^{**}(B[s])\}\}$$

Henceforth the interactive–integrative preferences emanating from the premise of unification epistemology described by the knowledge-based world view will be represented by $P_{N(s)}$. In this characterisation the following facts will be implied.

All inputs and outputs in this system are a continuous regeneration of knowledge emanating from and integrating towards the stock of knowledge (Θ) that forms unification epistemology. One thus makes an important distinction between stock defined in a primordial and cumulative sense, and flow of knowledge as regenerative knowledge of the temporal world (θ), evolving out of and increasingly cumulating to Θ. All policies and socio-economic variables evolving in this interactive–integrative knowledge-based system are characterised by a vector, say $y = g(x, p)(\theta \in \Theta)$. There are also recursions among variables of the type $x = h_1(x', p)(\theta)$, $p = h_2(x, p')(\theta)$, where x', p' denotes previously recursed variables influencing subsequent ones. Because of these recursions there will be similar recursions in the θ values, say $\theta = h_3(\theta')$, θ' being defined as for x', p'. Here g denotes a general function of x, p as vectors. h_1 and h_2 are implicit functions derived from recursions between the variables, as shown.

The world view is now defined by *WV*, as the nexus of all interactive–integrative preferences and reality evolving from the abovementioned system:

$$WV = \{(P_{N(s)}[\theta]); \ \theta \in \Theta; \ N \in \mathbb{N} \ (\text{or} \ \mathbb{R}), \ s \in \mathbb{N}\}$$

The subscripts will be deliberately suppressed unless they are required for analysis. Also, since *s* is specific to issues and *WV* is global inter- and intra-system while recognising the specificity of the problems across different systems, therefore, in the extended form within *WV*, *s* means inter- and intra-systemic interactions and integrations based on the uniqueness of $\theta \in \Theta$ in all systems. This is the essence of unification epistemology in terms of the textual laws and their comprehension, delivery and regeneration through knowledge.

Conversely, in the perception-based pluralistic (dualistic) system, P_{1i} and P_{2i} exist independently of each other. Consequently the role of knowledge as an interactive phenomenon is introduced as an exogenous input into the system of relations in $R^*(A)$. Now both P_i and $P_{N(s)}$ generate non-intersecting sets. If some form of knowledge is introduced into an interactive mode, as claimed by Drucker for his post-capitalist society, then too there will be dominance of agent-specific preference in the system, enforcing ethical, normative and systemic views. The result is negation of unification and the principle of simultaneity amongst all knowledge-induced possibilities, as otherwise intrinsic to the world view reality. Such dominance models are taken up by the ethical perceptor behaviour of utilitarian type additive social welfare functions formalised by Hammond,[37] the Eurocentric model of development,[38] and public choice theory of government behaviour based on utility maximisation of self-interests.[39]

RESOURCE ALLOCATION IN THE WORLD VIEW CONCEPT AND IN NEOCLASSICISM

This point is an important one in characterising resource allocation in the world view concept as opposed to that in neoclassicism. The logical conclusion is that the individuated model of neoclassicism must necessarily be premised on marginal substitution between competing ends. Global complementarity cannot exist as it would always be possible to group together complementary goods to substitute for other goods. In the world view concept the principle of simultaneity translates into a principle of global complementarity among goods. Likewise, in the complementation of realities this principle recognises that all 'bads' are complementary and there can be no substitution between 'goods' and 'bads'; rather there is complete rejection of 'bads'. Due to imperfect knowledge about a specific issue at hand, some 'goods' may be mistaken for 'bads' and *vice versa*. But this is seen as a temporary phenomenon and no global equilibrium can therefore exist in resource allocation. Neoclassicism, on the other hand, regards resource allocation to be generating equilibrium as long-run and globally stable states. Substitution and choice between acceptable levels of 'goods' and 'bads' thus persists in the neoclassical order in the long term.

FORMAL DEFINITION OF THE WORLD VIEW:
THE EPISTEMIC–ONTIC CIRCULAR CAUSATION AND
CONTINUITY MODEL OF UNIFIED REALITY

We will now take up the above formalisation of the world view concept
by means of philosophy of science. We will define the two concepts.

First, epistemic essence means the purely *a priori* nature of knowing,
and takes the form $S'(S)$ in disjunction with $F(R)$. By this the cognitive world is shown to result from a realisation of $S'(S)$ on $F(R)$, forming
a posteriori reality. But in the epistemic sense we do not have the
process of knowing any relationship emanating from the *a posteriori*
on to the *a priori*. That is, $F(R)$ through prior knowledge induction
does not generate conditions that can map it to a realisation of $S'(S)$.
Consequently a systems dominance exists in knowledge formation that
causes individuation and independence between the two integral components of total reality, that is the *a priori* and the *a posteriori*. The
purely metaphysical foundations of science were premised on the kind
of epistemic outlook explained here. The primacy of normative behaviour and its disjunction from positivity was the consequence of neoclassicism. Deductionism conflicted with inductivism, and this gave
rise to concepts such as Cartesian logical positivism and Popperian
falsificationism.[40] Thus epistemic refers here to the purely non-interactive realm of either reason or spirit in an otherwise total knowledge
formation, which is epistemology.

Second, ontic essence means the purely *a posteriori* origin of reality. Thus $F(R)$ maps onto $S'(S)$ and generates systemic dominance solely
by means of materiality. This approach has been customary in the
philosophy of science given by Descartes, Hume, Russell, Hobbes and
Bacon.[41] Matter–spirit individuation and independence are thus once
again made in the ontic premise as in the epistemic premise of philosophy of science. The ontic and the epistemic have different meanings
from the ontological and the epistemological, for these approaches point
to methodologies that reprieve each other via the processes of induction
or deduction, respectively.[42]

Is there a region of synthesis between the epistemic and the ontic in
the occidental philosophy of science? Husserl, Carnap and Whitehead
as philosophers, Godel as a mathematician, and von Mises and Boulding
as economists have attempted this exercise.[43] The conclusion remains,
that with the benchmark of primacy in reason alone, synthesis here
relies upon reason. Consequently the methodological problem of unification agenda caused by perception and plurality enters the synthetic

domain, and the problem of individuation, independence and systemic dominance appears once again. Consequently, in a purely reason-based or spiritual-based philosophy of science, *a priori–a posteriori* synthesis cannot be attained. This is the crisis of Western civilisation pointed out by Husserl.

The world view is thus a unique departure from the differentiated epistemic and ontic parts of an otherwise unified reality. It aims at the synthesis we are searching for here. Epistemic–ontic synthesis is both cause and effect of the interactive–integrative evolutionary epistemology. Only by treating knowledge as the input and output of all systems based on a unification epistemology functionalised by textual laws, their conceptual and institutional delivery and temporal regeneration, is it possible to link the knowledge-induced rules of life to the socio-scientific variables. This methodology rationalises the following epistemic–ontic circular causation and continuity model of the world view:[44]

$$\text{Simulate } (\theta \in \Theta)(y = g[x, p, \theta])$$
$$\text{subject to } x = h_1(x', p, \theta)$$
$$p = h_2(x, p', \theta)$$
$$\theta = h_3(\theta')$$

This simulative system applies to all interactions, such as between polity and the market order, and between knowledge topology and materiality. The emerging interactive system is then inter- and intra-systemically integrated, as in the case of unified field theory in physics and a theory of everything in the socio-scientific realm centred in knowledge.[45]

Note should be made here of the fact that endogenous recursions among the variables necessitate each variable to be functionally iterated by means of the other variables. Thus we have the functions h_1, h_2 and h_3, while simulation takes place over recursive Θ values, x values and p values.

THE NATURE OF EMPIRICAL ESTIMATION IN THE WORLD VIEW MODEL

Important recourse is made here to recursive and simulative quantitative models rather than to the maximisation model. The inductive methodology of econometrics as a perception-based model is replaced in the epistemic–ontic model by simulation of the coefficients of econometric models. Such simulation is caused by the inductive influence of θ variables as basic parameters of the system. The Bayesian method, Markovian processes and dynamic input–output coefficients are better estimation procedures for the non-linear simulative models emerging here. Yet the estimation procedure ceases to be a mechanical exercise. The interactions that arise are generated by feedbacks that are human responses measured by the ordinality of knowledge values and post-evaluation of corresponding socio-scientific variables that get induced by ordinal knowledge values, creating in turn newer ones through the polity–market interactions that proceed. Model formulations and their estimation are impossible without these polity–market inter-linkages. The models simply reflect the state of the arts that explains the epistemic–ontic circular causation and continuity process of knowledge generation.

The predictive power of the model rests on the interactions being monitored by two kinds of approach. One is to 'react' to the responses generated from the interactions as they arise. This is the learning-by-doing process. The second is to formulate feasible models of behaviour invoking $(P_{N(s)})$ on the basis of past experience of polity–market circularity in order to project alternatives.

One example of a predictive model of the latter type is given below. We assume here that total social welfare, $y(i + 1)$, is the product of attaining newer and improving policy variables, $p(i)$, and socio-economic variables, $x(i)$, both of which are induced in increasing returns to scale by knowledge values, $θ(i)$. These are subsequently evaluated in polity by post-evaluation of interactions. There also exist linear relations between the x, p and $θ$ variables, with coefficients such as $a's$, $b's$ and $c's$ determined in each interaction.

Note that the same kinds of recursion mentioned above now translate into the discrete case by introducing discrete iterations of i with a one-period lag.

$$\text{Simulate } (θ \in Θ)\ y(i + 1) = (x[i + 1] \cdot p[i + 1])^{θ(i+1)}$$
$$\text{subject to } θ(i + 1) = a_i θ(i)$$
$$x(i + 1) = b_{i1} x(i) + b_{i2} p(i) + b_{i3} θ(i)$$
$$p(i + 1) = c_{i1} x(i) + c_{i2} p(i) + c_{i3} θ(i).$$

Recursive substitutions for the x, p and $θ$ values in the objective function from the constraints yields the form in the case of a general adaptative lag taken over N iteration periods.

$$y(i + 1) = (f_1[b's, c's] x[i - N] + f_2[b's, c's] p[i - N]$$

$$+ f_3[b's, c's]\theta[i - N])^{f(a's)\theta(i-N)} (g_1[b's, c's]x[i - N]$$
$$+ g_2[b's, c's]p[i - N] + g_3[b's, c's]\theta[i - N])^{f(a's)\theta(i-N)}$$

We now have a non-linear estimation problem, and Bayesian assumptions on $f's$ and $g's$ are necessary. It should also be noted that the presence of ordinal knowledge induction in the reduced form of the model above makes knowledge an endogenous phenomenon in the model. Likewise x, p and y are all endogenous variables. The only exogenous variable that does not numerically enter the model is Θ. Hence ethics, morality and values are endogenous phenomena in the interactive–integrative world view.

Under interaction–integration it is expected that dynamic coefficients with Bayesian distributions will be well-behaved. Still the above formalisation of a non-linear model that can be estimated, points to the synthesis between normative roots caused by the conceptualisation and delivery of textual laws emanating from unification epistemology. Conversely, econometric methodology is based on a presumption of linearity and systemic non-interaction. Even when interactively generated dynamic coefficients are implied, the passage from theory to its model estimation remains either *a priori* set or the theory is developed and modified by recourse to empirical results.[46] The two occur simultaneously; such is a case that neither neoclassical economics nor econometric methods has addressed. These economic fields have evolved independently of each other. In the interactive–integrative system, on the other hand, the model is formulated from sources that arise from the circular continuity of the normative and positive parts of total theory.

The result of the epistemic–ontic model of unified reality, and the estimation of the corresponding model system, is to induce into such a system the deductive–inductive circularity that has gone into the model formalisation. Thus estimation ceases to be a purely inductive exercise. Likewise a model that reflects and guides behaviour is not a speculative construct of human nature, but a real response caused by the measured impact of $(p[\theta])$ on $(x[\theta])$, and of $(x[\theta])$ on $(p[\theta])$, as (θ) continues to derive its values from, and then accumulates to the stock, Θ.

THE CONGRUENCE OF THE *SHURATIC* PROCESS WITH THE EPISTEMIC–ONTIC MODEL

Finally we investigate where such an interactive–integrative knowledge-based world view can be found. In this respect we have already rejected occidental thought due to its unshakeable plurality and use of perception. In oriental thought too we have found that the metaphysics of 'one–many' logically contradicts unification epistemology. The pure reason at the foundation of postmodernism – perceptual, individuated and differentiating as it is – rejects divine authority in the scientific functionalism of knowledge. Thus in none of these systems is there a primordial source from which knowledge can emanate and unify to explain essential reality.

Qur'anic rule formation for the temporal order, called *Qur'anic Ahkam*, submits all creative origins in both the cosmological order and the microcosmic world to divine authority. All cognitions, including mathematical laws, are the result of knowledge made material. Materiality is then the result of perception to the mind. It is this knowledge-induced cognition that differentiates the 'good' from the 'bad'; it unifies all that is 'good' and recognises a similar affinity between the 'bads'. But since God himself does not represent physical forms, the only way that unification can occur is through the realisation of divine laws in life. In this respect the divine laws are translated into instruments of application and institutions of delivery to society. That society is one of believers (Muslims).

Thus rejecting the physical formism of God in materiality, replacing it with the permanence, immanence and extension of the divine laws as functional aspects of mind and action, the projection of knowledge from lower to higher degrees of excellence is brought about by derived felicities from the learning process. These are the signs of God, which the *Qur'an* repeatedly presents in the midst of the continuous creative process. Circular causation and continuity under unification epistemology is thus formed by the evolution of knowledge and its induction of all phenomena over time. This occurs through the continuous creative process that goes on between the primordiality of the stock of knowledge impacting upon the comprehension of the divine laws in mind and cosmos, and the affirmation of that process via the signs of God. The epistemic, which is God and his divine laws, is thus unified with the ontic, which are the signs of God and the new springs of knowledge flows so regenerated.

Within this epistemic–ontic circular causation and continuity model, functional results are gained by the examples of the Prophet Muhammad as the positive premise applying to the normative premise, which is the *Qur'an*. The two together form the core of the Islamic laws (*Shari'ah*). Yet the application of this unified core between *Sunnah* (Prophetic traditions as the positive) and *Qur'an* (normative) requires extensive study that is of the most embryonic and pervasive type extending over all faculties of knowledge (systems). This is the *Ijtihadi* discovery of *Qur'anic Ahkams* made possible by taking recourse to the core of *Shari'ah* (unification epistemology) and by extending them widely inter- and intra-systems.

The embryonic and pervasive nature of this continuously discursive process is the external manifestation of the divine laws. It is a process of confirmation of the divine essence in total reality. Hence it is centred on the following *Qur'anic* verse:

> And thus have We, by Our command, sent inspiration to thee [the primordial essence of knowledge on divine roots]: Thou knewest not [before] what was Revelation, and what was Faith [no creation without the divine laws]; but We have made the [*Qur'an*] a Light, wherewith We guide such of Our servants as We will; and verily thou dost guide [men] to the Straight Way [unification epistemology based on the *Qur'an* and *Sunnah*], the Way of God to Whom belongs whatever is in the heavens and whatever is on earth [functionalism of the divine laws]. Behold [how] all affairs tend towards God! [circular causation and continuity via the divine laws in the cognitive world and back to divine affirmation in higher levels of acquired knowledge]. (*Al-Qur'an*, Sura XLII, verses 52–3)

Since it is the embryonic and pervasive process of creation that is being mentioned here based on the divine manifestation of the epistemic–ontic circular causation and continuity world view, it becomes the centre of Islamic consultation. Thus the Islamic interactive–integrative process is the embryonic and pervasive domain of the *Shura* inter- and intra-systems. The *Shura* is not simply a grand political process. Rather it is manifest in the Islamic evolutionary epistemology leading to and springing from the divine stock of knowledge. The *Shuratic* process is thus synonymous with the epistemic–ontic circular causation and continuity model of unified reality. In the formalisation of the epistemic–ontic model we have thus drawn on the *Qur'an* and have logically reinforced the world view of the *Qur'anic* socio-scientific order.

CONCLUSION

This chapter has discussed a new and challenging methodology for Islamic socio-scientific investigation. This methodology, being deeply epistemologically centred, neither springs from nor leads to a mechanical view of the universe. Instead it is premised in functional ways on the unification epistemology established by the core of *Shari'ah*, namely the *Qur'an* and *Sunnah*. The rules of life and thought thus derived are then evolved through the discursive process of consensus formation or agreement called *Ijtihad*. The result is a methodology for the epistemic– ontic circular causation and continuity model of unified reality. This methodology equivalently describes the embryonic and pervasive nature of the *Shuratic* process. It is the unique world view established by the *Qur'an* and is seen here as universally applicable to all systems, not just the human system.

A comparative examination of occidental and oriental philosophies of thought and culture was undertaken to come up with the distinct form of methodology, inferences, concepts and institutionalism that are derived from the precept of the world view.

Hence the Islamic world view is seen here to be polar to and distinct from the occidental and oriental philosophies of science. A new approach, methodology and consequently inference and application are found to be embedded in the dynamically interactive and integrative relations arising from the epistemological foundations of the Islamic economic, social and scientific order.[47]

In the subsequent chapters we shall study the interactive–integrative methodology in greater depth. We shall take up specific areas of political economy and economic systems to illustrate the universality of this methodology.

2 Post-Marxian, Post-Humean and Post-Kantian Epistemology: Towards the Unification of Knowledge

The principal objective of this chapter is to illlustrate the fact that occidental scientific thought suffers from epistemological incompleteness. This is so inherent in occidental science that the problem cannot be overcome by a mere extension of discursive methodology of search, discovery and empiricism. What is needed is a theory of knowledge that is reducible to its ultimate form.

The evolution of knowledge in this search for ultimate roots has two fundamental consequences. First, the well-known *a priori* and *a posteriori* dichotomy in discerning the roots of knowledge, as philosophised by leading Western thinkers, becomes unacceptable and is replaced by a logical evolution of knowledge that integrates the *a priori* and the *a posteriori* through cause and effect. This phenomenon of evolutionary epistemology is also congruent with the idea of interactions among the verities of world systems, events and physical realities. The net result of interactions among systems is integration. Hence the search for, discovery and empirical verification of evolutionary epistemology involves systemic integration brought about by interaction. This is the essence of unification, while further irreducibility at the ultimate core of knowledge signifies unity of knowledge.

In a more substantive sense, we are searching for an endlessly evolutionary cause and effect interaction–integration between the moment-to-moment realisation of the epistemic reality and the cognitive or ontic reality. This epistemic–ontic process is circularly related by cause and effect and is both pervasive and continuous in nature. We shall refer to the emerging methodology that integrates the epistemic and ontic parts of total reality as the epistemic–ontic circular causation and continuity model of unified reality. This unique methodology will serve as the post-Marxian, post-Humean and post-Kantian answer to the distinct epistemology of unity and unification.

THE EPISTEMOLOGICAL PROBLEM WITH HEGEL AND MARX

It is doubtful whether Marx really had an epistemological approach to dialectical materialism. It is also doubtful whether Hegel – whose dialectical process relating to world spirit and freedom of discovery and search was emulated by Marx when building up the idea of economism – had an epistemology that was searching for unity and unification of knowledge through historicity.

Epistemological problems arise in Hegel by virtue of the perpetual transcendence of reason as the open-ended origin of knowledge and thought. This rationalism is associated with the occidental philosophy of historicism that arose in ancient Greece, wherein the realm of divine order is seen as incomprehensible. Only the humanly reasoned faculties of divinity, ethics, morality and truth are considered relevant to the social, political and economic realisation of civil order. Consequently, as only the divine order is complete and human reason is functional but incomplete, open-endedness here relates to the perpetual search for, discovery and empirical viability of Greek epistemology. Hegel followed this in his dialectics of the human mind and made it the centrepiece of occidental scientific perception.

Thus even as the evolutionary mind tries to relate the originary content with the genesis content and *vice versa*, all such evolutions remain within the domain of cognitive reason, independent of divine order, wherein the true essence lies. Furthermore, it is also in the divine order of reality where appearances are shaped, as reason assumes a cognitive consequence of divine creativity. Descartes called this essence *res cogitans*.

Hegel's evolutionary epistemology thus devolves into systemic tautology. For if genesis $\rightarrow$ appearance $\rightarrow$ genesis $\rightarrow$ etc., and since genesis $\in$ 'reason space'; appearance $\in$ 'reason space', and 'reason space' $\subset$ total space = 'reason space' $\cup$ 'divine space'; with 'reason space' $\cap$ 'divine space' = Φ, as argued in Chapter 1, 'reason space' being less dense than 'divine space' in the knowledge domain, then 'reason space' must be ultimately bounded. (The symbol $\rightarrow$ means evolution towards.)

If the reverse is true, then 'reason space' cannot attain general equilibrium without interrelating with 'divine space'. Thus only local equilibrium is acceptable in 'reason space'; global equilibrium is only possible by interrelating 'reason space' and 'divine space'. This is contrary to Hegelian dialectics. Hence the Hegelian philosophy of history, which creates modernism out of movement of the mind, is only a local perception of reality.[1]

Marx took Hegel's dialectics and focused it on the economic and material evolution of history. 'Reason space' became even more constrained in the total space of scientific reality. Consequently the nature of reality was further distanced in the localised consequences of Marxist thought on the socio-scientific order.

These gaps between the true perspective of what constitutes evolutionary knowledge unification and those arrived at locally, as in Hegel's and Marx's perceptions of reality, have serious implications for the realisation of knowledge in the socio-scientific order. The problems arise from the fragmentation of knowledge by differentiated systems, which, by the process of sub-setting within each larger space of cognition, develops a sequence of localised equilibria that do not interrelate. As a result there can be no transcendence between one system and another. The end result is categorisation of knowledge by systems. Knowledge in this sense becomes both a differentiated entity pertaining to individuated systems and a localised phenomenon of cognition. The mind too becomes simply a cognitive entity with no relation to total space, and each exists independently of the other. How then can there be a postmodern realisation of genesis → appearance → genesis as a historiographic process? In other words, if the limited knowledge denseness property of reason space means that this space becomes bounded, then what other can come after the abovementioned recursive sequence but convergence to a bounded reason space?

For these reasons it is suggested that Marx omitted from his materialistic interpretation of history the relevance of the great civilisations and institutions that framed the civil laws of European societies and of the entire Islamic world view.[2] It is therefore not farfetched to conclude that Marx's negation of the market process and of the nature of prices, money, resource allocation, exchange and profits led socialism and communism to their logical demise.

The flaw was in misconstruing and illogically trying to build a labour theory of value independently of what may be called the 'intrinsic value' in the state of nature imbued by divine order. Such a value concept causes sharing between the owners of capital and labour and induces mutual welfare. In this system of social contract, workers and capitalists can have no advantage over each other. Only the institutional framework, the textual laws and organisation of the social order to promote and realise the dynamics of intrinsic value, become reality in the interrelated domains of 'reason space' and 'divine space', with 'reason space' being increasingly encompassed by 'divine space' as knowledge evolves. Only in the context of knowledge can 'reason space' interact with 'divine space'. The two remain independent in the occidental (Hegelian) system. This alone makes it possible to transcend the values of the market by the ethical standards of society and *vice versa*. Without this overarching relationship, intersystemic interactions and integration logically cannot be construed, formalised, applied and realised. Consequently, in Marx as in Hegel, the desired universal relationship of genesis and appearance by cause and effect loses its validity.[3]

A CRITIQUE AND ALTERNATIVE TO THE LABOUR THEORY OF VALUE

We can now conceptualise a theory of intrinsic value that contrasts with the labour theory of value. The resulting view of the market mechanism can then be taken up.

In the labour theory of value two types of price exist.[4] First, there is the price that reflects the intrinsic value of labour embodied in the process of production. This is the true price of the product and reflects the pure unit cost of production, with labour as the primary variable factor. In Marxism such a price is seen to arise from the use-value of a good in exchange. Hence true price as value is seen to represent the objectified use-value of the labour directly or indirectly engaged in the production of socially recommended goods for exchange.

On the other hand Marx rejected market prices set by the pure mechanism of exchange as value reflected in the production of socially wasteful goods. Consequently the Ricardian theory of value, which integrates the role of capital, hence profits, into the effort of labour, is rejected by Marx as objectified value, because of the existence of capitalist ownership.[5] Consequently the entire relevance of market exchange as the interplay of demand and supply and preference formation in view of these, the resulting profits and unequal but not necessarily dehumanising exchange in the market venue, are all rejected by Marx through his conceptualisation of price as use-value. Prices as use-value are different from prices as exchange value in a market economy. Use-value can never realise itself, for market exchange must be accepted as the only true medium for value, as reflected in price as exchange value.

However, the socially requisite orientations in consumption and production in the generation of exchange value remain valid. But this cannot be taken up independently of the market mechanism. The inference then is that laws, institutional presence and the social transformation process must join hands with the market in order to realise social prices as objectified value within the ensuing domain of market-oriented interrelationships. The conclusion is that neither the Marxist nor the capitalist market order can deliver this type of social interrelationship, from which emanate measures of value as social price. In the Marxist system, exchange between labour and capital is impossible if socially objectified use-value is to be realised. In the capitalist market economy, market price does not reflect socially objectified value.

In the context of the systems-oriented formalisation we have taken up above, the dichotomy between use-value and exchange-value is just one example of the methodological individuation that must necessarily exist in the Marxist and other systems of economic transaction because of the assumed independence of moral values from economic ones. This process of methodological individualism is thus seen to pervade all the markets and institutions of Western epistemology. Genesis cannot emerge from the cognitive process of the market because of the unsocial nature of the latter. Appearance cannot reflect social values because of the impossibility of socially objectified exchange in the capitalist market order.

HUME'S ONTOLOGY AND ITS CRITIQUE

The literature on the philosophy of science presents the concept of ontology as a reprieve of the *a priori* approach of Kant.[6] Thereby a theory of origins is seen to lead to a cognition of being in the system under investigation. However, the process of cognition is now reversed, although the method of inference remains unchanged. In the ontological method the process towards reality leads from the domain of cognition (being) to the domain of inference; just as in the epistemological method it is from the domain of origin to cognition. While the ontological method explains an inductive process of inference, its derivative, 'ontic', is singularly applied to cognition of the act of being. Here we will take the concept of the epistemic to apply to the field of pure *a priori* relations, an act of rationality alone.

Using our previous formalisation of the impossibility of knowledge unification in the context of the independence of 'reason space' from 'divine space', we once again infer that the epistemic must remain independent of the ontic process. Consequently it is impossible to realise an evolving, pervasive and continuous cause–effect relationship, or genesis (*a priori*: epistemic) → appearance (*a posteriori*: ontic) → genesis (epistemic) → etc. In the absence of such a globalising inter-relationship, what emerges is simply human perception rather than essential reality relating to universal verities. Perceptions are lower conditions of the mind, and can only be included in 'reason space', according to our previous formalisation. They arise as individuated forms either in the deductive epistemological method or in the inductive ontological method, and the two generally contrast and conflict with each other.

David Hume characterised the perceptual category as being in 'reason space' in the following words:

> It has been observ'd, that reason, in a strict and philosophical sense, can have an influence on our conduct only after two ways: Either when it excites a passion by informing us of the existence of something which is a proper object of it; or when it discovers the connexion of causes and effects, so as to afford us means of exerting any passions. These are the only kinds of judgment, which can accompany our actions, or can be said to produce them in any manner.[7]

When such perception-based ideas of reality are applied to the socio-scientific order, a process of individuation, speculation and methodological incommensurability arises. To substantiate this point, let us look at a theory of money.

In the ontic sense, the quantity of money in the economy means the supply of monetary aggregates in relation to the perceived, that is, actual need to satisfy the demand for money in accordance with transactions demand. Therefore the value of purchases in the real goods sector equals the quantity of money needed to satisfy this volume of purchases.

Such a characterisation of money supply is reflected in the quantity theory of money, which Hume supported in answer to the question then posed to economists: 'What is the quantity of money that a given country needs?'[8] Hume's answer to this question was that the total demand for money, being influenced by transactions demand in an open economy, would be accordingly affected. In a closed economy, demand is determined by internal transaction demands in the real goods sector.

Yet, as so expressed, the quantity equation of money based on the inductive premise of the real sector transactions demand remains a tautology. It does not explain the relationship between price level and quantity of money; that is, which one of these affects the other. The quantity equation suggests that an increase in the quantity of money will increase the price level. But this may not be true if the additional money is chanelled into the production of social goods, wherein productivity and the distribution of resources and wealth are found to exist in harmony. Likewise the inference of quantity theory, that price increases push up the quantity of money through the transactions demand for goods in terms of higher prices, is strictly a condition of demand-push inflation as long as expectations are not built into the quantity equation.

The quantity theory thus leaves out the social attributes of money, which are better expressed by the social credit theory of money.[9] Money thus ceases to be neutral to ethical considerations of the social and economic order. As much as money supply remains a policy variable in the hands of banks, its function with regard to the nature of goods transacted in the market place and the distribution of wealth determined by the stock of money is now seen to be an ethical one. In this relationship of money to real goods transactions and to the policy-induced management of money directed towards social ends, there remains no clear-cut relationship between money and prices.[10] Hence the perceived relationship presented by the quantity equation on ontic grounds does not hold up in reality.

On the other hand an epistemic approach to money supply would invoke an exogenous and hence an expected supply perception that is vested as promissory notes solely with the central bank. Here the *IS–LM* relationship expressing monetary sector equilibrium corresponding to given levels of interest rates and national income becomes an *a priori* relationship of human behaviour, which was envisaged by Keynes on the basis of his income and money multipliers working in unison to establish full-employment levels of output and stable prices. Yet this epistemic formalisation of Keynesian general equilibrium fails to establish the full-employment level or to stabilise prices in a regime of exogenous money supply. International Keynesianism, as reflected in the Bretton Woods institutional paradigms and policies, is known to have contributed to a global de-equalisation between growth, spending and prices.

Finally, it may be noted that Keynesianism cannot be combined with monetarism: the full-employment output and employment conditions of the Keynesian model are shown to be non-inflationary or deflationary, whereas in the monetarist view, fiscal expansion to attain the required full-employment condition runs the risk of causing inflationary price spirals along the upward rising classical aggregate supply curve. Every full-employment point of output and price relationship in the Keynesian sense is associated with an inflationary regime of aggregate demand and supply in the monetarist view. The result then is complete irreconcilability between the epistemic and ontic views of relations governing the dynamics of the monetary sector. The disparate consequences here pervade both the behavioural side of liquidity preferences and the institutional side of monetary management.

In conclusion, the disparateness between the epistemic and ontic cause and effect of relationships in Hume's ideas of reality and relations are seen to result in the problem of non-integration between genesis and appearance. On the side of genesis, monetary theory under Hume's ontology is reduced to ontic reprieve of the *a priori* relations of the originary, now taken up at the inductive level of inference. On the side of appearance, the originary condition is vested in the ontic, without being able to prove the *a priori* relation of unified cause and effect between the monetary sector and the real goods sector, between Keynesianism and monetarism, between price level and quantity of money.

The institutional implications that these ontic consequences have on the political economy are pronounced in utilitarianism. The Benthamite utilitarian relation characterises the ontic concept of happiness in terms of material acquisitions, while Aristotle equated happiness with ethics, stating, 'Perhaps . . . it seems a truth which is generally admitted, that happiness is the supreme good.'[11] Thus either the carnal significance or the ethical equation of happiness with freedom and truth, centres the purpose of life and the meaning of individual and social relations, to the premise of material effects.

Conversely, if freedom is equated with happiness, then it is of temporal origin and material ends alone. Therefore happiness and hence freedom in this temporal domain suffer from the same methodological problem as that shown in the case of discontinuity between genesis and appearance, and between 'reason space' and 'divine space', in view of the overarching reality of total space, within which 'reason space' remains synthetically embedded and operational by cause and effect.

The legacy of the Aristotelian concept of happiness in utilitarianism led to the formalisation of a theory of morals and civil liberty for the occidental viewpoint, which remains bound by the ontic incompleteness of physical forms. In the epistemic sense the Aristotelian equation of ethics to happiness provides an epistemic but not a unified view of freedom through divine essence. The epistemic and the ontic thus remain distinct essences in all occidental thought. How then can the essence of knowledge as a unified reality be possible in such a dichotomous order?

A CRITIQUE OF KANTIAN EPISTEMOLOGY

Kant's theory of knowledge epitomises the dichotomy between the *a priori* and the *a posteriori* realms of total reality. For Kant, as a metaphysicist, only the *a priori* realm of pure and practical reason was capable of knowledge: 'This, then, is a question which at least calls for closer examination, and does not permit any off-hand answer: whether there is any knowledge that is thus independent of experience and even of all impressions of the senses. Such knowledge is entitled *a priori*, and is distinguished from the *empirical*, which has its sources *a posteriori*, that is, in experience.' Kant continues, 'In what follows, therefore, we shall understand by *a priori* knowledge, no knowledge independent of this or that experience, but knowledge absolutely independent of all experience. Opposed to it is empirical knowledge, which is knowledge possible only *a posteriori*, that is, through experience. *A priori* modes of knowledge are entitled pure when there is no admixture of anything empirical.'[12]

The realm of practical reason to Kant is an extension of the concept of pure reason to the area of sensible cognition. Thus cognition, according to practical reason, is determined by the primordiality of pure reason bearing upon the determination of practical reason in the world of sensibility. That is, according to the precept of practical reason, 'reason space' is imbued by the set of principles that guide theory and sensation in the *a posteriori* world of experience. On the other hand, the space of pure reason is imbued by moral law. Kant attached as high a value to moral law as the Greek philosophers writing on morality, truth, beauty and ethics in the governance of the household, state and political economy.[13]

Practical reason is further dichotomised into analytical and synthetic subspaces.[14] The subspace of analytical reason comprises the independent existence of an event, wherein the event can be fully described independently of any subsequent relations with other events. The subspace of synthetic reason comprises mathematical relations that can be extended to an event in connection with other events around it.

When the dichotomies between pure and practical reason and between analytical and synthetic reason are so observed, then a fundamental problem of inconsistency arises in the area of unification of knowledge. The question is posed as follows: if the space of practical reason is a subset of the space of pure reason, then there must be an empty area between the two, wherein practical reason does not function. In this area events have no practical relevance, and therefore remain unpurposeful for experience, observation and life. Mathematical relations become mere figments of the mind, without any analytical significance for observation or experience. The world as we must know it now in order to acquire knowledge, becomes systemically individuated, uncompromising between metaphysical nicety and useful knowledge.

Next, with regard to synthetic knowledge within the space of practical reason, a section of the total knowledge space remains integrative and interactive, whereas another subset remains independent. The latter is termed 'analytical knowledge in reason space'. The consequence is that unification of knowledge can happen only in the synthetic domain and cannot be extended to the analytical domain. The universal unification of knowledge then remains an impossibility in Kantian view of epistemology.

The consequences of dichotomising knowledge along lines of pure and practical reason and between the synthetic and analytical domains are examples of knowledge being split between independent, non-interacting subsets. The universe then becomes a totality of *a priori* mathematical relations that cannot integrate and interact with systems in the framework of a world view. This is a massive debility for the development of logical scientific processes aimed at intersystemic interaction and integration. Modern science and the ultimate scope of scientific pursuit is now steeped in the quest for unified field theory across disciplines and a theory of everything or a theory of unified field in physics remains halted in this individuated and non-interacting form of the universe.[15]

Because of the individuation consequences of Kantian epistemology, Kant may be said to be the enforcer as well as the perpetuator of the methodological individualism that has entered the length and breadth of occidental science. This root of individualism is intrinsic to the self, the institutions and the state. A strong example of this Kantian legacy is the neoclassical principle of gross substitution between goods in the utility framework of decision making. In this context, even goods such as distributive equity and economic efficiency become subject to trade-off, as do 'bads' such as inflation and unemployment. Thus in Kant's theory of morals, justice and law there is trade-off, gross substitution, individuation and non-integration. In Kant's writings the result of dichotomising the *a priori* and the *a posteriori* is felt in the disparity between the concept of duty and of doing good as a moral prerequisite in the *a priori* realm and of acting not in accordance to these essences in the *a posteriori* world. Goodness then becomes an *a priori* concept. It is not invoked in the *a posteriori* realm. Moral law is then divided into an essence that can be imagined but not realised except through an imperfect relationship in the empirical world, and another essence that remains imperfect when emanating from the empirical world. The ontic world thus loses any capacity to reflect the regenerative power of the pure moral law. Kant wrote in this regard,

> There must be a schema corresponding to the law of nature to which the objects we observe with our sense are subject; that is, it must have a general method for the imagination by which it can exhibit *a priori* to the senses the pure intellectual concept which the law determines. But the law of freedom, and consequently the concept of the unconditionally good, cannot be based upon any things-seen, nor upon any schema supplied for the purpose of applying the laws concrete. Consequently the moral law depends upon the intellect for its application to the objects of nature, certainly not upon the imagination.[16]

We note from the above that the *a priori* and *a posteriori* are utterly non-integrative and non-interactive, except by way of an imperfect relationship between the essentially synthetic domain of the *a priori* and the *a posteriori* domain of cognitive realism. What then is the utility of the essence of moral law for lived experience? What is the relevance of divine law in Kant's epistemology in relation to the evolutionary epistemology circularly interconnected between the regenerative processes of the *a priori* and the *a posteriori*?

Kant has no answer to such circularly interrelated processes. Divine laws, if taken up with the *a priori*, belong to the realm of pure or practical reason and are then subject to analytical thema, for Kant saw faith as the divine return for the best moral accomplishment of man.[17] Yet within the temporal limitation of 'reason space', morality in relation to faith would mean its finite equation to freedom and happiness, just as in Greek thought. This is a physical representation of moral needs and must therefore belong to the space of practical reason of the analytical type. Consequently, in spite of the high moral weight given to divine law, it is seen as a textual creation of the human mind and not as a divine act. In other words, the human mind is seen to determine the existence of divine law and not *vice versa*. Kant wrote, 'Faith, then, denotes trust in God that He will supply our deficiency in things beyond our power, provided we have done all within our power.'[18]

KANTIAN DUALISM

In the above sections, the derivation of ideas such as neoclassical gross substitution between goods, separation of the *a priori* and *a posteriori* domains in the subspaces of pure and practical reason with synthetic and analytical knowledge, and the determination of moral law on a scale of rationalism functionally distinct from the worldly impact of primordial divine laws, establish duality in the act of knowing. The *a priori* is the essence of laws; yet it exists only in the imagination and is not capable of being experienced. Hence its functional relevance is limited to 'reason space'. The latter is primary in the explanation of 'divine space', and not *vice versa*. Thus 'divine space' becomes a *non sequitur* in universal moral law. The cognitive treatment of divinity, within the framework of reason alone, bestows the divine order with the corporeal attributes of imagination, experience and appearance through the *a priori* impact on the ontic phenomena (*a posteriori*) but not *vice versa*. The universe and reality thus remain separate in all spheres. This is the essence of duality in Kant. It at once pervades as the individuation process and annuls the characterisation of divine essence by assuming the supremacy of 'reason space'. Kant wrote in this regard, 'But whence do we acquire the concept of God as the supreme good? Simply from the *idea* of moral perfection which reason sketches *a priori* and connects separately with the concept of free will.'[19]

Let us tackle a final question as a reprieve of Kant's epistemology: can *a priori* conditions pervade all events that occur, so as to establish the Kantian originary principle of knowledge? If we accept that this condition prevails and pervades universally, then the 'reason span' will finally span 'divine space' and total space universally. Thus the moral law of Kant being simply reason-determined, God takes a cognitive form. On the other hand, if divine moral law is equated with the *a priori*, then its essence remains outside the 'reason space' and can then never be sensed except by reason alone. Consequently such a characterisation of moral law is a *non sequitur* in Kant's epistemology.

In no way, therefore, is it possible to reduce Kant's epistemological methodology to an irreducible core of knowledge, and thereby to integrate its essence by a circular route of cause and effect between the epistemic (*a priori*) and the ontic (*a posteriori*). Hence a universally integrated field of reality cannot emerge from such a theory of knowledge. The inability to reduce knowledge to its most irreducible form points to the impossibility of knowledge in Kant's epistemology.

MARX, HUME AND KANT AND THE CRISIS OF SCIENCE

The abovementioned problem of duality, individuation and methodological incompleteness without the possibility of extension, reduction and unification in a universally interactive–integrative field is the crisis of occidental science. This crisis can be traced to the methodologies presented by Marx, Hume and Kant, which, it is contested here, do not differ from each other.

Marx, emulating Hegel, followed the dialectical process formulated by Kant solely within the 'reason space'. Freedom was thus equated with material happiness (economism for Marx). Dialectical historicism was then interpreted as a conflict between interest groups to acquire a greater share of this happiness or freedom.

However, the fact that Marx did not invoke an *a priori* concept makes him non-Kantian and non-epistemological. Neither was he ontological, which would have been the case if an *a priori* premise had characterised ontic experience. Marx was thus simply an empiricist. In this sense, the dialectical materialism in Marxist scientism cannot be taken up as an analytical process. We therefore find that, in the hands of dialectical materialism, occidental science has been delimited by a methodological bound of ontic phenomena that cannot be further extended by *a priori* analytics.

Hume, being an ontologist, provided a reprieve of Kant from the originary condition of the *a posteriori* to the terminal realisation of the *a priori*. The concept of material transcendence in reality subjects analytical reasoning to inductive methods. They thus become objects of individualistic preferences, character and interpretation. Randomness and incompleteness thereby prevail in determining how the universe evolves and learns. Hume's ontological approach has left a similar indeterminateness. It is based on a sheer materialistic interpretation of reality. Such a perceptual world can only be further compounded by individualism in the development of occidental science and its natural laws. Natural liberty, as opposed to moral origins, was a consequence of this materialistic approach to the study of occidental science.

In Kant's epistemology, the treatment of *a priori* as an originary phenomenon is similar to the treatment by Hume of the *a posteriori*. In addition this *a priori* realm is bestowed with the same degree of randomness and indeterminateness as a speculative process of inquiry in establishing reality. Duality and the absence of universally unified relations make it impossible to attain knowledge in its most irreducible form. The crisis suffered by occidental science in Kant's epistemology and Hume's ontology is one of failure to develop a unified field to explain reality by combining the *a priori* with the *a posteriori*.

Husserl noted the crisis of occidental science. He disagreed with Kant's dichotomy between noumena and phenomena, and argued that Kant's noumena was unattainable. Hence it bore no precise functional relation to the world of experience and knowledge could not be grounded on noumena, or in other words on Kant's *a priori* domain. Instead Husserl argued that in order to realise phenomena, the idea of noumena would have to be integrated with the experiential world. In this sense, then, Husserl's phenomenology came closer to Humean ontology. Consequently, although Husserl tried to argue in favour of a methodology of integration between the epistemic and the ontic, his rejection of the purely primordial domain of irreducible knowledge, the one which sees 'divine space' as the all-encompassing total space of reality, meant that it remained outside the realm of phenomena and was considered by Husserl to be unnecessary in scientific knowledge.[20] The crisis of occidental science – this intrinsic, non-unifying gap – was observed but not solved by Husserl.

A similar debility in the methodology of occidental philosophy can be discerned in the deductive process. If Kant's or Husserl's deductionism means the grounding of all events and observations on a previous set of laws, then the 'reason space', which randomises and dichotomises such laws, remains full of differentiated perceptions. Consequently there remain several sets of laws that are candidates for the deductive explanation of events and observations. The deductive premise in this sense is speculatively analytical or synthetic. The purpose of uniqueness in scientific explanation is lost in a quagmire of differentiated perceptions.

Reichenbach acknowledged this problem of occidental science emanating from methodologies of the Kantian type.[21] He pointed out that the *a priori* definition of space-time could only be applied to the macrocosm, not to the microcosm. Even if this were possible, the approach would have to be different. Consequently a unique set of laws would not be able to bring about unification within and between the macroscopic and the microscopic and the natural sciences and the social sciences. Differentiation in the name of the scientific hegemony of compartmentalised disciplines thus became the order of day in occidental science.

TOWARDS THE UNIFICATION OF KNOWLEDGE IN POST-OCCIDENTAL SCIENCE

Unifying knowledge across and within all scientific systems thus remains the ultimate postmodern challenge. Unification here means the determination of a set of laws that emanates from the irreducible truth that is fundamental to all systems. The need for irreducibility arises from the necessity of grounding all scientific laws, knowledge, observation and analysis on a moral premise. Such a moral world view is not one that is exogenously ethical, as in perceived science. Instead the treatment of ethics as part and parcel of the development of scientific laws is a centrally endogenous investigation emanating from and reinforcing the roots of moral law. When so comprehended, the endogenously moral premise of science cannot simply rest in the realm of a Kantian-type *numinous noumena* (*a priori*) and its prototype in Hegelian dialectics. Likewise it cannot be simply an experiential interpretation of reality by recourse to cognitive perceptions, as in the ontological conception of reality by Hume, Marx, Husserl and Reichenbach.[22] This corporeal delimitation has pervaded *all* of occidental science, beginning with Greek philosophy in terms of its equating freedom with happiness, and continuing in more recent times with the dualism between mind and matter set down by modern philosophers of science such as Russell[23] and Whitehead.[24]

In order to establish the renewal and continuity principle of a circularly interactive-integrative universal order, the primal and bounded 'reason space' falls apart and gives way to the universality of total space. This is identical to divine space, but with the distinct property that it is topologically functional between itself and reason space. The latter is then simply a cognitive occurrence of the topological action of divine space upon reason space. The actions reveal themselves as events in the midst of circular causation and continuity between the epistemic (*a priori*) and the ontic (*a posteriori*) phenomena of life and mind. In such a framework, every moment in the epistemic–ontic circular causation and continuity process is a creative moment, and hence must be a unique function of evolutionary knowledge derived and discursed on the premise of the cognitive influence of divine space (noumenal), followed by its effect on reason space and then recreated *vice versa* through reinforcement by the knowledge advancement.[25]

In this primal divine space where knowledged formation is interacted and integrated in discursively iterated manner with reason space, the emergence of scientific law follows the textual understanding and furtherance of the nature of epistemic–ontic circular causation and continuity process as a fundamental essence of creation. Knowledge simulation becomes functional only on this plane, as it derives from the primal stock of divine space and is transformed into flows in the evolutionary phase. All cognition then is the material or mental representation of the topological function of divine space on reason space through backward and forward continuity. The deductive thus becomes integrated with the inductive and dualism is annulled. Its manifestation in systemic individuation and non-interaction is destroyed. Moral laws become one with the physical world and are continuously comprehended through their relationship with its experience. Thus both dualism and the impossibility of noumena or of the originary randomness of the ontic perceptions of Hume and Marx, for example, are replaced by the universal principle of complementarity, interaction and integration across and within systems.

The endogenous nature of moral law in scientific knowledge is brought out by the interactive process of the epistemic–ontic circular causation methodology. All relations explaining inherent inter- and intrasystemic interactions are of a topological nature. The simulatively dynamic parameter of these relations, which endogenises all state and policy variables, is the knowledge variable. Hence all systemic relations, be they energy equations, pricing theory in ethicised market transactions and so on, are uniquely explained by knowledge centricity. This in turn is the cause and effect of the epistemic-ontic process in all systems. Only the specificity of the problems confronting different systems can vary.

To explain further, the energy equation is now determined by the interaction between flows of knowledge variables and their complementary material form, which in turn is induced by the knowledge-interaction process and generates the further diffusion of knowledge. Thus energy becomes the output of a series of interactions between the knowledge variables and the material world, augmented by the simulative knowledge formation process. The methodological orientation of this process is explained by the conservation and increasing generation of energy, as knowledge is always cumulative over evolutionary flows. The uniqueness of the methodology is explained by the epistemic–ontic circular causation and continuity model of unified creation. The moral perspective of the methodology arises from the generation of evolutionary flows of knowledge from a primal stock comprising the divine space. The certainty of the predictive capacity of this process is shown by precise mappings 'on to' and between the knowledge space and the material order.

Any topologically functional relation that does not satisfy the uniqueness principle, and is invariant up to a monotonic scalar transformation of the individuating processes, is a case of dualism, and thus cannot belong to the endogenous world view of the moral foundation of scientific knowledge.

The universal principle of complementarity between events now becomes the cause and effect of an interactive and integrative, inter- and intrasystemic world view. This, together with the primacy of knowledge in the simulative epistemic–ontic circular causation and continuity model, becomes the endogenous creative process integrating divine space with reason space. The latter is the material cognition of the former.

Such a moral world view has been absent from the philosophical structure of occidental science since the time of the ancient Greeks, because reason space was either made self-sufficient or divine space was placed outside purposeful creative activity. The result has thus been the moral irrelevance of occidental science, and the impossibility of attaining knowledge as the irreducible embryonic core of life and experience in this order. In this case of the role of a random search for unification of knowledge, occidental science takes its flight from and into the field of speculation and indeterminateness. Occidental science is thus individualistic, and does not focus purposefully on morality. This is the vagary of the culture of occidental science that does not provide the essence of reality. Holton refers to this as private and public science. It pursues a paradigm that is promoted and advanced by a school of adherents (a scientific research programme), a pursuit that can very well be politically and financially diverted from the search for essential truth (divine order). A meaningful explanation of divine space in the totality of scientific reality received its parting blow in occidental science with the arrival of the Age of Enlightenment and the fall of the Church's explaination of divine reality, when the Church was swept away by the metaphysical speculations of Greek philosophy.

THE ISLAMIC DERIVATION OF THE EPISTEMIC-ONTIC CIRCULAR CAUSATION AND CONTINUITY MODEL OF UNIFIED REALITY

The postmodern era of scientific revival is a return to the centrality of the endogenous moral foundations of scientific laws in the context of the epistemic–ontic circular causation and continuity model of unified reality. Its manifestation, combining the normative with the positive, the deductive with the normative, and divine (total) space with reason space, is to be found in the universal creation theory provided by the *Qur'an*. This text of the moral law includes a central reference to the normative function of knowledge and to the positivistic function of the traditions of Prophet Muhammad towards the understanding and operation of normative law. This creation theory, centred on the primacy of knowledge, presents the endogenous world view of moral law as the ultimate reality of life and experience.

The *Qur'anic* creation theory assumes topologically mathematical principles based on the unique methodology of a unified and justly ordered universe made possible by the pervasiveness and centrality of divine knowledge. This is also the epistemic–ontic circular causation and continuity model of unified reality. The physical, experimental, observational, synthetic and analytical positions of scientific knowledge are derived from the application of epistemic–ontic methodology to the material world. The reality and prediction, certainty and uniqueness of the knowledge-centred epistemic–ontic methodology are established by complementarity, unification and renewal. Thus topological mathematical relations become the medium for explaining simultaneously the *a priori* and *a posteriori* interrelationships in unified reality.

The *Qur'an* has many verses about the centrality of knowledge in universal unification, reorigination, mind–matter harmony and certainty, and provides methods to achieve these relations:

1. 'Proclaim! And thy Lord Is Most Bountiful, – He Who taught [The use of] the Pen, – Taught man that Which he knew not.' (chapter 96, verses 1–5) (centrality of knowledge gained incrementally)
2. 'Such is God, your real Cherisher and Sustainer: Apart from Truth, What (remains) by error? How then are ye turned away?' (chapter 10, verse 32) (universal certainty based on binary reality (truth and falsehood)
3. 'It is God Who originates Creation and repeats it: Then how are ye deluded Away (from the truth)?' (chapter 10, verse 34) (creations

theory: epistemic–ontic circular causation and continuity model of unified reality)

4. 'Your (real) friends are (No less than) God, His Apostle, and the (Fellowship Of) Believers . . .'. (chapter 5, verse 53) (combination of normative and positive methodology in scientific enquiry)

5. 'He rules (all) affairs From the heavens To the earth: in the end Will (all affairs) go up To Him.' (chapter 32, verse 5) (unification and pervasiveness of the knowledge-centred creation theory, inter- and intrasystem)

6. ' . . . He began The creation of man With (nothing more than) clay, And made his progeny From a quintessence Of the nature of A fuid despised: But He fashioned him In due proportion, and breathed Into him something of His spirit.' (chapter 32, verses 7–9) (interaction and integration of the noumenal (moral) with the phenomenal (physical) aspects of total reality)

7. 'Do they not reflect In their own minds? Not but for just ends And for a term appointed, Did God create the heavens And the earth, and all Between them.' (the principle of universal complementarity premised on the centrality of knowledge in moral law)

8. 'Glorify the name Of thy Guardian-Lord Most High, Who hath created, And further, given Order and proportion; Who hath ordained laws, And granted guidance.' (chapter 87, verses 1–2) (divine laws as the moral centre of the natural and social orders which can be treated by the essence of order signified by topological mathematical precepts)

9. 'Seest thou not how God sets forth a parable? – A goodly Word Like a goodly tree, Whose root is firmly fixed, And its branches (reach) To the heavens, – (the endogenous nature of the divine laws underlying universal reality and ensuing from its felicitous material benefits). It brings forth its fruit At all times, by the leave Of its Lord. So God sets forth parables For men, in order that They may receive admonition. And the parable Of an evil Word Is that of an evil tree: It is torn up by the root From the surface of the earth: It has no stability.' (chapter 14, verses 24–6) (this is contrasted with the endogenous nature of falsehood, which advances towards moral and material decadence in its own plane. The embryonic and per-petuating interrelationship between moral law (goodly Word) and material rewards (goodly tree) signifies the unifying process and certainty)

CONCLUSION

We have shown in this chapter, by recourse to a comparative study of the philosophy of science, that the epistemological quest has not reached its end in occidental science. As a consequence it is random, uncertain and speculative, and thus incapable of establishing knowledge as the irreducible limit of inquiry. Furthermore it is handicapped by the cultural orientations that have caused its individuated pluralism. The core of the problem is seen to be the dichotomised view of reality that has been entrenched institutionally in Western society by its philosophers of science since time immemorial. This dichotomy is found to be at work between divine space and reason space; between mind and matter; between the *a priori* and the *a posteriori* domains of knowledge; between noumena and phenomena; between the synthetic and analytical categorisations of reason. In general, this is tantamount to independence of the methodologies emanating from the purely epistemic and the purely ontic.

The crisis of postmodernism is essentially the debility caused by this non-interactive, non-integrative aspect of the occidental perception of reality. In order to break away from it, postmodernism and the ultimate emergence of new science is seen to be entrenched in endogenising the moral foundations of science. This brings us to the primacy of divine space, from which reason emerges harmoniously as a cognitive realisation, and thus generates the creative entirety encompassing observation, analysis, prediction and their continued furtherance.

The unification of knowledge in the methodology of the epistemic–ontic circular causation and continuity model of unified reality, seen here as the logical emergence of the primacy of divine space, is found uniquely to emerge from the *Qur'an*. The principles of unification, universal complementarity, uniqueness and certainty characterise the knowledge-centred world view that first emanates from the primacy of divine space over all subsequent phenomenology and then recreates itself.

3 Evolutionary Epistemology and Ethical Social Choice in the Islamic Perspective

The main objective of this chapter is to establish a knowledge-based social choice and social welfare function for the Islamic politico-economic order, wherein an altogether different concept of knowledge from that perceived in Western epistemology is invoked. In our progress towards this the precept of the unicity (oneness) of God (*Tawhid* in Islamic literature) will be thoroughly utilised. More conceptually, the unicity precept is taken up in this chapter to bestow meaning on the socio-scientific order. The emphasis is on unicity as God's oneness and spontaneously creative essence in the universe. The essence of unity is further substantiated through the world view of unification between the sciences of society and nature, and within different segments of society.

THE *TAWHIDI* PRECEPT

There is a substantive difference between the essence of what this author refers to as the field of unicity and the precept of unicity. The precept signifies the primordiality of all creations in a topological space of non-form, non-matter existence, unbounded by any initial condition. The field refers to the functional media for understanding and applying the primordiality of creation bestowed by the field. The field, being another highly sophisticated topic of study, is not the scope of this particular work. It is taken up in this author's *Epistemological Foundations.*[1]

It must not, however, be construed that the unicity field and the unicity precept are physical forms of the creativity of God, as was misconstrued by some of the early Islamic scholastic philosophers, following Hellenic metaphysical concepts. Rather these two concepts are unified. The field, being a function, is simply the spontaneous being or topological mapping of the primordiality of precept. There can be no room whatsoever for Kantian-type dualism or the Eastern philosophical mystification of multiplicity in the unicity precept.

56

THE STUDY OF EPISTEMOLOGY

To establish the building blocks of the social welfare methodology based on the knowledge plane of the Islamic ethico-economic system, we must first understand the concept of epistemology in this order. By definition, epistemology is the field of inquiry investigating the theory of knowledge. Its task is to study how knowledge is derived from its primal sources; how the sources of knowledge can be identified in different fields of scientific inquiry; and how that groundwork of knowledge can be disseminated. This approach to the study of epistemology has given rise to different categories of epistemology: an epistemology of science, an epistemology of religion, an epistemology of sociology and lately an epistemology of economics, starting with the Keynesian legacy in the economic literature.

While the attempts to study the epistemology of the sciences of nature and society were based on mankind's relentless pursuit of truth and rising from lesser to higher degrees of certainty, this pursuit was accompanied by growing independence and isolation between the sciences in the name of specialisation. A better understanding of the universe around us needs to be liberated from scientific narrowness and the hegemony of the disciplines and replaced by the universality of inter-relations among them. Such a methodology in a new epistemology of the sciences must result in the concept of a world view. It must negate the idea of political and cultural pluralism that pervades the dissected view of the modern sciences in particular. Social and scientific pluralism is thus replaced by the socio-scientific world view in the body of knowledge pertaining to some *a priori* realm. In this sense epistemology transcends the field of symbolic knowledge, as it investigates not only consistency in the relationships between phenomena but also seeks the true *a priori* roots of knowledge. Rationalism has thus become a mainstay of any epistemological inquiry. Yet the very concept of rationality and rationalism continues to defy a unique definition.

Kant's *Metaphysics of Morals* laid the foundation of an epistemology of Western thought that bases all sources of knowledge on individual reason unperturbed by any external influence.[2] This *a priori* bed of knowledge is treated as the sole source of knowledge, which then invokes human cognition in the *a posteriori* realm of experience. Yet the *a posteriori* or empirical realm is seen to have no substantive element for knowledge formation. Such a separation between the *a priori* and the *a posteriori* perception of total reality has given rise to dualism and multiplicity in Western and Eastern thought processes.

Thought processes mean here the entire set of relationships that bring about knowledge. The dualism and multiplicity in thought perception following the Kantian legacy have also been the cause of non-interactivity between the academic disciplines.

Kant's epistemology – being non-interactive between the two realms of knowledge, the *a priori* and the *a posteriori* – is essentially a non-evolutionary one. An evolutionary epistemology, on the other hand, is characterised by two features – growth in knowledge perception, and the presence of an interactive force that causes this knowledge perception to evolve over time.[3] Evolutionary epistemology develops knowledge comprehension through a sequence of interactions between the mental and sensory realms of experience. Through such interactions arises an evolving system of interrelationships between positive and normative views, between the *a priori* and knowable perceptions.

Although suitable for our purposes, this is not the perspective we obtain from Popper's conception of evolutionary epistemology. Popper's idea is based on the premise of scientific falsification whereby one paradigm supplants another in an endless sequence of scientific criticisability of the paradigms. In this way scientific knowledge is shown to proceed through the principle of falsification and criticisability in the knowledge domain.[4]

Popper's concept of evolutionary epistemology in the sciences leads to randomness of the knowledge domain, as no particular primordial knowledge base can be formulated that will standardise the scientific epistemology. Secondly, Popper's methodology is also subject to individual perceptions of reality. This in turn leads to multiple possibilities among all the individual approaches to knowledge perception. A uniquely well-defined, primordial foundation is impossible in Popper's concept of evolutionary epistemology. Indeed its subservience to random ways of acquiring differentiated knowledge raises the possibility of chaos rather than orderliness in the universe. There may be a long-run harmonisation of knowledge to bring about some form of order, but there is no specific methodological way of deriving order out of chaos.

Next we have the social Darwinian approach to evolutionary epistemology,[5] which draws on the Darwinian theory of natural selection to portray the growth of knowledge through well-ordered sequences of experience. Scientific knowledge is seen as imitating the biological world in that there is well-ordered natural selection between categories of knowledge in the various disciplines. Thus in social Darwinism the perpetuation of knowledge is seen as a perpetuation of mutually distinct but selected patterns of thought. In Social Darwinism, while the randomness of Popperian falsification is removed, the problem of non-interactivity between the realms of reality remains. The evolution of knowledge is thus a perpetuation of isolated patterns.

Between the Popperian and the social Darwinian approaches to evolutionary epistemology are the hierarchical selection models of knowledge formation.[6] Such models are based on the properties of bounded randomness in the criticisability framework of reference and the lack of complete well-ordering in the uncertainty framework of bounded rationality. However, the problem of leaving the primordial knowledge base and developing its *a priori* and *a posteriori* interactions still persists, for the essence of independence of group-specific knowledge premise, its consequential individualistic element, is not removed. This characteristic of all the paradigms of evolutionary epistemology makes it impossible for knowledge to be generated out of interactive experience.

We therefore find that, in the literature on evolutionary epistemology, non-interactivity remains between the groups of disciplines, although interactivity within these disciplines is maximised. This non-interactivity contradicts the essence of evolutionary epistemology in its alternative form defined above. For the fuller concept of evolutionary epistemology in the sciences, it is necessary not simply to derive the *a priori* field of knowledge but also to explain how the acquisition of knowledge proceeds towards that *a priori* primordiality through a series of interactions between the *a priori* and the *a posteriori* and between the group-specific disciplines.

In the unicity framework, the pluralism of thought processes in group-specific disciplines is replaced by the essence of unity and interactions. It is not derived from the vagaries of individualistic imagination. Thus the unicity precept assumes a world view and negates scientific, social and cultural pluralism among peoples. For the unicity precept to define the new concept of evolutionary epistemology, its comprehension must be based on the simplest of axioms. Such axioms must be easily accessible and comprehensible to all people.

But although the unicity precept is based on the axioms of its evident and immanent truth in the socio-scientific universe, its full comprehension is beyond realisation in the temporal world. Thus all knowledge perception in the unicity precept is a flight from the primordiality of God's unicity in the order of things to its discovery through the evolutionary process. Then there is the pervasiveness of this unicity premise in all things, which leads to the inevitable interdependence and unification among all knowledge premises through the evolutionary process. The *Tawhidi* epistemology thus reflects the gradual unfolding of the spring of knowledge from lesser to higher degrees of certainty as the quest for the Godly laws proceeds.

This is indeed how Ibn Al-Arabi explained his Islamic epistemology. Chittick writes in this regard, in his translation of Al-Arabi's *Al-Futuhat Al-Makiyyah* (the Makkan Revelations):[7]

> Two ways lead to knowledge of God. There is no third way. The person who declares God's Unity in some other way follows authority in his declaration.
> The first way is the way of unveiling. It is an incontrovertible knowledge which is actualized through unveiling and which man finds in himself. . . .
> The second way is the way of reflection and reasoning (*istidlal*) through rational demonstration (*burhan aqli*). This way is lower than the first way, since he who bases his consideration upon proof can be visited by obfuscations which detract from his proof, and only with difficulty can he remove them.

The universe, then, is seen in the *Tawhidi* world view as springing from the reality of God in the order of things, which is evolving in the midst of grand equilibrium and order, harmony and purpose. This *Tawhidi* precept is inexorable. The *Qur'an* presents it as an undeniable truth. Individuals and societies may or may not recognise it consciously, but the *Tawhidi* process manifests itself in reality. The conscious realisation of the *Tawhidi* epistemology from its roots of revelation, followed by its conversion into cognitive thought, marks the formation of knowledge.[8]

The evolutionary epistemology of the *Tawhidi* precept is thus laid down in the framework of the redefinition of this concept. This epistemology in the socio-scientific order is characterised by uniqueness of the knowledge base. It is evolutionary in the sense of mankind's perpetual movement towards realisation of the *Tawhidi* precept. It presents knowledge as being in the midst of order and certainty. It is based on an essentially interactive and unifying function.

EPISTEMOLOGICAL QUESTIONS

The unicity precept in the sciences of nature and society leads us to believe that realisation of this precept and its mobilisation in all spheres of thought invokes profound epistemological questions. First, what is the purpose of knowledge and learning? Second, what are the fundamental sources of knowledge that can help fulfil the purpose of knowledge? Third, is perfect knowledge attainable, and if so, how can it be attained? Fourth, how can this form of knowledge acquisition be used by society at large? How can such knowledge be organised to give it the quality of a human resource, and thus be used in development planning by national and world governments? The answers to these questions place the topic of human resource development within the perspective of the unicity precept.

Before answering the question of the purpose of knowledge we must first ask what knowledge is. To use Boulding's idea, knowledge is a cognitive structure of the mind that helps an entity attain its image in the midst of its environment. Boulding applies this image-base of knowledge to the human world and other living organisms. Thus while man builds his image through interactions within himself, with his society and with the universe around, all other living organisms attain their image by mutation and homeostasis with the corresponding interactive field of activity and its survival.[9] In both these realms, knowledge as image is seen to be a means of growth and establishment of a biological form.[10]

Thus knowledge is an innate quality in all living things that have the ability to grow and evolve in accordance with their environment. This idea of knowledge shares the perspective of the general equilibrium systems approach, in which a large number of interactive activities are going on. This contributes to the growth process of both the individual and the system at large. But being a system, there are necessarily initial conditions, checks and balances, choices and alternatives through which the players in the system proceed towards their goals. An evolutionary system of knowledge acquisition and the process of attaining identity – homoeostasis through knowledge – sets in.[11] However, a deeper question now arises. In the quest for image identity and reinforcing it in a systemic framework, do all players succeed together? Do they all fail together? Or is it that the system itself succeeds or fails, and some in the system fail or succeed as a result? The answer to this last question is a social one. Let us investigate this more closely.

A generalised systems approach in the social sciences, according to the Western schools of thought – the neoclassicists, the Keynesians, the dependency theorists, the world systems theorists – have always meant a trade-off between ethical values and economic efficiency. That is, if the systems are to be ethically oriented, then there must be a proportionate sacrifice in economic efficiency. The neoclassicists call this substitution between equity and efficiency in resource allocation,[12] while the Keynesians see it as a trade-off between unemployment and the price level. Keynes himself referred to such a phenomenon in his idea of the underemployment equilibrium.[13] While the classical economic school did not treat a general equilibrium framework of analysis, the new classicists, following Milton Friedman, see the fiscal side as price elastic, and the unemployment rate as rigid at the long run rate.[14] Thus a price-unemployment trade-off of classical economic theory exists among the monetarists.

Then there are the dependency development theorists, who see the process of development as a conflict between the core, which thrives, and the periphery, which is perpetually subjected to the economism of the core. Thus the development of the core determines the development of the periphery.[15] The world systems theorists see global dependency as a historical process. Thus the rise of capitalism and the impoverisation of the Third World are seen not so much as particular cases of the core–periphery debacle, but as the result of conflict between two historical systems of development.[16]

Turning now to the implications of all these approaches to certain human phenomena in the systems theory of knowledge using Western models, we arrive at the following conclusion. All such systems involve a trade-off, which in the systems approach to the study of knowledge must imply that the overall growth of the knowledge system may not mean growth of each of its components. There are those who will win and those who will lose – not simply because of their differential skills and successes, but because of the conflict in the power structure of the system. This is the unsocial view of the systems model of knowledge in spite of the profound value placed on knowledge acquisition as a medium for acquiring and perpetuating a cognitive structure. Consequently much of the knowledge base and its purpose is lost. First, if knowledge as cognitive structure for perpetuating an image denies that possibility in the Western systems framework, then there must be two mistakes in this concept of knowledge. Either the concept of knowledge is that of a cognitive means of ensuring social and economic survival, or its definition misses a more profound epistemological truth. If knowledge is a cognitive means towards social and economic power, then such knowledge simply enhances the power struggle, which is pervasively de-equalising.[17] On the other hand, the absence of a more profound basis of knowledge in the Western systems approach makes it standardise knowledge of conflict within the power structure.

The second problem with the Western system of knowledge is its structural inability to reduce the knowledge base to anything more elemental than a means of acquiring material forms of the cognitive structure. This problem is seen as a historical fact that dawned in the eighteenth century in the wake of scholasticism and the industrial revolution in Europe. It brought material plenty and the liberal freedom to question and choose. Individualism became the expression of these various attributes of human liberty. The acquisition of truth through knowledge thus became individualistic determinism.

The events that led to this individualistic rationalism in the understanding and application of knowledge were mixed. First there was the inability of the Church to explain the relevance of Christianity in the realm of rationalism. The great minds of the time – Newton, Kant, Descartes, Leibniz, Spinoza – were all religiously inclined but vehemently disputed the relevance of the Church on matters of freedom in scientific inquiry, and thus the scientific community pronounced its independence from the religious domain. That was the beginning of the dualistic concept between God as a teleological myth and science as a rational, cognitive phenomenon. Ever since – in the sciences, society, economics and polity – this concept of dualism has prevailed in some ineradicable form to sustain the power structure and growth of the Western system. The knowledge base of the Western order began at this parting point of Church and science. Knowledge in such a system thereby perpetuates, first, its cognitive structural philosophy, and second, its functional, if not *a priori*, independence from a deeper epistemological root.

Hence we can come to three conclusions with respect to the treatment of knowledge in the Western framework. First, the concept of knowledge is one of a cognitive power structure enforcing individual images within a system of conflict between individuals. Second, there is the indelible concept of dualism. Third, there is the absence of an epistemological premise for precisely conveying the meaning of knowledge. The concept of knowledge therefore needs a meaning and a new hierarchy of organisation in an alternative general systems approach.

EASTERN EPISTEMOLOGY

Now let us turn to the Eastern philosophy of knowledge, as found in Confucianism, Buddhism and Hinduism. In each of these systems there is a hierarchical notion of reality. There is a constant effort to discover the final unity of life, but this is based on pluralism. According to Capra:

The most important characteristics of the Eastern world view – one could almost say the essence of it – is the awareness of the unity and mutual interrelation of all things and events, the experience of all phenomena in the world as manifestations of a basic oneness. All things are seen as interdependent and inseparable parts of this cosmic whole; as different manifestations of the same ultimate, indivisible reality which manifests itself in all things, and of which all things are parts. It is called Brahman in Hinduism, Dharmakaya in Buddhism, Tao in Taoism.[18]

Thus we find that in the Eastern philosophies too there is a systems concept of thought processes. Yet the blur in the concept of knowledge comes through the emptiness of the concept of oneness as a speculative metaphysical entity, not well-defined, and therefore incapable of imparting precise form and order to the mental construct.

It leaves open the definition of space and time as variant concepts of reality, and is therefore incapable of defining reality. Accordingly no precise foundation of the knowledge premise can be established. The epistemological foundation of thought is reduced to an empty premise. Besides, the premise of duality is now extended to multiplicity, for the mathematical 'union' of 'all' things as representations of the 'one' is not the same thing as the representation of the 'one' in everything. In the context of the absolute and intuitionist infinite set structure, we cannot define in this case uniquely inverse mappings between the 'one' set and the multiple sets.[19]

SUMMARY

The meaning of knowledge cannot therefore be based simply on its cognitive structure as a means of enhancing the image of a power structure in a systems framework. Instead, there is a real possibility for such a system to admit of consistency between efficiency and equity, in the sense that no one single player in the system perpetuates its power over another in asserting its image. If this is possible, then the systems model of knowledge denotes a stock of knowledge wherein each of its players is made well-off simultaneously – not through a trade-off among the goals and agents of competition. The growth of such a system ensues not from aggressive competition, but through complementarity and integration. These are in fact the attributes of cooperation.

While it is substitution that plays the key role in the allocative and growth processes of the Western system of knowledge, in the unicity precept it is goodwill, participation and complementarity in the division of labour that provides the income multiplier effect to the growth processes of the system, with simultaneity between efficiency and equity prevailing. The rate of growth of such a system, through the incentive effect of participation and the greater mobilisation of knowledge as a resource, is expected to be much faster than in the competing system. This is supported on grounds of the economy of scale effect caused by the sum total of pecuniary and non-pecuniary benefits of the knowledge base.[20]

APPLICATION OF THE UNICITY PRECEPT TO A THEORY OF KNOWLEDGE

To the systems model of knowledge with equity–efficiency simultaneity we now add the epistemological base of unification to understand the meaning and observe the manifestation of reality. Such a unified knowledge base must be capable of a unique set of interrelationships between the unified set and its representations in reality. The same set of representations must be capable of generating a string of evolutionary regeneration of the unified set.

Let A_i ($i = 1, 2, \ldots$) be subsets of T. In other words, each A_i is a flow of knowledge in the experiential order arising from the divine law, which is T. Now since T is the unified set, its subsets are all perceptions of the T-set in an evolutionary phase. Now the mapping of T to A_2 can be seen as a composition of the mappings of T to A_1 and A_1 to A_2. Likewise the mapping from T to A_n is a composition of the mappings T to A_1, A_1 to A_2, \ldots A_{n-1} to A_n. This hierarchy of mappings and their interrelationships mean that the unified set maps itself 'on to' the sets A_i in such a way that it preserves the inverse mapping only through an evolutionary relationship between the A_i sets.

Now, $\lim(n \to \infty)UA_i = T$, in the sense of equal cardinalities of these two infinite sets. In other words the primordial T in the first epistemology (divine origin: *Lauh Mahfuz*) becomes cardinally completed by the optimal realisation of the full stock of knowledge in *Akhira* (the hereafter). Thus the stock T evolves 'on to' itself ($T \to T$) through the process of temporal flows, A_i. The knowledge base in this generalised system has now come to attain its epistemological goal: to mobilise all knowledge towards greater comprehension of the T set of

morals and values, and to accomplish this through an evolutionary interrelationship between realities. The same epistemological basis in turn
provides the springboard for perpetuating a cognitive structure in the
real world out of an efficiency–equity perspective of complementarity
in the evolutionary process. In such a system the inconsistencies of
the one–many problem is resolved by the unique existence of simultaneity and unification between the axioms and functions of the knowledge system.

TOWARDS AN ISLAMIC THEORY OF KNOWLEDGE BASED ON THE UNICITY PRECEPT

What we have thus accomplished in the system of unified knowledge
is essentially the unicity basis of knowledge. The concept of Islamic
knowledge is a strong example of this unicity precept being applied to
its epistemology. It is based on the following key premises: the acquisition of obligatory knowledge (*Fard Ayn*), which is then supported by
requisite but not obligatory knowledge (*Fard Kifaya*). This Islamic
perspective of knowledge negates learning, as in the case of the Western defined cognitive structure, simply for image formation, to form a
medium for social superiority. It is rather an understanding of the purpose of knowledge that comes with the unicity precept (*Tawhid*), which
forms the differentiating tiers of social cognition among men. But this
fundamental root of knowledge, according to the *Qur'an*, is pervasive
and is acquired by all individuals by simple recourse to reason and
observation: 'Do they not look at God's creation, (even) among (in-
animate) things. . . . And to God does obeisance all that is in the heavens
and on earth, whether moving (living) creatures or the angels: for none
are ignorant before their Lord' (chapter XVI, v. 48–9).

EPISTEMOLOGICAL QUESTIONS ANSWERED BY THE UNICITY PRECEPT

Once we have explained the knowledge base in the Islamic framework, it is clear how our earlier questions have been answered. The
basis of the Islamic concept of knowledge has been shown to be the
unicity precept. The purpose of this knowledge base is to perpetuate a
two-fold evolutionary growth process in the systems model of knowledge
for Islamic society. This was explained above. The *Tawhidi* (unicity)

basis of knowledge defines *Fard Ayn*, to be derived from the understanding and application of the *Qur'an* and prophetic traditions (*Sunnah*). The *Fard Kifaya* base adds to this the institution of authoritative Islamic research with the consensus of the community or of the Islamic learneds (*Ijtihad* or *Qiyas*, respectively), which itself requires pursuit of the requisite knowledge for the exercise of interpretative power and technical matters according to the *Qur'anic* and *Sunnatic* understanding.

In this sense, then, the primary source of knowledge in Islam, the one that defines the epistemological basis of thought, is revelation. The scope of revealed knowledge is much broader than reason alone – revelation includes reason. The *Qur'an* says in this regard, 'And those who believe in God and His apostles – they are the sincere lovers of truth, and the witnesses who testify, in the eyes of their Lord: They shall have their reward and their light' (chapter VII, v. 19). *Ijtihad* as a means of applying reason to the understanding of revelation is derived from the *Qur'an* and *Sunnah* through consensus and analogy – *Ijma* and *Qiyas* respectively. It cannot be an abrogation of the revealed message. If this were to happen, the part and parcel of the *Tawhidi* precept in the socio-scientific order would be disturbed. The thought process would then encounter the problem of inconsistency, of one–many in its epistemological context. This would totally destroy the meaning and purpose of knowledge in Islam, as explained above.

REVELATION AND REASON IN *TAWHIDI* EPISTEMOLOGY

We now turn to the third of the questions asked earlier: can knowledge be attained, and if so, how? We have demonstrated with the T set and the A_i subsets of the T set that their interrelationships manifest an evolutionary process. In this the T set cannot be attained absolutely but can only be approximated to, in the sense of set-theoretic cardinalities for the $\lim(i \to \infty)UA_i$, and of the T set. This means that revealed knowledge is so vast that it cannot be fully comprehended by the simple exercise of human reason. However, in the set-theoretic cardinal sense, the greater the pursuit of the unicity precept in society, the nearer society will come to a perfect Islamic state. The power of that limiting set is then very large.[21] During the time of Prophet Muhammad this limiting value was exemplified by the state of Madinah, which can be seen as an ideal Islamic state. The Islamic State of Madinah thus becomes the epistemological spring of all the principles of the Islamic world view. This is true even though the material conditions of future Muslim

States were to advance beyond that of the City State of Madinah.

The pursuit of knowledge to establish the unicity base in its comprehensive sense must be done through the application of educational planning that is instrumental in this type of model. It is at this stage that knowledge becomes a human resource in the sense that it is promoted through a planning process. This planning process involves the allocation of educational expenditure according to priorities that reflect the socio-economic development of the world nation of Islam with respect to the integrative premise of unicity in the practical and moral values of society. This is the idea of consistency between economic efficiency and social equity discussed earlier. It is here that we see the evolution of fields of substantive inquiry such as Islamic political economy, Islamic sociology, Islamic sciences and so on.

FROM KNOWLEDGE TO HUMAN RESOURCE

Insofar as Islam places great value on individual freedom within the social context, the choices as to type of education and its financing is left to a mix of public and private-sector policies. Education investment decisions depend upon the monetary and spiritual returns that are expected to be gained by the individual.[22] This means there must be an appropriate labour market demand for the type of graduates being trained, and suggests that an Islamic system of human resource development must be supported by the overall evolution of the world nation of Islam. There must be an adaptive process to realise this planning goal. Post-evaluation of education expenditure by the public authorities in accordance with the overall Islamicisation process will depend upon the success and vitality of the *Shuratic* process (the embryonic and pervasive inter-active–integrative interrelationship between Islamic polity, *Shura* and the ecological order in the particular sense, and universally in the general sense). Such a process essentially establishes the polity–market interactions for regenerating the ethico-economic transformation of the Islamic socio-economic system.[23] Thus the passage from knowledge premise to human resource development in the Islamic framework provides a unison among theory, planning and methods.

FORMALISATION OF THE KNOWLEDGE-BASED SOCIAL WELFARE FUNCTION IN ISLAM

Now we will bring together the elements of the *Tawhidi* epistemology to establish the Islamic social choice and welfare function. We will then go on to show how such a social welfare function can be used to study human resource development in the Islamic perspective.

We defined earlier the primordial ethical vector $\theta(T)$, corresponding to the ultimate *Tawhid* set T, and based on Islamic law, towards which all knowledge development moves in the *Tawhidi* epistemology. While such a set and vector cannot be fully attained, subsets of T, such as A_i, $i = 1, 2, \ldots$, are temporally attainable. Corresponding to these knowledge subsets are vectors of knowledge parameters, such as (θ_i), where $\Theta_i = (\Theta_{i1}, \Theta_{i2}, \ldots, \Theta_{in}, \ldots)$, for $i = 1, 2, \ldots$, corresponding to phases of evolution of the subsets.

Note that in Islamic polity (*Shura*), decision makers (*Sharees*) assign ordinal values to θ_{ij} collectively out of a discursive process, $i, j = 1, 2, \ldots$. Therefore at any point of decision making there is a set-theoretic 'denumerable' valuation of these parameters. On the other hand, the realisation of the T-mind space comprises an infinite class of subsets. Thereby we have an infinite sequence of vectors of ethical parameters, each corresponding to a given level of knowledge comprehension, denoted by $(\theta_1, \theta_2, \theta_3, \ldots)$. Since this is an infinite set-theoretic 'denumerable' sequence there is a real-valued limiting point in it, say θ^*. That is, $\lim(i \to \infty)(\Theta_1, \Theta_2, \ldots, \Theta_i, \ldots) = \lim(i \to \infty)\lim(n \to \infty)(\Theta_{i1}, \Theta_{i2}, \ldots, \Theta_{in}, \ldots) = \Theta^*$. We can formalise the last result as follows:

$$\Theta_1 = \lim(n \to \infty)(\Theta_{11}, \Theta_{12}, \ldots, \Theta_{1n}, \ldots),$$

$$\Theta_2 = \lim(n \to \infty)(\Theta_{21}, \Theta_{22}, \ldots, \Theta_{2n}, \ldots), \ldots$$

$$\Theta_n = \lim(n \to \infty)(\Theta_{n1}, \Theta_{n2}, \ldots, \Theta_{nn}, \ldots)$$

Hence $\Theta^* = \lim(n \to \infty)(\Theta_1, \Theta_2, \ldots, \Theta_n, \ldots)$. For brevity, such vectorial cases we will write $\Theta^* = \lim(i \to \infty)(\Theta_i) = \lim(i \to \infty)\lim(n \to \infty)(\Theta_{in})$.

Next, to integrate polity-market interactions in the knowledge forming framework, we recall the simultaneity of actions between socio-economic variables, x_i, and policy variables, P_i, in the ith stage of knowledge evolution. The latter case is primordially driven by θ parameters. But through this the socio-economic variables are also influenced by the same ethical parameters. Here, without loss of generality, we are assuming that the ith socio-economic vector is influenced by the jth policy vector at an ith stage of knowledge evolution to the *Tawhidi* set.

In the above sense, the concept of interaction between polity and the ecological order (market as a specific subset) is defined by the primordial influence of θ on both the socio-economic variables and the policy variables. There are well-defined, two-way mappings as follows.

Mappings from Polity to Market System

If $\theta_i \geqslant \theta_i'$, then $P_i(\theta_i) \geqslant P_i'(\theta_i')$, and in the space of socio-economic variables we will have by the property of scalar monotonicity of knowledge, $x_i(P_i[\theta_i]) \geqslant x_i'(P_i'[\theta_i'])$. Note that allowance for ethically neutral market consequentialism, temporary though in the face of ethical action, is allowed for by including all forms of preference ordering.[24] But it remains the objective of Islamic polity to reach social consensus on policy issues, which in the sense of polity–market interactions must be established by ethical market actions. Consequently $x_i(P_i[\theta_i]) \leqslant x_i'(P_i'[\theta_i'])$ must ultimately be eliminated.

We note the following three cases:

1. $x_i \sim x_i'$ is a case of progressive evolution. No social consensus is attained as the possibility exists for further improvement as a result of interactions at a given stage of evolution.
2. $x_i \sim x_i'$ is the case of social consensus, as no further improvement is possible in this state within a given stage of knowledge evolution in the sense of interactions.
3. $x_i < x_i'$ is the case of either rejection or revision. When rejection is upheld by polity, the principle of 'irrelevant preferences' is applied in the light of Islamic law.[25] When revision is sought, the ethical action of polity is subject to a further learning process in the *Shura* until the x_i' bundle is induced into the x_i bundle.

In cases 1 and 3 the θ_{ij} parameter is augmented by a further learning parameter, say θ_{ik}. That is, $\theta_{ij} \to \theta_{ik} \, o \, \theta_{ij}$. This is due to the compound relationship denoted by o, between θ_{ik} and θ_{ij} as shown here. Now the mapping from (θ_i) to (x_i) continues as follows:

$$\theta_{ik} \, o \, \theta_{ij} > \theta_{ij}, \Rightarrow P_i(\theta_{ik} \, o \, \theta_{ij}) > P_i(\theta_{ij}), \Rightarrow x_i(P[\theta_{ik} \, o \, \theta_{ij}])$$
$$> x_i(P_i[\theta_{ij}])$$

For simplicity, let $\theta_{ik} \, o \, \theta_{ij} = \theta_{kj}$. Now the following cases can hold (see the notations on Θ_j^* and Θ_i above):

1. $(\theta_{kj}) \cap (\theta_i) = \Phi$ when social consensus is partial, Φ, when 'irrelevant preferences' exist and cannot be any further induced by changes in θ_{jk}. Hence, (x_i) is rejected from the social menu.
2. $(\theta_{jk}) = (\theta_i)$. Now unanimity exists in polity and (x_i) is accepted without further ethical induction.

The above relationship forms a complete correspondence in the polity set but does not define polity–market interaction. The correspondence is complete because the mappings $T \rightarrow (\theta_{ij})$ and $(\theta_{ij}) \rightarrow T$ are continuous and bounded in the small in the *Tawhidi* set, T.

Mappings from Market System to Polity

The reverse mapping of the polity–market interaction is defined by

$$x_i(P_i[\theta_i]) > x_i'(P_i'[\theta_i']), \text{ then } P(\theta_i) \geqslant P_i'(\theta_i'), \text{ then } \theta_i > \theta_i'$$

Here too one notes the initial inclusion of non-reflexivity between market preferences and polity preferences for the same reason of generalising ethically neutral market consequentialism in adverse cases of x_i bundles that are non-conformable with Islamic law. By the same process of eliminating 'irrelevant preferences' and incorporating both partial and unanimous social consensus, we come to the case of $(\geqslant)$ ordering.

Polity–Market Interaction

Polity–market interaction can be defined by integrating the two mappings shown above. Hence

$$\theta_i \geqslant \theta_i', \text{ then } P_i(\theta_i) \geqslant P_i(\theta_i'), \text{ then } x_i(P_i[\theta_i]) \geqslant x_i(P_i[\theta_i']), \text{ then}$$

$$P_{i+1}(\theta_{i+1}) \geqslant P_{i+1}(\theta_{i'+1}), \text{ then } \theta_{i+1} \geqslant \theta_{i'+1} \text{ and so on}$$

Note that, because of the interrelationship between policy variables and socio-economic variables, a measure-theoretic function v_P, defined on the set of all P_i in polity (hence x_P) to preserve the order $i \geqslant i'$, will yield $v_P(P_i[\theta_i]) \in (x_i)$. Likewise, for a measure-theoretic function, v_M on x_i (market system) will yield $v_M([x_i]) \in (P_{i+1}[\theta_{i+1}])$ and so on. In other words, by describing the compound mappings (functionals) by the symbol, o, we write, $v_P \ o \ v_M \in (x_i)$; $v_M \ o \ v_P \in (P_i)$, by generalisation over i evolutions.

Hence $(\geqslant)$ must affect both polity and the market system. The polity–

market interaction, I, is now defined by the ordered set $I = ([P, M], \geqslant; [\geqslant_P] \cap [\geqslant_M] \neq \Phi)$.

Note that in a situation of social consensus (partial or unanimous) it is possible for x_i to evolve dynamically. But the θ_is are related to each other by a specific relationship as long as that social consensus is not supplanted by newer phases of knowledge evolution. All randomness in the relationships is removed in this situation. Hence the sequence $(\theta_1, \theta_2, \ldots, \theta_n, \ldots)$ has a limit, θ^*. The interaction, I, is now explained by the mathematical correspondences

$$\theta^* \to \theta^{*\prime}, \text{ then } P_i(\theta^*) \to P_i(\theta^*), \text{ then } x_i(\theta^*) \to x_{i+1}(\theta^*)$$

$$\to \text{ and so on}$$

By the fixed point theorem, each of the sets (θ_i), $(P[\theta_i])$ and (x_i) has an equilibrium point of its own. But because of the possibility of x_i influencing P_{i+1} and so on, the equilibrium point will hold only locally, not globally.[26] Because the existence of local equilibrium is possible in each of the above sets, it is possible to define a social welfare choice by means of knowledge-valued variables determined in the interaction set. Corresponding to such an interaction it is possible to define a symmetric measure-theoretic function. This is given by $v = v_P \ o \ v_M = v_M \ o \ v_P$. The notation o for compound mapping was defined earlier.

The condition of local equilibrium must suggest that social choice is as fluid as the interactions. The knowledge set, policy set and socio-economic set are thus perpetually disturbed to reach higher stages of knowledge evolution. Consequently the optimisation criterion for the social welfare function must be replaced by a 'satisficing' (simulative) welfare criterion in the Islamic political economy with ethico-economic preference behaviour.[27] The following is one such. Simulate $v = v_P \ o \ v_M$, where

$$v_P = \{v_P(P_i[\theta_i])\}$$

$$v_M = \{v_M(x_i[P_i(\theta_i)])\}$$

$$v_P \ o \ v_M = (v[P_i, x_i, \theta_i])$$

subject to

$$\theta(i + 1), j = a_1 + b_1 \cdot \theta'_{ij}$$

$$P(i + 1), j = a_2 + b_2 \cdot P'_{ij}$$

$$x(i + 1), j = a_3 + b_3 \cdot x'_{ij}$$
$$i = 1, 2, \ldots; j, j' = 1, 2, \ldots n$$

The derivation of these implicit functions follows the endogenous, knowledge-based arguments and their induction on socio-economic variables given earlier.

RECAPITULATING EVOLUTIONARY EPISTEMOLOGY IN ISLAMIC SOCIAL CHOICE AND WELFARE

Polity–market interactions leading to simultaneity in policy and socio-economic realisation is an example of the unification of ethical laws in political economy. It totally negates the neoclassical notion of substitution and marginalisation in resource allocation. The central role of ethical values derived from the *Tawhidi* epistemology through the dynamic evolution of Islamic law is the essence of knowledge formation leading to social consensus formation in the polity–market interactive framework. It is this essence of knowledge formation that endows the Islamic social choice and social welfare function with the essence of evolutionary epistemology in Islam.

The question of simultaneity versus substitution between the goals of the political economy, the most important of which are social (distributive) justice and economic efficiency, is addressed here within a systems framework. Unlike knowledge in the Western systems framework, Islamic knowledge in social choice formation is shown to be simultaneous and continuous. This negates Boulding's conception of knowledge as a system in the socio-economic order. This we examined earlier. The epistemology based on dualism (the Western case) and multiplicity (the Eastern case) is negated in the Islamic approach as the ethical parameters are central and immutable. This means that the core of Islamic law, from which the Islamic theory of knowledge derives, remains unique. It is only humanity's understanding of those precepts that varies continuously. This ceaseless pursuit takes humanity to higher levels of development in which greater levels of comprehension are inculcated by a discursive method of inquiry.

THE HUMAN RESOURCE FACTOR IN THE ISLAMIC SOCIAL WELFARE FUNCTION

The human resource factor is simply an instrument of knowledge. It helps to regenerate knowledge. So the quantity of human resource development, signified by expenditure on education, productivity gains, the social effects of public education and so on, is included in the x_i vector.

Otherwise, as a policy variable, human resources are included in the $P_i(\theta_i)$ variable. One way of incorporating the knowledge-augmenting effect of the human resource variable, H_{ij}, would be to take it as an augmenting factor of θ_i. Then, over phases of knowledge evolution, θ_i is transformed into $H_{ij} \, o \, \theta_i$. This expression also shows the compound mapping between H_{ij} and θ_i. But since H_{ij} is not independent of θ_i, the sequence $(H_{ij} \, o \, \theta_i)$ must be a power sequence of the θ_i values. This shows that the speed of convergence of the θ_i values to θ^* is enhanced by the $(H_{ij} \, o \, \theta_i)$ values. On the other hand, the long-run value of $z^* = (x^*, P^*, \theta^*)$ is increased by the power sequence of the θ vector into z^{**}, say, with $z^{**} > z^*$. Hence human resource development enhances polity–market interactions.

However if z^{**} is independent or weakly related to θ_i, then it becomes a constant scalar addition to the social welfare function. This neither alters the speed of convergence to z^* nor enhances the long-run value of the z^* vector.

The former example of H_{ij} is a balanced pursuit of the *Shariatic* sciences. H_{ij} could also denote pursuit of non-*Shariatic* but socially requisite sciences. H_{ij} must therefore be based upon simultaneity between ethical precepts and socio-scientific factors. The only way to do this, as shown in our knowledge-based social choice and social welfare function, is through polity–market interactions. These interactions lead to the growth and adaptation of knowledge in polity and the ecological order (a subset of which is the market system). That process finally leads to dynamic social consensus formation. In the Islamic politico-economic order such a social consensus is essential for the primacy of Islamic law in society at large.

CONCLUSION

In this chapter we have shown that Islamic epistemology is essentially a ceaseless evolutionary quest for the unicity precept in the order of nature and society. In the politico-economic order such a precept of unicity can be explained by interrelationships between the primordial world of moral and ethical rules and the real world of ecological and market phenomena. Unification is achieved by harnessing these two together in the evolving interactions between polity and the ecological order based on Islamic law. It is through the latter that Islamic society, polity and the socio-scientific order acquires its knowledge base and its capacity to unify through interactions, and thus evolve.

In the milieu of this *Tawhidi* epistemology, the social choice and social welfare model was introduced as a way of evaluating polity–market interactions. Here the principal idea was seen to rest on the dynamic behaviour bestowed on the Islamic ethico-economic and knowledge-based social welfare function by the essence of polity–market interactions.

This leads to a criterion function that does not lend to optimisation rules of the neoclassical methodology. By the same token, the substitution and marginalisation of the neoclassical school, which leads to a trade-off between social (distributive) justice and economic efficiency, is replaced in Islamic social choice by simultaneity between the two. The proper quantitative methodology to use for incoporating these features of interactions and simultaneity in the Islamic social welfare model was shown to be that of 'satisfycing' behaviour.

4 A Theory of Renewal and Continuity in Islamic Science

This chapter is a follow-up of an interesting article by Nezameddin Faghih on the topic of renewal in the *Mathnawi* of Jalal al-Din Mawlawi Rumi.[1] Here is his translation of a verse from the *Mathnawi* on the subject of renewal and continuity:

> Every moment the world is renewed, and we are unaware of its being renewed whilst it remains (the same in appearance). Life is ever arriving anew, like the stream, though in the body it has the semblance of continuity.[2]

Faghih shows that Rumi put many scientific facts into his famous and elaborate body of poetry, this being the style of scientific inquiry of his time. Thus one finds that Rumi tackled such problems as universal gravitation, atomic energy, elementary fundamental particles, matter and antimatter, the uncertainty principle and the renewal process. Faghih claims that this established a scientific legacy for Islamic thinkers long before such ideas dawned in Western science.

A MATHEMATICAL SUMMARY OF THE RENEWAL PROCESS PROVIDED BY THE LAPLACE TRANSFORMATION METHOD

Briefly, the thoughts expressed in Faghih's paper are as follows. There is continuous regeneration of cause and effect over the lifetime of the universe and of every denizen of that universe. Using the Laplace transformation for a finite sequence of time-related state variables (broadly, all kinds of explanatory variables, s, and specifically, socio-economic variables in the social sciences), the author established the following result for a recursive event related to the number of times it is renewed.

If (t_i) denotes the time periods of renewals and $N(t_i)$ the number of times an event renews itself over these time periods, and if $P(t_i)$ denotes the probability of $N(t_i)$ occurring in (t_i), then the total probability of an event occurring in (t_i) is given by the product of the probabilities that the event can occur at any moment over the periods (t_i). Hence $P([t_i]) = \Pi_{s \in (ti)} P(s)$, $s \in (t_i)$. Under the specific assumption that all such period-specific probabilities are identical, the above expression reduces to $P([t_i]) = \{P(s \in [t_i])\}^i$, $s \in (t_i)$.

Next, the expected number of renewals using the continuous analogue of the above expression is given by

$$g(t) = \int_{-\infty}^{+\infty} s_i \cdot P([s_i]) ds_i = E(s_i \in [t_i])$$

By applying the Laplace transformation to both sides of the last expression we obtain the following relations.

$L\{s_i \cdot P([s_i])\}$ denotes the Laplace transform of the integrand.[3] By definition $L(f[t]) = \int_{-\infty}^{+\infty} f(t)e^{-st}dt = E(e^{-s})$, if $f(t)$ is a probability distribution, and i-times the Laplace transformation of $P([s_i])$ can be written as

$$L\{P([s_i])\} = (P[s])^i$$
$$L(g[t]) = E(e^{-st}) = E(e^{-g(s) \cdot t})$$

That is, $g(t) = s \in (t_i) = E\{N(t \in [t_i])\}$ over the lifetime. This expression means that the expected number of renewals equals the lifetime.

It can be seen that the last equality mentioned above is due to the substitution of time by events, with $s \in R$, the real number system. Hence $s = N(t_i)$, implies the conversion of time into events through the relations that can be defined between these variables over the real topological space in general (not strictly the real line), R^n.

Finally, with $t \to \infty$, the convergence of the process $N(t)$ in $t \in (0, \infty)$ establishes the global equivalence between time and momentary sequences of renewals of events over time, when both of these are mapped 'on to' the real space, R.

The result so derived is of crucial importance in the understanding of the conversion between events and time for purposes of explaining renewal through the process of such an equivalence. The essential point to note here is that $s = N(t)$ and (t) are both mapped 'on to' the real space, R. Furthermore R is a complete space (bounded and convergent in subsets known as Cauchy sequences),[4] and therefore, through $s = N(t)$ and (t), the real space is mapped 'into' itself. In addition, in every subset of R, where such mappings are defined, there exist limiting points, sometimes also referred to as fixed points.[5] The equivalence among $(s = N[t])$, (t) and subsets of the real space where Cauchy completeness can be defined and a fixed point thereby identified, can be shown by the compound mappings in Figure 4.1.

In Figure 4.1, consider the mappings $f_1: N(t) \rightarrow R$, and $f_2: t \rightarrow R$. Then $f_2 = f_1 \, o \, f_4$; $f_1 = f_2 \, o \, f_3$. By substitution between these expressions we obtain, $f_3 \, o \, f_4 = I$. f_3 and f_4 are therefore inverse images of each other. This result establishes the equivalence between $(s = N[t])$ as event and (t) as time. For reasons of continuity along with renewal, we need to consider similar equivalence mappings from R to $(N[t])$ and (t). These mappings are shown in the lower half of Figure 4.1. Now $g_1 = g_2 \, o \, g_4$; $g_2 = g_1 \, o \, g_3$. Consequently $g_3 \, o \, g_4 = I$. This implies that there is a unique way of mapping subsets of R on to $(N[t])$ and (t), with g_3 being the inverse image of g_4.

It can finally be seen that $g_3 = f_3$; $g_4 = f_4$ up to a scalar multiple. This is so because, if the contrary were true, then the condition of completeness in R via the mappings would be violated. The real space would then cease to be Cauchy complete. This would a contradict the metric property of R.

PROBLEMS ASSOCIATED WITH LAPLACE TRANSFORMATION IN THE THEORY OF RENEWAL AND CONTINUITY

The problem relating to the Laplace transformation of time into events and *vice versa* to establish the theory of renewal and continuity is encountered at the terminal points. As $t \rightarrow \infty$, the terminal value of $N(t)$ has to assume one of two possible values. Either $N(t) \rightarrow \infty$, as $t \rightarrow \infty$, and then this would be an indeterminate relation in the explanatory power of a theory of renewal and continuity; or, $N(t) \rightarrow N^*$ as a limiting value based on completeness of R. N^* must then become independent of t, and hence independent of events. In other words N^* is a final state, which cannot reproduce other events. At best it can only repeat itself as a tautological case. Such a tautological convergence loses explanatory power in a theory of renewal and continuity.

Thus the problem of equivalence among $N(t)$, (t) and R cannot be fully explained by the Laplace transformation, neither can it be related to the concept of temporal or spatial infinity.[6] For if $s = N(t)$ is a state variable that increases monotonically with t, then $t \rightarrow \infty$ must make $N(t) \rightarrow \infty$, and vice versa. Hence both temporal and spatial infinity are

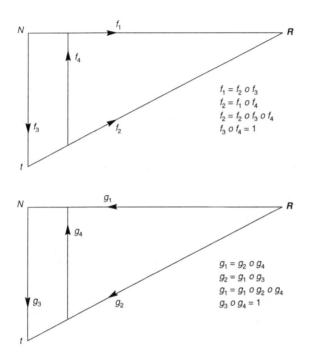

Figure 4.1   Equivalence between events ($N[t]$) and time (t) in real space R

unable to provide an explanatory theory of renewal and continuity. It was the commensurability between temporal and spatial variables that resulted in the conflicting discourses on the nature of infinity by Kant, Hilbert and Einstein.[7] Kant thought that an infinite temporal and spatial dimension was the essence of reality; Hilbert refuted this and tried to base all mathematical truths on finite structures; Einstein considered an infinite yet bounded universe in his theory of relativity.

FORMALISING A UNIVERSAL THEORY OF RENEWAL AND CONTINUITY BY MULTILINEAR METHODS

To resolve this problem of incommensurability between time and event at the terminal value of infinity, an alternative is to take recourse to the cardinality concepts of set theory given by Cantor.[8] The task then is to convert all time into a particular essence of events. We approach this problem as follows.

We replace all reference to time in the renewal process by the primal precept of knowledge flows as events. In this perspective of a knowledge-centred universe, knowledge as a description of events is seen as leading to recursive relations between cause and effect premised on socio-scientific phenomena. Thus there exists a primal mapping of (θ) on to (t). Thereby $(s = N[t])$ is transformed into the knowledge-based event through such a mapping, and $(N[\theta])$ now represents a subset of evolutionary relations formed by interactions between knowledge variables and the socio-scientific order.

Formally, we represent such a knowledge-induced interactive space as follows: $(\theta, s[\theta]) = (f_i)$, $i = 1, 2 \ldots$; such that $\theta_0 \rightarrow_{f0} s(\theta_0) \rightarrow_{f1} \theta_1 \rightarrow_{f2} s(\theta_1) \rightarrow$ and so on. The subscripts here mean 'by means of the functional transformation', as shown.

Even though (f_i) may not be order-preserving in the long run, it can be enclosed into two disjoint sets. We may call these sets $A_1 = f_{i1}(\theta_{i1})$, with (θ_{i1}) being *knowledge* vectors, and has limiting values, say (θ_i^*), in each of the (θ_{i1}) vectors, $i = 1, 2, \ldots$

The important point to note with these limiting knowledge vectors is that they shift with evolutionary changes. Such changes are due to the intensity of the interactions shown by (f_{i1}). The interactions themselves are shown by cause and effect of the circular interrelations.

Like the set A_1, there is a set of *de-knowledge* vectors defined by a subset of the general set, $(\theta, s[\theta])$. This set is denoted by $A_2 = f_{j2}(\theta_{j2})$, (θ_{j2}) being de-knowledge vectors, and has limiting values, say (θ_j^*), in each of the (θ_{j2}) vectors, $j = 1, 2, \ldots$; $i \neq j$. There are limiting de-knowledge vectors that shift with evolutionary changes. Such changes are due to the intensity of interactions in the de-knowledge set, (f_{j2}).

In the long run $A_1 \cap A_2 = \phi$. This means that $(f_{i1}) \cap (f_{j2}) = \phi$, $i, j = 1, 2, \ldots$; $i \neq j$. But this being a long-run phenomenon, it is necessary to recognise the intermediate interactions between hybrid sets of in-complete knowledge in order to describe the evolutionary interactions embodied in the process of renewal and continuity. Thus we treat the set $A_3 = f_{k3}(\theta_{k3})$, with $(\theta_{k3}) \cap (f_{i1}) \neq \phi$, $(\theta_{k3}) \cap (f_{j2}) \neq \phi$, for $i, j, k = 1, 2, \ldots N$.

By implication then, for a finite number of interactions, $(f_{i1}) \cap (f_{j2}) \cap (f_{k3}) \neq \phi$. Consequently, complete independence between the knowledge and de-knowledge sets can occur only among the limiting vectors in these spaces. Then $\lim(k \rightarrow \infty) ([f_{k3}]) = 0$.

So far we have managed to redefine the concept of renewal and continuity in socio-scientific phenomena by replacing Laplace's transformation with topological algebra. There remain two further points to emphasise here: (1) the characterisation of knowledge and de-knowledge sets as forms of topological algebra; and (2) the empirical viability of such an approach to the theory of renewal and continuity must be established to give this alternative approach scientific credence.

We shall start with the limiting vectors of the knowledge set, for which

$$(\theta_1^*) = (\theta_{11}^*, \theta_{21}^*, \ldots, \theta_{n1}^*); \ (s[\theta_1^*]) = (s_{11}^*, s_{21}^*, \ldots, s_{n1}^*)$$

Then the interdependence between these vectors can be explained by their bilinear mappings, that is, by means of all possible monotonic transformations of these vectors 'on to' the other sets of vectors by means of contravariant and covariant vector relations.[9] The bilinear relation between, say, θ_{11}^* and $s(\theta_{11}^*)$ is represented by

$$B(\theta_{11}^*; s[\theta_{11}^*]) = \sum_p \sum_q (a_{pq} \cdot \alpha_p \beta_q)_{11}$$

(See Appendix 4.1.)

Here α_p, $p = 1, 2, \ldots, m$, denotes the coordinates of the vector (θ_{11}^*); β_q, $q = 1, 2, \ldots, m$, denotes the coordinates of the vector $(s[\theta_{11}^*])$; and a_{pq} denotes coefficients of scalar transformations of the vectors, $A = \|a_{pq}\|$ being the matrix of the transformation.

Interactions between (θ_1^*) and $(s[\theta_1^*])$ necessitate interdependent transformations between the linear combinations of all the vectors shown; that is, between (θ_1^*) and $(s[\theta_1^*])$, along with their possible scalar transformations. This yields multilinear transformations of the type

$$1(\theta_1^*, s[\theta_1^*]) = \sum_p \sum_q \ldots \sum_u \ldots \sum_w \ldots a_{pqr\ldots}^{uvw\ldots} \alpha^p \beta^q \gamma^r \ldots$$

$$\mu_u \nu_v \omega_w \ldots; \ p, q, r, u, v, w = 1, 2, \ldots, n$$

(α^p) being coordinates of the vector (θ_{11}^*); (β^q) being coordinates of the vector (θ_{21}^*); (γ^r) being coordinates of the vector (θ_{31}^*) and so on. (μ_u) are coordinates of (s_{11}^*); (ν_v) are coordinates of (s_{21}^*); (ω_w) are coordinates of (s_{31}^*) and so on. $A = \|a_{pqr\ldots}^{\quad uvw\ldots}\|$ denotes the matrix of multilinear transformation of the vectors.

It can now be seen that the set of multilinear transformations comprises a continuous and closed knowledge-based space. In this sense all subsets of such a space comprise relations in the knowledge space. The extension of such a space to the total knowledge-induced space makes it a topological space, with A_1, A_2 and A_3 being its subsets and ϕ being a limiting null subset of this space. The unions and intersections of all subsets of the general knowledge space are members of this space. Any subset of such a topological space is also a topological space; any linear combination of vectors in these spaces also forms a topological space. Indeed, because of the circularity between the knowledge and state variables, the topological spaces remain continuous.[10] Interactions in these spaces explain renewal amidst continuity. We have thus methodologically replaced the Laplace transformation with the methods of tensor algebra.

Next we address the second requirement, namely the empirical viability of the new method. When the mapping $(\theta) \to (s = N[\theta])$ via the primal transformation $(\theta) \to (t)$ is seen as bounded mapping of (θ) 'into' itself, then the multilinear functions assume finite measures. Such processes can be simulated in cybernetical systems.

The problem to note particularly is the relation between (θ), $(s[\theta])$ and (t), corresponding to $t \to \infty$, assuming monotonically increasing transformations in both the A_1 and A_2 subspaces. To get away from the problem of indeterminateness caused by infinity at the terminal points, we apply the Cantor cardinalistic measure to A_1 and A_2.[11]

The idea here is that no matter how many subsets of the set of multilinear topological space are generated, they can be arranged ordinally and made to correspond to the natural number system. This large ordinal assigned to the number of subsets is denoted by ω. Subsequently, any meaningful transformation (not necessarily linear) of ω, say $C(\omega)$, can be treated as an extension of ω. Hence there is always a way to ordinalise all possible arrangements of the number of subsets of the infinite set of multilinear forms. The largest of all these sequences of cardinalities through all possible extensions by means of $C(\omega)$ can then be assigned an upper bound. Such a bound may be referred to as the supercardinality, $SC(\omega)$.[12]

The boundedness of the infinite number of subsets of multilinear forms makes the set of knowledge-based multilinear forms amenable to empirical cybernetics under all conditions. The same argument cannot be made and the boundedness result cannot be established if time variables are treated as independent variables in the system. The monotonicity of the knowledge-based interactive relations (f_{ii}) would cause these functions to become unbounded at the terminal point, $t \simeq \infty$. Renewal and continuity cannot then be explained at such a terminal point.

By the same token, if one considers what Kant referred to as transcendental time (in which the universe was created) as different from the Newtonian concept of receptacle time,[13] then there is no meaningful explanation of the genesis of the universe if the time variable is treated as the independent variable, as in the Laplace transformation. The explanation of a truly universal theory of renewal and continuity becomes impossible in such a treatment of time in the recursive, knowledge-based, interactive processes of the socio-scientific order. Thus it is the overall boundedness of multilinear spaces of transformations under all conditions within a knowledge-based universe that enables a thorough explanation of the theory of renewal and continuity.

What is true of the knowledge-based order is equally true of the de-knowledge order. But the two processes yield different measures of cardinality. The superiority of the measure of cardinality of knowledge space over that of the de-knowledge space, can be taken up by an entropic theory of conflict between these two systems of disjoint cardinality.[14] However, this topic is outside the scope of this book.

The nature of events in the knowledge-based space can be understood now. Events are defined in the above formalisation of the interactive system by the recursive functional relations $(f_{i1}[\theta_{i1}])$ in terms of the primacy of the knowledge-based variables (θ_{i1}). Thus neither time nor event as ontological observations are isolated from the primacy of knowledge. Yet knowledge is iteratively evolved through interactions as well. Thus the equivalence principle between time, event and real space, which we formalised earlier, must now be recast within the framework of the primacy of knowledge. In this system events cannot exist independently of knowledge. Thus by subsuming time and event within the primal knowledge stock and its evolution, the socio-scientific system presented here to explain a theory of renewal and continuity can also be termed the epistemic–ontic circular causation and continuity model of unified reality.[15]

It is then also recognised that the functional interrelationships using the unifying essence of knowledge variables cannot be systemically differentiated. Otherwise the essence of renewal and continuity cannot be seen as a universal reality. Thus the functional relations must be extended across systems as well as within systems in the socio-scientific order. This means that there is a unique law that explains the theory of renewal and continuity in the natural sciences as in the social sciences, and so on. Such an extension methodology also proves the non-substantive nature of events and time as primal facts. They are replaced by knowledge alone as the unifying epistemic–ontic essence of these interactively integrated systems.

Such an extension methodology cannot be explained by the Laplace transformation. Indeed Faghih mentions the difficulty of addressing such interactive–integrative problems, and the treatment of renewal theory by Laplace transformation in the name of nicety but at the expense of realism.

SUMMARY

In summary, a universal theory of renewal and continuity in socio-scientific systems necessitates the reduction of all systemic relations to the primacy of knowledge and its regeneration. In this primal set of relations all phenomena, such as events, time and time-events, must reduce to the unifying epistemic–ontic order of intersystemic interactions and integration through knowledge. When so formalised, the knowledge-based socio-scientific system becomes a bounded one. All relations in it and their transformation to higher levels, inter- and intra-system, assume bounded solutions and treatment. This methodology totally removes the problem of indeterminacy caused by the existence of infinity.[16] The normative and positivistic viability of a universal theory of renewal and continuity is thus made possible in such knowledge-based socio-scientific systems.

APPLICATION OF THE KNOWLEDGE-BASED THEORY OF RENEWAL AND CONTINUITY TO ISLAMIC POLITICAL ECONOMY

In this section we will apply the theory of renewal and continuity developed above, to the realm of Islamic political economy.[17] But first let us explain what we mean by Islamic political economy.

Islamic political economy is the study of ethico-economic relations between polity and the ecological system. Within this grand ecological system resides the market subsystem. But the Islamic market order is neither severed from the socio-political system nor is it overly interrupted by institutional policing. Islam has great respect for the market process, but requires its moral actualisation.

The polity of the Islamic politico-economic system is called *Shura*. The *Shura* is constituted of decision makers who are learned in the tenets of Islamic Law (*Shari'ah*) on specific socio-economic and scientific issues. These decision makers come from very decentralised areas of life with democratic privileges and arrive at collective decisions through voting (complete or partial social consensus) in the *Shura*. The *Shura* formulates market-friendly policies for ethicising the market. This generates polity–market interactions, with the market system responding to the policy regimes instituted by the *Shura* on the basis of knowledge of specific areas of *Shari'ah* (the formation of *Ahqam* from fundamentals, *Usul*).[18]

The power structure of polity–market interactions of the ethico-economic type in the Islamic concept of political economy is aimed at bringing about integration through interactions between the *Shura* and the market system (ecology) in accordance with the precepts of the *Qur'an* and the strictly authentic and revelatory traditions of the Prophet Muhammad (*Sunnah*). The appeal of these sources of knowledge in Islamic political economy is based on the belief that humans naturally comprehend the inevitability and perpetuation of truth as premised on God's unity in the order of things (*Tawhid*). This unicity precept forms the primordial realm of *Shari'ah*. It guides the embryonic and pervasive *Shura* (not simply the political *Shura*) in deriving knowledge from the foundations of *Shari'ah* (*Usul*) and in developing policy prescriptions on specific issues (*Ahkam*). A knowledge-based process of transformation is thus generated by the socio-scientific thinkers in the *Shura* (*Sharees*), in the institutions that such knowledge development influences, and in society at large, which the above two integrate to realise social transformation. In this knowledge-forming process the unicity precept, as the unifying world view for understanding and inculcating truth through interrelationships between God (*Shari'ah*), man (the socio-economic order, *Istihsan* and *Muamalat*) and nature (the scientific order, *Khalq*), is regenerated and enforced.

It has been formalised elsewhere[19] that the unicity precept, once derived from the tenets of the *Qur'an* and the strictly authentic *Sunnah*, reflects itself in the principles of justice and entitlement (*A'dl* and *Haqq*, respectively). We can now denote the knowledge of the unicity precept by the ordinal (θ_1). The principle of justice is denoted by the ordinalised knowledge value (θ_2), and the principle of entitlement is denoted by the ordinalised knowledge value (θ_3). Because of the continuously evolving, circular cause and effect relationships among these variables, we denote their interactions and integration by $(\theta) = (\theta_1) \cap (\theta_2) \cap (\theta_3)$. The (θ) values are evolutionary in the context of renewal and continuity as a result of the interrelationships among the component knowledge values.

First, when we consider (θ) intra-system, it appears as a vector space with an infinite number of vector co-ordinates, each of which denotes knowledge formation within a given system through interactions. Integration is denoted by the convergence of the vectors into limiting points as the interactions proceed. Thus we have the concept of interaction–integration.

Second, when we consider (θ) not merely intra-system but also inter-system, then it appears as a set of vectors, each corresponding to a vector of the abovementioned type for the corresponding system under consideration. In this sense (θ) becomes a vector space. Between the system of Islamic political and economy and the extended socio-scientific order, the inter-systemic extensions are realised by the invariance of the principles of unicity, justice and order. The last principle is identical to the principle of entitlement through the process of realising unity and justice by means of laws, institutions and enforcement. This aspect of inquiry is common to all sciences.

The principles are guided by the instruments, institutions and policies of an Islamic political economy based on *Shari'ah*, including the elimination of interest (*Riba*), the institution of profit-sharing under economic cooperation (*Mudarabah* and *Musharakah*), the institution of wealth tax (*Zakah*) and the avoidance of waste (*Israf*).

The interrelationships among the principles and instruments form an elaborate system. These can be explained in terms of various interactions and priorities relating principles to instruments, as the Islamic political economy evolves to higher stages of its development. These possibilities are shown schematically in Figure 4.2. The point to note is that while the principles remain circular in the direction shown, the instruments can interact with and regenerate the principles in many ways.

FORMALISATION OF THE THEORY OF RENEWAL AND CONTINUITY

To cast the interactive–integrative interrelationships in the theory of renewal and continuity, we proceed as follows.

The knowledge vectors or vector space are defined by

$$(\theta) = (\theta_1) \cap (\theta_2) \cap (\theta_3)$$

The vector of instruments is denoted by $(X) = (R, Z, M, I)$, with R denoting the abolition of interest (*Riba*), Z the wealth tax (*Zakah*), M profit-sharing under economic cooperation (*Mudarabah* and *Musharakah*) and I the avoidance of waste (*Israf*). The numerical values of these economic instruments can be assigned as simulational targets relating to issues in these areas.

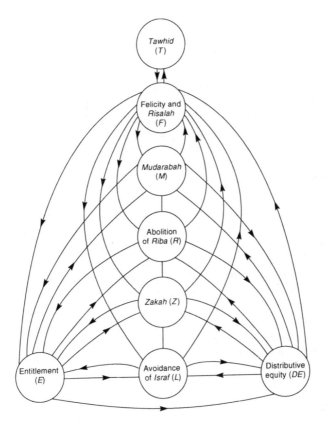

Note: In this figure it can be seen that a great many possible combinations can be formed among the Islamic principles and instruments. The only aspect is the return of all such circular flows (shown by arrows) to the crowning principles of *Tawhid*.

Figure 4.2   Principles and instruments of Islamic political economy

As for the knowledge variables, there are interactive and simultaneous relationships among the components of this vector. Each interrelationship is driven by mappings of the type formulated earlier: $(\theta) \to_f (X) \to_g (\theta) \to$ and so on. The meaning of the subscripts was provided earlier.

Let one such relationship corresponding to the value of (θ) formed along a specific chain of interrelationship be $y = f(X, \theta)$. Furthermore, let the following be the coordinates of the vectors shown: $R = (R_1, R_2, \ldots, R_n, \ldots)$; $Z = (Z_1, Z_2, \ldots, Z_n, \ldots)$; $M = (M_1, M_2, \ldots, M_n, \ldots)$.

The occurrence of these coordinates depends on the influence of interactions, and hence the (θ) values on them. $\theta = (\theta^1, \theta^2, \ldots, \theta^n, \ldots)$. Whichever alternative is chosen, that is, proceeding from R to M or vice versa, from Z to M to I to R, or other directions of priorities, there must always exist preference maps associated with the particular choice of priorities by polity, $\mathcal{P}$. That is, $\exists (\succcurlyeq_i^{\mathcal{P}} (X, \theta])$, $i = 1, 2, \ldots$, so that the following interactive preference map is well-defined: $(\succcurlyeq^{\mathcal{P}})$ $= \cap (\succcurlyeq_i^{\mathcal{P}}[X, \theta])$. For each such preference map there exist circular cause and effect relations of the type shown above. Hence $y = f(\theta; [\succcurlyeq^{\mathcal{P}}])$ is a well-defined form over the range of preference maps and the corresponding choices of knowledge-induced instruments in polity (*Shura*).

Renewal and continuity in Islamic political economy necessitate not only the existence of polity-specific preferences, but also that these polity preferences interact with those formed in the market order (ecological order) under the influence of the knowledge-induced socio-economic instruments mentioned above. Hence market preferences must exist, for example ($\succcurlyeq^m$), as must interactive preferences: $(\succcurlyeq) = (\succcurlyeq^{\mathcal{P}})$ $\cap (\succcurlyeq^m)$. For the market order, socio-economic variables are denoted by (S), so that the preferences ($\succcurlyeq^m$) are well-defined over (S), and ($\succcurlyeq$) are well-defined over (S) $\cap$ (X, θ). Thus there are well-defined relationships on such interactive knowledge-induced preferences of the form $z = g(S, X, \theta)$.

The (y) and (θ) vectors can be expressed in bilinear form with respect to the basis vectors of the contravariant vector (θ), as follows:

$$B(y', \theta) = \sum_i \sum_j a_{ij} y_i \theta_j; \quad i, j = 1, 2, \ldots$$

$A = \|a_{ij}\|$ is the matrix of the bilinear transformation. $(y') = (S, y)$ and all linear or monotonic combinations of these vectors. (y_i) are coordinates of (y'); (θ_j) are coordinates of (θ). Next, with the transformation $f_1(y', \theta)$ we obtain yet other bilinear transformations according to the circular cause–effect interrelationships. Now $f_2(y') \rightarrow$ (θ), $f_3(\theta) \rightarrow (y')$ at higher values (lower values for de-knowledge) of these interrelated transformations. This establishes the principle of renewal and continuity between all linear combinations and monotonic transformations in polity–market (ecology) interactions in an Islamic political economy.

Inter-systemic extension of the above vectors links the principles of Islamic political economy to those of other systems, as the unicity precept, the principle of justice and order must remain invariant across systems. The instruments may, however, change. Now the vectors are replaced by vector spaces. Multilinear transformations replace the bilinear transformations. In this case the expressions for the knowledge-induced polity–market (ecology) interactions are as follows:

1. $1(\theta^1, \theta^2, \ldots; y'_1, y'_2, \ldots) = \Sigma_a \ldots \Sigma_\gamma \| \ldots c_{abc\ldots}{}^{\alpha\beta\gamma\cdots} \| p^a \cdot q^b \cdot r^c \ldots$
   $u_\alpha v_\beta w_\gamma \ldots, C = \|c_{abc\ldots}{}^{\alpha\beta\gamma\cdots}\|$ is the matrix of the multilinear transformation.
2. $(p^1, p^2, \ldots)$ are the coordinates of θ^1.
3. $(q^1, q^2, \ldots)$ are the coordinates of θ^2.
4. $(r^1, r^2, \ldots)$ are the coordinates of θ^3.
5. $(u_1, u_2, \ldots)$ are the coordinates of y'_1.
6. $(v_1, v_2, \ldots)$ are the coordinates of y'_2.
7. $(w_1, w_2, \ldots)$ are the coordinates of y'_3.
8. $a, b, c, \alpha, \beta, \gamma = 1, 2, \ldots$

Finally, any monotonic and linear transformation of the vector space extends the basis vectors from contravariant to covariant spaces in the circular causation and continuity model of unified reality.[20] This is the essence of renewal and continuity in Islamic science. In all these formalisations, the independence of the system from time relegates the dynamic properties to knowledge as the primal essence. Such a primordiality replaces the idea of relativistic time–event equivalence, known as the principle of simultaneity in relativity physics,[21] with the essence of certainty embalmed in the justice, balance, order and felicity of the universe. The *Qur'an* says in this regard: 'Verily, this is the Very Truth and Certainty' (chapter LVI, vs. 95). And in regard to the principle of renewal and continuity the *Qur'an* says 'See they not how God originates creation, then repeats it: truly that is easy for God' (chapter XXIX, vs. 19).

CONCLUSION: EXTENSION OF THE THEORY OF RENEWAL AND CONTINUITY IN RUMI'S *MATHNAWI*

The interpretation of the verses of *Mathnawi* in terms of modern scientific discoveries, presumes the correctness of these scientific theories. This is an inductive way of reasoning that the truth of the Islamic laws and the *Qur'an* and the positivism of *Sunnah* are reflected by the assumed finality of the scientific theories. This is both a dangerous and an inconsistent method for an independent quest for truth within the primal origins (*Usul*) of the *Qur'an*. Consequently we find that Faghih has not been able to dissociate his interpretation of the scientific elements of *Mathnawi* from its claimed dependence on the primacy of time in the Western scientific constructs of a theory of renewal and continuity. The reason for this is obvious. Modern science has not been able to dissociate itself from the notion of independence of time in scientific phenomena. Thus even in the theory of relativity this equivalence is ontological, based on the simultaneity of time and event. The independence of time also appears in dynamic neoclassical economic analysis.

Islamic scientific methodology must therefore emanate independently of those formulated and construed by occidental philosophy. Any coincidence of methods would be accepted, but only under the test and critique of the independent Islamic world view, methodology, interpretation and application.[22]

In this chapter we have tried to liberate the theory of renewal and continuity from its reliance on modern scientific concept of receptacle time. The proposed alternative bases all phenomenology on the premise of knowledge. The universe can then be truly seen as a recreative realm of knowledge-based relations within and across all systems. This appears to be the *Qur'anic* scientific *Ahkam* on the the principle of temporal reorigination of events and the transcendental (*Akhira*) recreation. Both of these together establish the distinct theory of renewal and continuity as a theory of creations in Islam.

APPENDIX 4.1 RENEWAL THEORY BASED ON LAPLACE TRANSFORMATION

Laplace transformation of the function $f(t)$, $L(f[t])$ is defined by

$$L(f[t]) = \int_{-\infty}^{+\infty} p(t)e^{-st}dt$$

As a special case, $p(t)$ can be taken as probability density function, so that $0 \le p(t) \le 1$. Let the probability distribution function, $\Phi(t)$, be given by

$$\Phi(t) = \int_0^t p(t)dt$$

Hence $L(d\Phi/dt) = L(p[t])$, since $d\Phi/dt = p(t)$ everywhere, not simply in $(0, t)$.

Let the number of renewals up to time t be denoted by N_t. N_t is then also the total survival time. Let the number of renewals at time t be denoted by r. Then

$$E(N_i) = \int_{-\infty}^{\infty} r \cdot p(r) dr$$

$$= \int_{-\infty}^{\infty} r \cdot (d\Phi/dr) \cdot dr$$

$$= \int_{-\infty}^{\infty} r \cdot d\Phi$$

$$= E(r)$$

Thus the expected survival time (lifetime) equals the expected number of renewals over the lifetime.

Principal Equations of Linear, Bilinear and Multilinear Transformations

Let $x \in \Re$, $y \in \Re^-$ (the dual of $\Re$ with the same or linearly transformed basis vectors).

Then $x = \Sigma_{i=1}^{n} \xi_i \cdot e_i$, relative to the basis vectors (e_i). Generally, x can be a new basis vector generated by (e_i). x can also be y. Hence the possibility of transforming (e_i) vectors and of expressing c_i vectors in terms of the (e_i) vectors or their transforms. $(\xi_1, \xi_2, \ldots, \xi_n)$ are coordinates of the x vector. Therefore generally, if f is linear, $f(x) = f(\Sigma_{i=1}^{n} \xi_i \cdot e_i) = \Sigma_{i=1}^{n} \xi_i \cdot f(e_i) = \Sigma_{i=1}^{n} \xi_i \cdot a_i$; $a_i = f(e_i)$ are linearly transformed basis vectors of (e_i).

Define a linear form as $(e, c) = \Sigma_{i=1}^{n} \Sigma_{j=1}^{n} \xi_i \cdot \eta_j$; where, $(\xi_1, \xi_2, \ldots, \xi_n)$ are coordinates of c; $(\eta_1, \eta_2, \ldots, \eta_n)$ are coordinates of e. (e, c) is the inner product of the vectors e and c. Because e and c are dual vectors, they are transformable as dual vectors.

Define a bilinear form (functional) as as linear form in ExC space: $A(e;c) = \Sigma_{i,j=1}^{n} a_{ij} \cdot \xi_i \eta_j$; $e = (\eta_1, \eta_2, \ldots, \eta_n)$; $c = (\xi_1, \xi_2, \ldots, \xi_n)$. $|a_{ij}|$ forms a matrix of coefficients a_{ij}, $i, j = 1, 2, \ldots, n$.

Define a multilinear form (functional) as an extension of a bilinear form with multiple vectors $(e_1, e_2, \ldots, e_n)$, $(c_1, c_2, \ldots, c_n)$: $l(e_1, e_2, \ldots, e_n; c_1, c_2, \ldots, c_n) = \Sigma_{a,b,c\ldots} A_{abc\ldots}{}^{rst\ldots} \xi^a \xi^b v^c \ldots \iota_i \theta_s \mu_i \ldots \|A_{abc\ldots}{}^{rst\ldots}\|$ is the matrix of the transformation of the contravariant basis vectors $(e_1, e_2, \ldots, e_n)$ relating the consumption vectors $(c_1, c_2, \ldots, c_n)$ to these transformed basis vectors.

5 What is Islamic Political Economy?

REVIEW OF DEVELOPMENTS IN ISLAMIC ECONOMICS

About fifty years ago some Muslim economists started to write on what they claimed to be Islamic economics. These writers were predominantly of Indian, Pakistani or Egyptian origin, and many of the early works were religiously or politically motivated. They were meant to support popular Islamic political movements such as Jamat-e-Islami in Pakistan, the Deoband and Aligarh Islamic movements in India and Ikhwan al-Muslimun in Egypt. We thus find works by Maulana Maududi (leader of Jamat in Pakistan), Khurshid Ahmad (a translator of the works of Maududi), Nejatullah Siddiqi (of Aligarh in India), and Hasan al-Bannah and Syed Qutb (of Ikhwan in Egypt) on a whole range of Islamic economic and social consciousness.[1] All these writings stemmed from a religious fervour to awaken Muslims to a new way of thinking about the management of their own destinies in accordance with the tenets of the *Qur'an* and the traditions of Prophet Muhammad (*Sunnah*), which together comprise the foundation of Islamic Law, *Shari'ah*.

These two fundamental sources of Islamic knowledge were invoked to derive Islamic economic precepts. This was an important development in the annals of Islamic studies, for the *Qur'an* and *Sunnah* are richly endowed with economic and social prescriptions that address social justice and invoke divine laws on human affairs in relation to the environment, in the broadest sense of this term. Yet these invocations continued – indeed by the very universal message of the fundamental sources of Islamic knowledge – to be *Deenic* (of the essence of the divine conduct of life) prescriptions. It was thus not felt necessary for these prescriptions to be spelt out in scientific and analytical depth. However, both the *Qur'an* and *Sunnah* vest this latter responsibility on humankind to discover their meanings in the midst of the vastness of knowledge-seeking and analytical reasoning.[2]

SOCIO-ECONOMIC THOUGHT IN ISLAMIC HISTORY

In addition to the abovementioned beginnings of Islamic economic thinking there was the socio-economic thinking of Ibn Khaldun, who imparted to the world of learning the philosophy of history and the science of culture as the essence of societal change. Ibn Khaldun's scientific/empirical investigation rested on the central precept that man acts not simply according to reason but also needs, and is indeed supported by revelatory knowledge. Thus the primacy of reason in Greek philosophy was used by Ibn Khaldun to determine the pre-existence of revelatory knowledge. Rather, it must be revelatory knowledge that controls and enriches reason in the first place.[3] To Ibn Khaldun the revelatory premise of knowledge was what beauty, truth, justice and harmony were to the Greeks – the *Ghaia*.[4]

Other important social, legal and political thinkers have contributed significantly to Islamic economics. Among these was Imam Ghazzali, who wrote on epistemology and showed how individual needs and wants are created, avoided and managed by following the divine revelation.[5] Imam Ghazzali's ideas were an early form of the ordinal utility function and of the ideas surrounding individual relations with his environment through the knowledge created by revelation and enhanced thereafter by reason. To the extent that Imam Ghazzali's theory of knowledge tied revelatory knowledge to reason and perception, this may have been the background against which the physiocrats later developed the concept of *jus divinum*, the interconnection between the divine laws of balance and the conduct of the social economy at large.[6]

Yet another mastermind of socio-ethical and legal thinking was Imam Shatibi, whose theory of public purpose (*Maslaha*) and basic needs precept of human development are well known.[7] According to Shatibi it requires both an intellectual understanding and physical realisation to establish the worth of things that humans desire. Of these, justice is uppermost. Shatibi then set a hierarchy of consumption priorities: (1) the consumption of needs (*Dhururiyath*), (2) the consumption of conveniences (*Hajiyyath*) and (3) the consumption of wants (*Tasiniyyath*). The third category was a matter of exception rather than rule. These ideas laid the groundwork for the basic needs regime of development and Maslow's idea of self-actualisation.[8]

MODERN DEVELOPMENTS IN ISLAMIC ECONOMICS

In recent times, Islamic economics has been vigorously pursued by Islamic and non-Islamic thinkers alike.[9] The need arose as more and more Islamic nations gained their independence from colonial powers after the Second World War and began to face the challenges presented by development and the need for self-reliance. Oil exporting countries came to accumulate huge capital surpluses and established institutions that, it was claimed, would be run according to Islamic principles. In general, the claim was made that Islamic Law (*Shari'ah*) would form the centrepiece of Islamic management. Yet the practices adopted by Islamic financial institutions have had two questionable consequences.

First, while Islamic financial institutions are politically motivated to use certain *Shari'ah* precepts, they have functioned in imperfect Islamic environments at home and abroad. For example, there is a need to mobilise the resources of Muslim individuals and nations according to the precepts of *Shari'ah*, but these resources have been put to uses that are not Islamic in character, such as interest-bearing assets or stocks that generate interest-bearing returns.[10] Interest-bearing transactions are unequivocally forbidden by *Shari'ah*.

Second, the emerging Islamic economists took note of the fervour aroused by the establishment of Islamic financial institutions, and viewed the economics of financial markets as foremost in the formulation of Islamic economic ideas.[11] As a consequences theses and scholarly papers have tended to concentrate on money, banking, investment, savings and resource mobilisation, plus some focus on development financing. This bias has continued to prevail, and a considerable proportion of the research funds for the study of Islamic economics today flow either from capital-rich countries or from grants set up by capital-rich countries or wealthy citizens.[12] Thus Islamic economists and institutions have become subservient to the research field of financing resource mobilisation of the Islamic individuals and countries by means of the Islamic commercial and financial developments that have sprung up in the last two decades.

The main areas of interest for Islamic economists are finance, money and banking; financing development and resource mobilisation; theory and application of *Shari'ah* in developing secondary capital market instruments; macroeconomic models of Islamic systems, monetary and investment relationships; Islamic economic history; and international Islamic economic cooperation.[13] Islamic microeconomics, growth and comparative systems enjoy limited but growing attention.[14] Nonetheless neoclassical or Keynesian methodologies remain firmly in place in Islamic economic analysis. In other words, Islamic economists have continued to use existing economic models, logical premises and world views to address Islamic values and institutional norms, rather than develop a distinctive form of Islamic economics. Islamic economics is thus simply mainstream economics with value judgements added to the analysis. This approach is similar to social economics, institutionalism and socio-economics, all of which are value-laden economic analysis in the neoclassical and Keynesian (post-Keynesian) mould.[15]

In Islamic socio-economics, however, questions of economic epistemology have been raised. The best work in this area has been carried out by the sociologist Shariati.[16] The works of Baqir as-Sadr, on the other hand, are of a populist nature and compare Islamic economic thinking with the capitalist and socialist systems. Islamic economics is seen as a middle way between the capitalist and socialist economic doctrines, with a good deal of state intervention.[17]

FROM ISLAMIC ECONOMICS TO ISLAMIC POLITICAL ECONOMY

It is therefore important to investigate whether Islamic economics can be logically pursued within the existing methodologies and axiomatic bounds of mainstream economics, or whether Islamic socio-economic analysis should be based on a completely new epistemological premise.

It would be wrong to treat Islamic economics as Islamic political economy, as the former is simply the theoretical and empirical study of economic phenomena, but using the correcting policies and behavioural norms prescribed by Islam. Islamic economic history can then be seen in this area to represent an exogenous treatment of unified reality. This at best conveys the historical ways in which Islamic norms have been understood and implemented. Such an approach to the study of Islamic economics necessitates no demand for or development of the epistemological foundations of morals, ethics and values that essentially endogenise the Islamic system of socio-economic reasoning.[18] It is not sufficient for values to be drawn from the *Qur'an* and *Sunnah*, and then subjected to rigorous scientific investigation. It is also necessary for such an intellectual inquiry to be universally acceptable among the scientific community and institutions. The ideas so discovered and developed must then be capable of intellectual dissemination in classrooms, scientific fora and through national and international institutions.

In this second approach to the study of Islamic socio-economics, such a discipline must cease to be classified as 'economics' and be replaced by the idea of political economy. But this political economy would be very different from those of the classical, neoclassical, Marxist and institutionalist persuasions, including the Keynesian idea of political economy. The reason for this difference is that Islamic political economy is essentially a study of ethico-economic relationships between polity and the ecological system. Within this grand ecological system is the subsystem of the market.[19] But the Islamic market is neither severed from the social and socio-political system nor overly interrupted by institutional policing. Islam has great respect for the market process, but requires it to be morally ordered.

The polity of the Islamic economic system is called *Shura*. The *Shura* is constituted of decision makers who are learned in the tenets of *Shari'ah* on specific socio-economic and scientific issues. These decision makers come from very decentralised walks of life enjoying democratic privileges and come to collective decisions through voting (complete or partial social consensus) in the *Shura*. The *Shura* formulates market-friendly policies for ethicising the market. This generates polity–market interactions, with the market system responding to the policy regimes instituted by the *Shura* on the basis of knowledge of specific areas of *Shari'ah* (the formation of *Aham* from fundamentals, *Usul*).[20] The power structure of polity–market interactions of the ethico-economic type in the Islamic concept of political economy is aimed at bringing about integration through interactions between the *Shura* and the market system in accordance with the precept of the *Qur'an* and *Sunnah*. The appeal of these sources of knowledge in Islamic political economy is based on the belief that humans comprehend the inevitablity and perpetuation of truth, as premised on God's unicity in the order of things (*Tawhid*). The unicity principle forms the primordial precept of *Shari'ah*. This guides the *Shura* in deriving its knowledge from the foundation of *Shari'ah* (*Usul*) and developing necessary policy prescriptions on specific issues (*Ahkam*). A knowledge-based process of transformation is then generated by the socio-scientific thinkers in the *Shura* (*Sharees*), in the institutions that such knowledge development influences, and in the society at large, which the above two integrate to transform. In this knowledge-forming process the unicity precept, as the unifying world view for understanding and inculcating truth through interrelationships between God (*Shari'ah*), man (the socio-economic order, *Istihsan* or *Muamalat*)) and nature (the scientific order, *Khalq*), is regenerated and enforced.

ISLAMIC POLITICAL ECONOMY DEFINED: A COMPARATIVE STUDY

In short, then, Islamic political economy is the study of interactive relationships between polity (*Shura*) and the ecological order (market subsystem). These interactions develop human comprehension, social receptivity and institutionalisation of *Shari'ah* in the conduct of life. Such a world view of ethico-economic relations is developed through the primacy of the unicity of God, as substantively understood in the socio-scientific order. Thus the *Shura* perpetuates its existence in the midst of this unifying realisation. It is not the objective of the *Shura* to promote institutional intervention, but neither does it permit irresponsible market pursuits. Values are thus the endogenous engine of Islamic transformation in the interactive and integrative polity–market system.

The above perspective of political economy is very different from that in the standard literature. In the latter, political economy is the study of conflicting relationships between the structure of power and the structure of wealth and its distribution.[21] Liberal political economy does acknowledge the relevance of collective action to mitigate social conflict, but advocates minimum government intervention in the resolution of such power relationships.[22] In this category are the perspectives forwarded by Benthamite utilitarian ethics, the neoclassical study of the state that legitimises and enforces its preferences through policies that serve the power structure of interest groups.[23] In institutionalism we find the concerns of the Fabian socialists, the moral philosophers and the philosophers of the welfare state on the need for moral control of the market by the state.[24] But neoclassical orientation in new institutionalism remains a significant departure due to its reliance on the world of optimal organisations.[25]

Keynesian political economy or institutionalism is ethically benign in its aggregative analysis. These cannot explain and resolve power conflicts to bring about social change.[26] Keynesianism does not address institutional behaviour *per se*. Rather it is an analysis of the consequences of aggregative economic activities that institutions undertake in the economy. The market and its effect on wealth formation and distribution is replaced in Keynesian economics by the analysis of fiscal policy in relation to growth and income determination. Therefore while neoclassical economics accepts the role of the market in social determination and treats government institutions as a reflection of the preferences of the market system, Keynesianism does not concern itself with the forces that form power.

Rational choice theory is yet another politico-economic development based on neoclassical theory and extended to institutional behaviour. Rational choice applied to governments and institutions can be explained as follows.[27] The political economist views a political situation, at least in democracies, as affording exchange possibilities among citizens, political parties, governments and bureaucracies. Voters are treated as 'buyers' of collective goods while governments and political parties are considered as alternative 'suppliers' competing to produce public policies (goods and services, or promises thereof) in return for the support of voters at elections. The basic conceptual schema for the economist is a 'political market' that is roughly analogous to the regular marketplace.

Likewise public choice theory uses neoclassical methodology to determine social choice functions through collective action. But the neoclassical concept of economic rationality, given consumer preferences and self-interest, causing methodological individualism to reign supreme, are all assumed. Thus over the years, the rebirth of political economy has become a paradigm of economic reasoning pursuing the neoclassical precepts.[28]

In Marxist political economy we find for the first time explicit treatment of the conflict between political (institutional) power and wealth (accumulation and distribution) in epistemological terms. It was the Hegelian concept of world spirit that motivated Marx to think of freeing humanity from capitalist bondage and formulate his concept of human equality.[29] But being more of an ontologist than an epistemologist, Marx based all his ideas on economic equality. Thus for Marx economism became the fundamental basis of all social behaviour. Within this milieu, Marx pursued his study of the nature of production and distribution of wealth and the social conflict that characterises distribution in the capitalist order. But by ascribing an unsocial role to profits, Marx complicated the notion of perceived market prices in his dichotomous theory of value and prices.[30] This rendered the market system, as we perceive it, non-existent, and hence unusable in the generation of ethics and values, social equalisation and human transformation.[31]

Hayek and von Mises argued vehemently against the concept of 'the social' in Marxist thinking.[32] They argued that the market as a vast collective institution does not acknowledge the concept of 'unsocial', as prescribed by Marx. This is due to the consequentialist response of the market system, which according to Hayek remains socially neutral. This is also the perception developed by Sen.[33] Market systems therefore may or may not respond to specific policies in spite of people's good intentions with respect to policing the economy. Because such policies must inevitably fail in the face of the consequentialism of the market system, then to act under the pretext of 'the social' is seen as costly and unwarranted. Policy intervention is thus seen to be an inefficient way and misconstrued premise for determining a social act out of the market order. This is also the view of the minimalist state held by Nozick.[34] Thereby Hayek's arguments are seen first as a defence of a liberal philosophy of economics that makes all values exogenous to the market phenomenon. Second, it is seen as a refutation of socialist philosophy, which in the name of the social opposes resource allocation through free market exchange.

Von Mises rejected the Marxist argument that all societies would inevitably and relentlessly move towards international socialism. Von Mises argued that the basis of human reasoning would be thwarted by a Marxist political economy based simply on *modus vivendi*, explaining reality in terms of the historical relationship of productive processes to society. Thus von Mises argued that Marx missed the finer regress into the realm of thought in order to realise the ultimate spring of human reason. This, according to von Mises, was overly to rely on observed historical processes of change. The quest for theoretical construct must prove to be a universal and unifying experience of the mind. According to von Mises, 'Theory as distinct from history is the search for constant relations between entities or, what means the same, for regularity in the succession of events. In establishing epistemology as a theory of knowledge, the philosopher implicitly assumes or asserts that there is in the intellectual effort of man something that remains unchanged, viz., the logical structure of the human mind.'[35]

Among the arguments presented by von Mises in support of economic epistemics is a deeper message for the nature of political economy than that found in Hayek's critique of the social element and in Marx's dialectical materialism. Von Mises integrated the premise of reason with the open-ended system of human capacities that is built up in a relational way with the epistemology of perfect knowledge. It is through the perpetual voyage of the human mind through such interrelationships, recognising the limits of human volitions, while experiencing the potential for growth through the advance of epistemological roots tied with ontic experiences, across which the human mind is seen to progress. Theoretical conditions are made to take shape. Societies and institutions evolve. Political economy, in the substantive sense of the study of interactions between the laws and norms of society (of nature) and the realities of market, is born. This is the discursive reasoning

process towards the discovery and advancement of truth, according to
von Mises.

THE KNOWLEDGE-BASED INTERACTIVE PROCESS OF
ISLAMIC POLITICAL ECONOMY

Von Mises' ideas on the process of social action are profoundly help-
ful in comprehending the nature of Islamic social economy. In the
latter, while epistemological foundations are sought in the springs of
Shari'ah, knowledge formation is evolutionary and discursive, with the
unicity of God as an axiomatic truth that can lead to and be established in the midst of interactive relations. It is through such interactive relationships, which establish the unicity of God in the order of
things, that the epistemic premise of knowledge becomes circularly
integrated with the ontic premise of knowledge. In this evolutionary
continuity, epistemic and ontic distinctions to comprehend and relate
to socio-scientific reality eventually disappear.[36]

   The structure of relationships that brings about epistemic–ontic integration is based on the theoretical understanding that morals, ethics
and values are the most fundamental elements of social and economic
reality, and form the basis of a meaningful socio-economic and institutional (political) structure. Even ideas regarding the monetary and
currency numeraire are formed on the basis of the fundamental ethical
numeraire.[37]

   Such a socio-economic reality requires, first, that the preferences of
institutions and markets (households, individuals) are not fixed at any
moment of the interactive relationship. Second, social preferences are
formed and continuously changed through the interactive preferences
of polity and markets. Third, each such state of joint but dynamic
preferences should generate an interaction of the discursive type. Critical
knowledge is formed when such joint preferences result in social consensus (majority voting or unanimity) on given issues. The cycle of
interactive and discursive relations continues to evolve thereafter. In
such interactive relations we must assume the primacy of *Shari'ah*,
given an existing state of its comprehension in *Shura*, at a given stage
of knowledge in the plane of evolutionary epistemology.[38] The interactions send responses back to the *Shura*. Such responses thereby form
knowledge from the ontic experience. The continuous evolution of joint
preferences of polity and the markets represent the integration between
the epistemic and ontic phases in the unification of knowledge. In the

Islamic political economy, such a process of interaction may be termed the *Shuratic* process.[39]

The significance of market response to polity implies the importance placed on the market process and the minimality of institutional intervention in Islamic political economy. Institutional presence is necessary for moral guidance of the market system. An example of social regulatory institutions for markets is *Al-Hisbah*, which was recommended by Ibn Taimiyyah.[40] Consensus formation is known in Islamic legal theory either as *Qiyas* (when the *Shari'ah* ruling is made by the Islamically learned, known as *Mujtahid*, in the absence of a viable Islamic community) or *Ijma* (complete consensus). In my case both of these may also constitute majority rule, but not necessarily unanimity. This is a valid Islamic principle, and is known to have been upheld by Ibn Hazam.[41] It also appears to have been promoted by Imam Ghazzali with respect to maintaining a minimum number of axioms and rules for the formulation of essential knowledge on specific issues. Ghazzali considered that the details are better left for secondary determination.[42] The integration of preferences, signifying epistemic–ontic continuity in socio-economic knowledge formation, forms the essence of unification of knowledge in the unicity precept of God as presented in the *Qur'an* and explicated by the *Sunnah*.[43]

Note how Shackle's contemporary critique of economic theory on grounds of its 'pre-reconciliation of actions' and the assumption of optimal knowledge come close to the precepts of Islamic political economy. Shackle argues against the possibility of complete rationality in the understanding of things, and thus in analysing them. He goes on to show that only in the midst of time variations of multiple-value, characteristic of economic things, can a dynamic meaning be formed. Such arguments lead to a vehement rejection of the received concepts of economic rationality and optimal knowledge, and hence the concept of static equilibrium in partial equilibrium analysis within the general equilibrium framework. Shackle writes, 'Equilibrium is a solution, and there is, in the most general frame of thought, no guarantee that a problem which presents itself, unchosen and undesigned by us, will have any solution, or that it will not have an infinity of solutions. In either case, there is no prescription of conduct.'[44]

FORMALISATION OF THE *SHURATIC* PROCESS: EPISTEMIC–ONTIC CIRCULARITY

The decentralised (domain of decision making) and the democratic (individual preferences) nature of polity (*Shura*) must lead to the *Shuratic* process. A polity is then defined by $P^* = U_{i,t} \cap {}_j P(\theta)(i, j, t)$, given $\geqslant_j$, $\theta \in \mathbb{R}$. As throughout this book, the appearance of variables, functions and indices such as $P(\Theta)(i, j, t)$, $W(X[\Theta], P[\Theta])(i, j, t)$ and so on means that each of the inner arguments in these variables or functions is governed by the variables in the (.) bracket, that is, over i: socio-economic systems; j: participants in the interactive process; t: number of interactions over time. Here $i = 1, 2, \ldots, n_1$ signifies a socio-economic system that is influenced by the preferences of polity within a given range of knowledge (i); $t = 1, 2, \ldots, n_2$ denotes the time variable allowing rounds of interactions to take place (i); $j = 1, 2, \ldots, n_3$ denotes the number of participants in a decision-making process in the *Shura*. (θ) denotes a vector of ordinal values signifying the level of comprehension of the primordial ethical premise for (i, j, t). $\theta(i, j, t)$ takes values in the real number system by virtue of the monotonic ordinal relationship that must exist between $P(\theta)$ and θ.

P^* thus means that at any stage of knowledge formation and in any period of time, polity presents its preferences to the socio-economic system on the basis of majority consensus, signified by the preference ordering $\geqslant_j$, subject to the assumption of bounded uncertainty in the formation of such preferences. Such a bounded uncertainty arises because of the existence of simple majority rule and the lack of full knowledge at any stage of the evolutionary epistemology of the system.[45]

The next point to study is how the evolutionary knowledge base is established in the *Shura*. Since the generalised system comprises interactions within and across polity and the ecological subsystems, the ethical policies of the *Shura* must have an impact on the socio-economic variables. This impact is optimal when the socio-economic system is allowed to respond freely, without institutional intervention in the market system, apart from maintaining moral responsibility. The first part of knowledge formation in polity thus consists of ethical policies, as formulated by a consensual outlook on existing knowledge of the Islamic laws (*Shari'ah*).

This first part of knowledge formation in polity is formalised as follows. There exists a well-defined mapping, f, from the polity domain, P^*, on to the socio-economic domain, X, such that,

$$f: P^* \rightarrow X, \text{ with } f(P^*) \subseteq X$$

Now, just as there is a sub-process at work in the formation of ethical policies, so is a sub-process at work in ethically inducing such policies in the socio-economic domain. As the above correspondence shows, there is a transmission of $\theta(i, j, t)$ 'on to' X via the effect of $f(P^*)$. That is, $X = (x[\theta][i, j, t], \theta \in \mathbb{R})$ given $\geqslant_i, \geqslant_j, i = 1, 2, \ldots, n_1$; $j = 1, 2, \ldots, n_2; t = 1, 2, \ldots, n_3$.

The impact of ethical policy $(\theta[i, j, t])$ on $x(\theta)(i, j, t)$ results in the acceptance, rejection or prevalence of such polices. Thus a preference mapping, shown above by $\geqslant_i$, is induced in X by P^*, and a consensual process exists in X to form these preferences. Consensus in the X subsystem is based on evaluation of its social welfare function objective (or in terms of the payoff function in an n-person cooperative game). Individual (group) preferences $\geqslant_i$ are formed in an environment of market response to policy variables. The consensual $\geqslant_i$ preference is conveyed by the observed ethico-economic transformation in the market system. But while evaluation of the ethico-economic policy impact is left to the market system, post-evaluation of the degree of ethico-economic transformation of socio-economic variables realised is left to polity. A circular interrelationship is thus established from polity to market system to polity, and so on. A process is established in the sense of a nexus of polity–market interrelationships, the totality of which represents the evolution of knowledge in society at large.

The principal Islamic policy vector (P^*) indicates the following priorities: progressive elimination of financial interest (*Riba*), institution of profit sharing under economic cooperation (*Mudarabah/Musharakah*), the institution of wealth tax (*Zakah*) and the elimination of waste in consumption and production (*Israf*). Some of the socio-economic variables (X) to look at are income distribution, property ownership, elimination of poverty, price stability, economic growth, productive investment and so on[46] (see Appendix 5.1 for details).

A social welfare objective function can explain this process. Let the social welfare function be denoted by

$$W((X[\theta], P^*[\theta]), (\geqslant_i \cap \geqslant_j)[i, j, t])$$

The preferences $(\geqslant_i \cap \geqslant_j)$ are determined on the basis of the principal goals of Islamic political economy. These are establishment of *Shari'ah* and through this the realisation of social justice, as well as bringing about entitlement formation (universal property rights) through work and productivity. Clearly an optimisation process cannot exist for W, as any maximal position for W with respect to economic efficiency (one of the $x[\theta][i, j, t]$ variables) would not necessarily establish the approval of $\geqslant_j$ and vice versa. The choice of $\geqslant_i$ with respect to $x(\theta)[i, j, t]$ is left to $\geqslant_j$, and hence to the θ values in transforming the preferences of the socio-scientific order. Only when there is monotonic mapping between the $\geqslant_i$ and $\geqslant_j$ preference mappings will $X(\theta)$ and $P^*(\theta)$ assume monotonically related values. But this does not necessarily optimise the social welfare function, since the monotonicity between $X(\theta)$ and $P^*(\theta)$ now represents only one of all possible relationships and is subject to changes in i, j, t and in the consequential perceptions of θ, and so on. The knowledge domain is dynamic and this introduces bounded uncertainty in preference formation. The fuzzy set of $(X[\theta], P^*[\theta][i, j, t])$ values does not define unique, optimisable correspondences from the polity domain 'on to' the socio-economic domain. Also, no unique and optimisable correspondences can be expected from the socio-economic domain on to the polity domain.[47]

THE OBJECTIVE CRITERION FUNCTION OF THE POLITY–MARKET INTERACTIVE PROCESS

The objective criterion function of the polity-market interactive process is formalised as follows (such an iteratively determined implicit function system was explained earlier).

$$\text{Simulate}_{\theta(i, j, t)} \ W(X[\theta], P^*[\theta])(i, j, t)$$

$$\theta(i, j, t) = g_1(\theta)(i', j', t - 1),$$

$$X(\theta)(i, j, t) = g_2(X[\theta][i', j', t - 1])$$

$$P^*(\theta)(i, j, t) = g_3(P^*[\theta][i', j', t - 1])$$

$$\theta(i, j, t) \in \mathbb{R} \ (\text{or} \ \mathbb{N}); \ X(\theta)(i, j, t) = (x[\theta][i, j, t], \geqslant_i, \geqslant_j);$$

$$P^*(\theta)(i, j, t) = (\cup_{i,t}, \cap_{j}. \ P[\theta][i, j, t], \geqslant_j) \cdot i, \ i' = 1, 2, \ldots, n_1,$$

$$i \neq i'; j, j' = 1, 2, \ldots, n_2, \ j \neq j';$$

$$t = 1, 2, \ldots, n_3;$$

$$(\geqslant_i \cap \geqslant_j) = (\geqslant)(i, j, t)$$

Clearly now, because of the fuzzy nature of the set $A = \{(X[\theta], P^*[\theta]) (i, j, t)\}$,[48] there is no unique solution to the above simulation problem. However, the question of equilibrium, optimality and stability of equilibrium still arises when there is systematic evolution of knowledge in polity and its integration with the socio-scientific order. In this case the functions g_1, g_2 and g_3 assume systematic relationships of the Markovian type. However stable relationships can hold only locally about the points of equilibrium. In this localised region of equilibrium values $(X[\theta], P[\theta])(i, j, t)$, one may expect preferences to be unchanging. This is simply to convey bounded uncertainty, and thereby to convey predictiveness in the behaviour of polity and the socio-scientific system with respect to given preferences. But globally about the point of equilibrium, preferences are bound to change, although there will be monotonicity between the preferences. As knowledge evolves, these preference changes will cause policy changes and changes in socio-economic perceptions. Consequently $\lim(t \to T) (X[\theta][i, j, t]) = X(\theta)(i', j', T)$, where T denotes the global region around the temporary equilibrium point. Hence we have the global instability of relationships via the media of preference changes in i, i', j, j'. The reverse is the case for local equilibrium. Similar results hold for $P^*(\theta)(i, j, t)$, and hence for $W(X[\theta], P^*[\theta])(i, j, t)$.

We have now established that all correspondences in the fuzzy set A have temporary equilibrium points locally, but have neither unique nor stable equilibrium points globally.[49] The strength of the polity–market system lies in ethical transformation through a learning process between polity and the ecological subsystems of this total social system. In this general framework of ethical endogeneity, the concepts of justice, entitlement, resource allocation and distribution can all be taken up in the sense of simultaneity of occurrence, rather than as trade-offs of the neoclassical economic system.[50] This of course is not to say that during the evolution of the polity–market interactive system there will not be discord between the ethical preferences of polity and the neoclassical preferences of the market system. But the results of consensual and monotonic preferences in this system must necessitate the attainment of simultaneity between the variables. Economic efficiency and distributive justice must now be simultaneously attainable, as must redistribution and entitlement formation, and distributive justice and social justice. Resource allocation is simulated over consumption and production bundles that are formed out of dynamic consensus in polity–market preferences.[51]

EPISTEMIC–ONTIC CONTINUITY OF EVENTS

The epistemic–ontic circularity of polity–market interactions is the most distinctive characteristic of Islamic political economy and differentiates it from all other political economy orientations. It also provides Islamic political economy with distinct new dimensions of inquiry and makes it a normative–positive whole. This principle of unification can result in a broadening of the field of scientific reality. Unlike the ontological formalisation presented by Ramsay and Carnap, in the above principle[52] the following scientific form will hold. If $\exists X_1 \rightarrow \exists X_2 \rightarrow \exists X_3 \rightarrow \ldots$ etc. $\rightarrow (X_i \rightarrow X_j) \rightarrow (X_j \rightarrow X_i)$, $i, j = 1, 2, \ldots n, i \neq j$, then a meaningful relationship can be defined amongst these variables by $F(X_1, X_2, \ldots, X_n) = 0$.

Since each of these variables, and hence the relationship among them denoted by $F(..)$, is parametrised by the knowledge variable, θ, it is not necessary for any of the perceptions conveyed by these variables to start from a perfect state of knowledge, and therefore from a well-defined, axiomatic premise. In Islamic political economy this must mean giving allowance to any level of comprehension of *Shari'ah* as the starting point of an Islamic transformation process. It is therefore possible to constrain $X_i (i = 1, 2, \ldots, n)$ by the condition of minimality of axioms to establish an initial point of Islamicisation of knowledge.[53] X_i and X_j $(i, j = 1, 2, \ldots, n; i \neq j)$ thus form isomorphism (topological mappings) between the epistemic premise and the ontic premise, and *vice versa*.[54]

FORMULATING RESOURCE ALLOCATION IN THE *SHURATIC* PROCESS

The above formalisation can also be applied to resource allocation, in contradistinction to the neoclassical idea of optimal allocation of resources. In general social contracts (polity–market interactions) and resource allocation loci can be represented by the trajectories $0A$, AB and so on, where points such as a, b and so on indicate consensus in polity–market interactions. These points are unique with respect to attained preferences $\geq_i$, $\geq_j$. Points such as a', b' and so on denote similar consensus with respect to other preferences. But since any move from a to a', from b to b' and so on alters preferences, these points cannot lie on a convex to the origin optimal consumption or production surfaces. Likewise, for the same reason of perturbations transmitted by interactions and changes of joint preferences around such points, there are fields of localised possibilities generated around these points. The trajectories can best be considered as random ones, stable in the short run (locally) but unstable in the long run (globally). The allocation of goods in the Islamic political economy is illustrated in Figure 5.1.

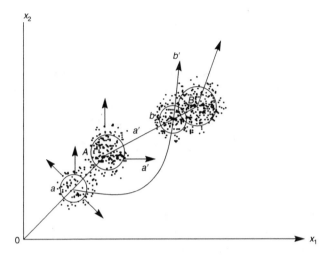

Figure 5.1   Resource allocation trajectories (locus of social contract points) in Islamic political economy

In the above type of resource allocation trajectories where knowledge parameters are instrumental in moving the trajectories from point to point as an essential character of Islamic political economy, it remains to be seen how prices are formed. In the knowledge-based system, a move towards more efficient resource allocation must mean the simultaneous allocation of 'goods' and avoidance of 'bads', in contradistinction to the concept of gross substitution between 'goods' and 'bads'. Hence on this positivistic level of Islamic transformation, the formula for price formation must be given by $dX_1/dX_2 = p_1/p_2$, where X_1 and X_2 are 'goods', and p_1 and p_2 are the price of X_1 and X_2, respectively.

Note here that the general relationship is $dX_1/dX_2 = f_1(p_1[\Theta])/f_2(p_2[\Theta])$. When complementarity between X_1 and X_2 exists, then f_1 and f_2 are monotonic to each other under the influence of recursive θ values. Only in the perverse case of neoclassical resource allocation will $f_1(p_1) = p_1^{-1}$, $f_2 = p_2^{-1}$. Now $dX_1/dX_2 = p_2/p_1$, the usual optimal result under marginal rate of substitution between X_1 and X_2.

Note, however, that since evolution towards the perfect Islamic political economy is not being assumed, perturbations around the resource allocation points show the existence of neoclassical-type resource substitution between 'goods' and 'bads'. But these must be of a temporary nature, or the Islamic politico-economic system will cease to exist and give way to a neoclassical system.

This points to two facts with regard to the knowledge-based evolutionary system depicted here: first, that the neoclassical is an incorrect representation of the general form of the knowledge-based system; second, there can be no coercion in the *Shura* to perpetuate an Islamic political economy when the democratic will calls for other systems. It is therefore only the clarity of the message and axiomatic basis of accepting the unifying truth of the unicity of God, along with the *Shari'ah* and institutions this invokes, that constitute the *raison d'être* of Islamic political economy.

CONCLUSION

We conclude this chapter by pointing out the important issues raised in it. First, the most important epistemological essence is absent in the field that has come to be known as Islamic economics. This makes this field of inquiry nothing more than a value-oriented conceptualisation and application of neoclassical theory. It may be said to have pursued the path of a Beckerian type analysis of a gamut of socio-ethical issues in Islamic perspectives.[55] It is therefore difficult for Islamic economics to evolve as a new dimension in economic reasoning out of this neoclassical snare of 'mono-economics'.[56]

On the other hand it is becoming increasingly clear that Islamic economic theory should rest on the unicity precept of God as the epistemology of a knowledge-based model of political economy. Here we find that Islamic political economy has a new field of inquiry to contribute within its analytical framework of the epistemic–ontic circular causation and continuity.

Islamic political economy as a knowledge-based system is a field of inquiry that has universal academic appeal. To restrict the study and pursuit of Islamic political economy to the Islamic community would be in contradiction of the knowledge-based system. Once this model is conceptualised, developed and applied to society at large, then various socio-economic issues are subsequently evolved and given theoretical and positive orientation, in contradistinction to mainstream economics. Examples of fields that could be included in the new system are the endogenous theory of money, ethico-economic development theory, the regeneration of social institutions, price theory and market complementarity, international development cooperation based on an ethico-economic framework of development, and so on.

Finally, it is seen that the formalisation of the nature of Islamic political economy brings it nearer to the way that the Islamic thinkers in the history of Islam thought of the unity between mind and matter. They were as interested in developing a theory of political economy as laying down the conceptual foundations of a unifying system of thought. When so understood, Islamic political economy does not present a rigid theory. It represents a purview of evolutionary epistemology based on the *Tawhidi* precept. Beyond this lies the development of various systems that can all qualify as candidates for the global system.

APPENDIX 5.1 INTERACTIONS AMONG THE PRINCIPLES AND INSTRUMENTS OF ISLAMIC POLITICAL ECONOMY

The objectives of this appendix are first, to show how the principles and instruments of Islamic political economy are derived from the *Qur'an* and *Sunnah*. Second, we will identify the epistemic–ontic relationship in the system of interactions between the principles and instruments. The socio-economic variables cannot be precisely identified because of their diversities. The *Qur'an* is emphatic on one kind of socio-economic variable, however. That is, spending in a varied number of directions, for purposes of generating goodwill amongst others, felicity amongst all, spending freely in the good cause, and in oneself.[57]

The Principles of Islamic Political Economy

It is commonly agreed by Islamic thinkers that one of the prime attributes of God (and hence of the unicity precept) is justice (*A'dl*).[58] The concept of justice is expressed in the *Qur'an* and *Sunnah* broadly in terms of balance, which in the socio-economic system becomes distributive justice. But since political economy encompasses both society and the economy, in Islamic political economy the narrower concept of distributive equity is replaced by the idea of social justice. Besides, as there is no difference between the antecedentalist and consequentialist phases of social justice in the sense of continuity between the epistemic and ontic, so the ideas of social justice and distributive justice must remain inseparable in Islamic political economy.[59] Hence the unicity precept, which is the principal premise of knowledge in Islamic political economy, must fully define the laws governing social justice in this comprehensive sense.

The *Qur'an* and *Sunnah* also emphasise the central need to guarantee and protect property rights or entitlement.[60] Thus we find the high value given to market process in Islamic political economy, and to the non-legislative power of *Shura*, which really acts principally as a knowledge-forming agency for the guidance of society in accordance with *Shari'ah*, and brings socially unacceptable behaviours under control through its supportive agencies, for example the *Hisbah*. In addition, because of the unifying concept of social justice in Islamic political economy, the concept of property rights must embrace *all* forms of property, as well as human welfare.[61]

Work and productivity must be considered as a subset of the principle of entitlement (property rights, *Haq al-Mal*). Such a sub-principle cannot be elevated to a fully fledged principle because social productivity and entitlement must also mean caring for and protecting the needy, the weak, the old, the young and the underprivileged. An Islamic economy may have a significant profit-sharing and co-operative sector. In this case the concept of work is not understood in terms of wage payments; neither is the contribution of output interpreted as average or marginal productivity as in the neoclassical sense. In any case, since this aspect of social justice and subsequently, universal formation and protection of property, cannot be realised in the absence of productive work and capital formation, the sub-principle of work and productivity is an implied subset of the principle of entitlement. We have thus established the minimum set of three principles of Islamic political economy: the unicity precept of God (*Tawhid*, which is supported by the *Sunnah* of the Prophet Muhammad); the principle of social justice; and the principle of entitlement (which is a sub-principle of work and productivity). To this minimum set can be added other sub-principles such as prayers, responsible behaviour, generosity, kindness (*Ehsan*), duties to God (*Huquq al-Allah*), duties to man (*Huqūq al-'Ibadah*) and so on. But these attributes are obviously included in the relationship of *Tawhid* with the formation of laws (*Shari'ah*) governing both social justice and entitlement. It is seen as well that the three principles circularly interrelate with each other.

The Principal Instruments of Islamic Political Economy

Next we examine the field of instruments of Islamic political economy, which are based on and serve the above fundamental principles. All Islamic economists agree that the abolition of interest (*Riba*) is a mandatory injunction of the *Qur'an*. The argument is both of a moral and economic nature. The *Qur'an* considers that interest, no matter how large or small, is an undue charge that is taken by the rich from the poor.[62] There is, however, considerable debate among the Islamic learned (*Fuqaha*) as to what constitutes interest – both in the physical exchange of items and in trade in monetary assets.[63]

Profit sharing is implicit in the *Qur'an*, but is directly invoked in the *Sunnah*.[64] This instrument is known as either *Mudarabah* or *Musharakah*. Profit sharing at all levels of the Islamic political economy is the principal alternative to interest-bearing transactions. Hence, since the abolition of *Riba* is a fundamental condition for the attainment of social and economic welfare and justice, the institution of *Mudarabah* and *Musharakah* must be equally important instruments for the elimination of *Riba*.

The *Qur'an* places the highest importance, along with prayers, on the duty of the wealthy to pay the wealth tax (*Zakah*) for the rehabilitation of the needy. *Zakah* revenues should be collected and disbursed in an organised way. In early Islam this method of managing *Zakah* funds was known as *Bait al-Mal*, the public treasury. *Zakah* marginalises other forms of direct taxes in the Islamic political economy, for the government comes to assume minimal function in such a system, while the responsibility to generate economic activity is predominantly passed on to the market economy with a *Shuratic* guidance. The market process is induced by spending that can be promoted by regimes of lower tax rates.

Zakah, along with the elimination of *Riba* and its replacement by *Mudarabah/Musharakah*, can be seen as a form of enhanced spending in the economy. The absence of interest on personal loans, along with the gift of *Zakah*, generates a type of grants economy, with an emphasis on investment and spending through human solidarity and goodwill.[65]

Finally, the *Qur'an* is emphatic about the elimination of ostentatious consumption and wasteful production (*Israf*).[66] The elimination of *Israf* links logically to the efficiency of *Mudarabah*, which then provides the impetus to eliminate *Riba*. *Riba* itself is considered as a form of *Israf* in the Islamic sense. But since *Zakah* disbursement is a positive function of absolute poverty, its volume depends on population size of the absolutely poor. *Zakah* disbursement per capita would increase either by an increase in national incomes or by a reduction of the target population size. Hence, an effective reduction of waste followed by its consequential relationship with *Mudarabah* would mobilise capital into productive investments. This will have an enhancing effect on *Zakah* to combat poverty and generate more distribution.

We have now established the minimum number of instruments needed for the Islamic political economy. These are the abolition of *Riba*, the institution of *Mudarabah/Musharakah*, the institution of wealth tax (*Zakah*) and the elimination of waste (*Israf*). There are other instruments, but they are not independent of the minimum set listed here. Foreign trade financing with mark-up (*Murabaha*), rental (*Ijara*), leasing (*Ba'y Muajjal*), interest-free loans (*Qard-e-Hasanah*), endowments (*Waqf*) and a range of *Shari'ah*-prescribed secondary market instruments can be added to the minimum list, but actually belong to the *Mudarabah/Musharakah* category and are mentioned neither in the *Qur'an* nor in the *Sunnah*.[67] Hence the latter instruments are details rather than principal instruments. They are also subject to options, unlike the instruments of the minimum set, which form the principal category.

Interactions Between the Principles and Instruments

It can now be seen how these instruments link up with the principles of Islamic political economy. The universal application of *Shari'ah* (and thus *Tawhid*) inculcates a social responsibility to establish justice and property rights for all. In order to realise this social objective, the instruments must be activated. This direction of relationship establishes the epistemic to ontic realisation in knowledge formation in Islamic political economy. Conversely, starting from the premise of politico-economic instruments, the activation of socio-economic activity (in conjunction with the exercise of the instruments) leads to better comprehension of *Shari'ah*. This is established in response to the realisation of socio-economic efficacy attained by the prescribed instruments. The ontic–epistemic cycle of knowledge formation is thus generated. Hence the interactions between the principles and instruments in the *Shura*, along with the responses from the socio-economic variables (most importantly the spending variable and its socio-economic effects) that are affected by such knowledge formation, establishes the epistemic–ontic circularity as the basis of evolution of the Islamic political economy.

Figure 5.2 shows the interactions between the principles and instruments of the Islamic political economy. The interaction of these principles and instruments with the socio-economic order is implied, for reasons that there are no

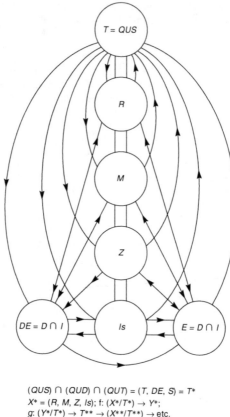

$(QUS) \cap (QUD) \cap (QUT) = (T, DE, S) = T*$
$X* = (R, M, Z, Is)$; f: $(X*/T*) \rightarrow Y*$;
g: $(Y*/T*) \rightarrow T** \rightarrow (X**/T**) \rightarrow$ etc.

Figure 5.2   Interactions between the principles and instruments of Islamic political economy

Notes: Q = *Qur'an*; S = *Sunnah*; T = *Tawhid*; D = syllogism; I = *Ijtihad*; DE = distributive equity (social justice); E = entitlement (property rights); R = abolition of financial interest (*Riba*); M = profit-sharing in economic ventures (*Mudarabah*) or equity participation (*Musharakah*); Z = *Zakah*; Is = avoidance of waste of all kinds (*Israf*).

exact socio-economic variables that can be identified, except the important one: namely, the spending variable in the good cause, which the *Qur'an* has constantly emphasised. All other socio-economic variables are derived from such a broad understanding of spending in the good cause. More detailed forms of interactions in the Islamic political economy can be developed from the above basic principles and instruments.

In Figure 5.2, $(Q \cup S) \cap (Q \cup D) \cap (Q \cup T) = (T, DE, S) = T^*$ as a convergent state of knowledge formation in the iterative system. $X^* = (R, M, Z, Is)$ is a corresponding state of knowledge derivation pertaining to T^* for the institutional order, as shown; $f: (X^*/T^*) \to Y^*$ is a functional mapping from the range of X^* given T^* to the socio-economic (political economy) Y^*. In $g: (Y^*/T^*) \to T^{**} \to (X^{**}/T^{**}) \to Y^{**} \to$, g is a map similar to f through iterations in the knowledge-formation process, T^{**} and so on, and the institutional–socio-economic transformations through circular causation and continuity.

APPENDIX 5.2 TECHNICAL APPENDIX

In reference to Figure 5.2 we define $\Omega = (T \cap E \cap DE)$. Θ_i is a specific relationship of Ω values, hence, $\Theta_i \in \Omega$.

Let $P^* = (R_i, M_i, Z_i, I_i)(\Theta_i)$. These are suitable policy variables. For example $R_i = \rho/r$, where ρ is the aggregate profit rate and r the interest rate; $M_i = \pi/Y$, where π is the value of profit and Y the aggregate income level; Z_i is taken in value terms of *Zakah* expenditure; $I_i = B/L$, where B is expenditure on basic needs and L is expenditure on luxuries. $f: P^* \to X$ ($=$ of the spending variable Sp_i; economic growth Q_i, entitlement A_i). Let $f(P^*, X) =$ constant, $i = 1, 2, \ldots, n$.

For simulational conditions we can formulate equations derived from the above functional relations, as follows:

$$R_i = f_{1i}(M_i, Z_i, I_i, X_i)(\Theta_i)$$

$$M_i = f_{2i}(R_i, Z_i, I_i, X_i)(\Theta_i)$$

$$Z_i = f_{3i}(R_i, M_i, I_i, X_i)(\Theta_i)$$

$$I_i = f_{4i}(R_i, M_i, Z_i, X_i)(\Theta_i)$$

$$X_i = f_{5i}(R_i, M_i, Z_i, I_i)(\Theta_i)$$

$\Theta_i = f_{6i}(\Theta_i')$, Θ_i' denote iterated values of Θ_i. Given $(\geqslant) = (\geqslant_P) \cap (\geqslant_M)$; $\Theta_i \in \underline{?} \subset \Omega$.

The objective criterion to simulate now is $W = W(X, P^*)(\Theta_i)$, subject to the above simulational relations. It is the objective of simulation to come up with the correct signs of the coefficients of variables in the above relationships. At that point a convergent iterated value of $\Theta = \Theta^*$ is established, for which $X = X^*(\Theta^*)$, $P^* = P^*(\Theta^*)$ and $W^* = W(P^*, X^*)(\Theta^*)$.

6 Why Cannot Neoclassicism Explain Resource Allocation and Development in the Islamic Political Economy?

Resource allocation is central to the study of the role of the private and public sectors in economic development. By the latter we mean structurally transforming the economy in order to attain economic efficiency and distributive equity. In the Islamic approach to socio-economic matters, the focus on these targets assumes a precise and methodological content. The issue then is: is it possible to realise both economic efficiency (material welfare) and distributive equity (moral worth) in an Islamic economic framework using neoclassical methodology?

Our objective in this chapter is to answer this question in an analytical and empirical light. However, we cannot provide an exhaustive critique of the neoclassical doctrine; neither can we formulate the methodology of Islamic political economy. For these matters the reader may refer to the literature.[1] The neoclassical methodology will also be implicated with the capitalist and socialist/communist doctrines while examining the approach to privatisation adopted in the capitalist transformation of the Muslim Commonwealth of Independent States (CIS). The neoclassical premise of these doctrines is well documented in the literature.[2]

THE ETHICAL CONSTRAINTS OF NEOCLASSICAL ECONOMICS

According to Phelps, distributive equity is not the focus of the neoclassical economic order, because under rational choice the maximisation of profits, utility, output and productivity renders the ethical goal of distributive equity less attractive and more costly to attain.[3] The same rational choice argument can be applied to moral targets. Here the rational individual (firm) has two choices. If less rather than more equity is chosen, this implies an unethical choice, since equitable distribution cannot be realised. If more equity is chosen rather than less, then economic efficiency must be sacrificed somewhere in the economic system. In a multisectorial economy, such a trade-off between greater distributive equity and reduced economic efficiency becomes untenable in a market of output-optimising firms and utility-maximising consumers.[4]

This market-directed response to agent-specific behaviour in neoclassical economics has been explained by Sen in terms of what he calls 'market consequentialism'.[5] This is the idea that market orientation depends upon the types of consumer preferences that are possible in it. In a neoclassical economic system, market consequentialism cannot favour distributive equity, as scarce resources are allocated for competing ends in order to optimise output and utility. Market consequentialism assumes even more aggressive hedonic proportions when utilitarianism is introduced in preference formation in a market setting.

WHAT IS NEOCLASSICAL ECONOMIC METHODOLOGY?

We are now ready to formalise the meaning of neoclassical economic methodology. The axioms of neoclassicism are (1) the existence of full information, (2) the existence of transitivity among alternate choices, and (3) strictly positive marginal utility/product if and only if non-zero inputs exist. The immediate consequence of the full-information axiom is to enable rational choice. This rational choice is then instrumentalised by the axiom of transitivity. In fact many economists are prone to identify the concept of economic rationality solely with the axiom of transitivity.[6]

Other consequences follow from these axioms. With the existence of full information in either perfect or imperfect competition it is assumed that agents are able to maximise their own self-interests and their individual rational choices. This leads to independence among rational agents, thus establishing a causal relationship between economic competition and the degree of agent-specific independence attained. That is, competition is realised in the presence of the axioms. Besides, if competition exists, then optimal information must be available to agents. This result is a classical one in the theory of perfect competition.[7]

In neoclassical oligopolistic behaviour, two contradictions appear. First, full information for individual agents does not exist, but the same first-order optimisation methodology is maintained to explain resource allocation.[8] Second, in the case of oligopolistic (including duopolistic) collusion, interdependence among agents is explained in terms of competition between colluding firms.[9]

Thus in all cases an optimisation methodology is maintained, although the absence of full information would prevent this from occurring in the case of interdependence. The result of this is that there can be no global interdependence among agents in the neoclassical framework. Oligopolistic firms appear as groups of competitors, as Lindbeck points out.[10] Inter-agent independence thus becomes the standard feature of neoclassical methodology. This causes resource allocation to depend on the substitution principle applied to the entire choice set. That is, although complementarity can exist between goods (as in the case of oligopolies), there is still competition between groups. Hence there is substitution in resource allocation between such competing groups. The concept of global complementarity therefore loses validity in neoclassical resource allocation methodology.

Independence, competition and substitution as causal relations arising from neoclassical axioms also generate equilibrium states of resource allocation. Such equilibrium states depend on the assumption that independence is the long-run, *ex post* consequence of historical interactions that remain exogenous in the determination of equilibrium condition. Economic competition, in the methodological sense, leads to independence of states in the long run. This is often referred to in the literature as the state of methodological individualism:[11] the agents now having gone through a series of interactions arrive at a long-run state of competitive choice, wherein equilibrium is possible. In this perspective of competition and equilibrium, resources are treated as scarce. Consequently marginal substitution becomes the logical tool of analysis for neoclassical economics.

Methodological individualism and methodological optimisation are logically inseparable consequences of the neoclassical school. They present the individual as self-seeking (not simply self-interested) and pitted against others for the optimal share of resources in order to enhance economic efficiency in the midst of market consequentialism. The resulting competition now explained by the neoclassical principle of substitution is a picture in duality of preferences and agents, with respect to the trade-off between economic efficiency and distributive equity. There likewise exists duality between the moral and material aspects of human welfare.

With regard to the methodological concept of competition, there remains duality between non-interacting agents. In choices between 'goods' and 'bads', between 'goods' and 'goods', and between 'bads' and 'bads', there must remain a neoclassical basket comprising all these categories as independent possibilities of choices. Thus a logical place is given to legitimise 'bads' over goods, etc. Thus the principle of substitution permits the choice between ethical and unethical bundles as a *permanent* possibility. This legitimation of the choice of 'bads' does not change in the long run with the advance of knowledge respecting the choices in neoclassical resource allocation.

THE SOCIAL AND ECONOMIC CONSEQUENCES OF NEOCLASSICAL ECONOMICS

The literature on social welfare, social choice and public choice economics is seen as neoclassical methodology extended to the political and social domains. As a result, what arose as a methodological problem of neoclassical microeconomics is transmitted to institutions, governments and the political economy as well. Thus political cycles are explained by the self-seeking behaviour of politicians near election time.[12] New institutionalism is a study of transaction cost minimisation, seen to result from the optimising behaviour of stakeholders seeking to minimise social conflict.[13] Formalisation of the social welfare function is a neoclassical aggregation of communal utilities. It is subject to the first and second order conditions of welfare optimisation, extended globally over a larger economic space.[14]

In all such economic states, households, factor markets, product markets and governments/institutions reflect the aggregative rational behaviour of individuals and firms. Thus neoclassicism is made to apply to institutions at large. In this extended sense too, methodological individualism, methodological optimisation and competition, followed by their hidden dualistic consequences, cannot attain moral–material simultaneity. Resource allocation of all kinds is subjected to these dualistically substituting consequences.

The underlying dualism of matter and spirit conveyed in the impossibility of moral-material simultaneity, and in *permanently* allowing bundles of good–bad/bad–bad/good–good choices to arise out of substitution, is not resolved by the neoclassical optimal choice on the production frontier. It is also not resolved by imputing technological advance to the neoclassical production and consumption functions.

In the case of determining choice on the optimal production frontier (or portfolio set),[15] such a point is seen as the result of the long-run consequences of competition, full information, methodological individualism, optimisation and equilibrium. They appear as choices intrinsically benign to the process of interactions among agents. The interactive learning processes become redundant as exogenous factors in neoclassical decision making, once the above types of long-run implications of optimality-equilibrium are assigned. This is also true – in a contradictory way – of perfectly and imperfectly competitive firms.

Next consider the result of technological induction on resource allocation in the neoclassical framework. Neoclassical optimal choices are long-run phenomena. Hence evolution of the optimal production frontier under technological induction means the evolution of allocative points over the long run. Within all such periods the axioms, conditions and socio-economic implications of neoclassical resource allocation characterise the entire technologically induced trajectory of growth.

Technology, as a long-run condition that abides by the optimal-equilibrium state of rational choice in the neoclassical order becomes interactively benign. This socially non-interactive nature of technology makes it dynamically evolutionary over time but not over states. The cause and effect process that should be instrumental in technological evolution is therefore absent in the neoclassical version of technological change. Thus neoclassical technological change remains exogenous to resource allocation. Hence the neoclassical evolutionary growth trajectory is simply the repetitive exogenous induction of technology over time.

SUMMARY

The preceding sections show that there is a one-to-one correspondence among optimality, equilibrium, substitution, methodological individualism and economic rationality. All of these are instrumental in establishing an intrinsically non-interactive socio-economic model of reality. It is the non-interactive nature of neoclassical methodology that makes it ethically neutral, socially benign and technologically exogenous, in an otherwise morally centred social, economic and political reality. Non-interactive technological induction in neoclassical methodology is damaging because of its inability to address social, political and economic problems and processes in an interactive and integrated way.[16]

The moral–material dualism of neoclassical methodology in terms of resource allocation, both in the tangible and the moral plane, is the principal cause of actions having no social sensitivity. Dualism here arises from a deeper philosophical belief in the occidental culture. It equally affects the occidental conception of modernity and science.

THE PHILOSOPHICAL ROOTS OF NEOCLASSICAL DUALISM

Neoclassical dualism is derived from the Hellenic culture, which treated the laws of the universe as divinely embodied in *telos*, and as a physical representation of divinity in lived experience.[17] This Hellenic perception of reality means that cognition is an *a priori*, one-directional determinism of the divine laws. But there exists no reverse causality from the *a posteriori* to the *a priori* world. Thus cognitive phenomena in this order are unable to unravel the unfolding knowledge of divine *a priorism*. Hence cause–effect evolutionary knowledge formation of the uniquely unified universal reality is structurally impossible in the Hellenic roots of rationalism. This renders the divine laws inactive, and hence unable to explain the real world and its socio-scientific symbiosis.

In the Age of Enlightenment this separation between the divine laws and lived experience spilled over into the Church and resulted in an intellectual backlash from the scientific community. This sounded the death knell of religious hegemony over scientific matters and gave rise to the rationalistic eighteenth-century philosophy of life that separated science from the divine precepts. (The rationalist movement was led by Newton, Kant, Descartes, Hume, Heidegger, Adam Smith, Bentham and Leon Walras.)[18] Duality between the moral and material essences of an otherwise unified reality was thus rendered complete in the Western world.

When we come to neoclassicism, the same dualism manifests itself in mutual independence caused by non-interactive benignity and by its principle of substitution globally. It is also caused by the absence of cause and effect through the circular interrelationship between the epistemic and ontic forms in the market. We therefore find the sole primacy of the market to be based in its ethically neutral consequentialism; and the sole primacy of individuated consumer preferences to be instrumental in moulding the entire system of consumption–production–distributional activities. Consumer preferences, like technology and the epistemic *praxis* of human reason, remain exogenously given as datum in the neoclassical order.[19]

The epistemic versus ontic *praxis* of neoclassicism can be explained as follows.[20] The product market determines its supply of goods by supply prices and outputs, which in turn are determined not by demand, but by the marginal cost conditions of firms in either perfect or imperfect conditions. Consumer demand (hence market demand) in the product market is determined by the prevailing conditions on the demand side of price formation, as given by the marginal utility of goods. Supply price is equated with demand price to establish equilibrium price and output in the context of these two independent sides of price determination. Subsequently costs are minimised, profits are optimised and individual utilities are maximised. This applies both to the partial and to the general equilibrium conditions of markets. Such a methodology is applied to both perfect and imperfect equilibrium in neoclassical economics.

The first methodological problem to arise from the above market exchange is the incompatibility of the underlying perspectives of prices in the two cases of demand and supply. For if exchange is demand driven, then demand prices must predominate. Hence all supply prices, p_s, must be determined by all demand prices, p_d. Thus as a function, $p_s = p_s(p_d)$. Furthermore the supply function, $S(.)$, is such that, as a function, $q_s = S(p_s) = S(p_s[p_d])$, where q_s denotes the quantity supplied at price p_s. Likewise it can be argued that, for the demand side, $q_d = D(p_d[p_s])$.

From these relations we obtain the excess demand function, $E = E(p_d, p_s)$. For our purposes $E = S - D$, so that as S increases with p_s, D decreases. Therefore, $\partial E/\partial p_s > 0$. For the same reason $\partial E/\partial p_d > 0$. Subsequently $dE/dp_d = (\partial E/\partial p_s) \cdot (dp_s/dp_d) + (\partial E/\partial p_d)$. We rewrite this as follows: $dE/dp_d = (\partial E/\partial p_s)(dp_s/dp_d + [\partial E/\partial p_d]/[\partial E/\partial p_s]) > 0$, since all terms on the right-hand side are positive. Now since $(\partial E/\partial p_s) > 0$, $(\partial E/\partial p_d) > 0$ and $dp_s/dp_d > 0$ – all because of the market equilibrating condition – it is impossible that $dE/dp_d < 0$, the condition required for market equilibrium to exist. Likewise it can be shown that it is impossible that $dE/dp_s < 0$.[21] Therefore the only way for market equilibrium to exist in the Walrasian or the Marshallian sense is to assume that a market equilibrium price exists, without explaining the problems of its existence.[22] The existence of market equilibrium and the underlying behaviour of pricing and objective functions thus become axiomatic premises of neoclassical economic theory. This rules out the possibility of integrating the demand and supply price mechanisms, when one predominates over the other from the price and quantity sides. Hence the underlying behavioural relationship in all neoclassical economics is methodological individualism of maximising behaviour.[23]

The above indeterminacy of market equilibrium in the ontic sense is found to occur in the factors market and the monetary sector. In the factors market a Pareto optimal general equilibrium result means that consumers' rate of commodity substitution between supply of factors and demand for commodities must equal the corresponding factor-specific marginal products. That is, factor prices are proportionate to the consumers' rate of commodity substitution. Hence factor prices become indeterminate, corresponding to the indeterminacy between the demand and supply prices of goods, as explained earlier.[24] This point also implies that the marginal productivity of factors remains unobservable. Hence factor prices cannot be determined in terms of marginal products, as suggested by the general equilibrium result.

In the monetary sector the price of money is taken to be interest rate, which includes in its measure a speculative value of risk and uncertainty, whereas money is used to transact goods/services with actual prices. Thus the return on money must be the return on the good/ service, which is its price. How then can the interest rate be taken as the price of money replacing the objective economic value in terms of the prices of goods/services? There is a problem of inconsistency here, which is not resolved by the quantity theory of money or by the Keynesian demand for liquidity preferences and the *LM* curve.[25]

Indeed with such an axiomatic assumption, market prices (like consumer prices) cannot be observed. We thus encounter the problem of not observing an *a priori* axiomatic entity.[26] Conversely, given the different types of pricing and exchange behaviour in the market system, for example cooperation, competitive cooperation, the 'satisfycing' behaviour of consumers and firms, and polity–market interactive decision making, it becomes impossible to explain the theoretical and institutional experiences of the economic competition of neoclassical economics. Here the ontic philosophy does not convey reality. Thus both the epistemic and the ontic experiences of the market economy, as perceived by mainstream economics, are foreign to the otherwise interactive and integrative functions of agents in alternative market systems.[27]

WHAT IS DIFFERENT AND NEW IN THE ISLAMIC POLITICO-ECONOMIC WORLD VIEW?[28]

Formulation of the Knowledge-Based Model of the Polity–Market Interactive World View

It is now clear that, to break away from the trade-off between the goals of social justice and economic efficiency, the neoclassical doctrine applied to the capitalist or socialist doctrines of structural transformation does not work out. Such an entrenched root of marginalist substitution between felicitous and productive alternatives in these doctrines also causes the notion of prices to appear as certain values in both these systems. Prices turn out to be optimal exchange values in the capitalist system and conjectured use values in the Marxist system. But in both, the intrinsic worth imputed in the goods by divine providence is epistemologically ignored. Thus the moral and ethical basis of all epistemologies cannot exist in these systems because of their very design.

To get away from this epistemologically empty premise of moral–material worth in the goods transacted through the market, substitution must be replaced by the principle of universal complementarity (simultaneity). To realise this principle an entirely new epistemological world view must be invoked. This is the interactive, knowledge-based Islamic world view.

In Figure 6.1, the polity box shows components of this view in terms of epistemological roots based on the precept that the divine laws emanate from a balanced, purposive, just and felicitous order of existence. Subsequently they aim at interactively integrating the various systems of existence in their minutest detail on the premise of the divine laws. This is the precept that asserts that the unity of God is the cause and effect of the interactively integrated process of the universe and finds its expression in both the realm of comprehension and in the order of cognitive reality. Thus in the epistemology of the unicity precept the difference between the Kantian *a priori* and *a posteriori* is annulled. Likewise the ontic difference between form and reality is rendered unsubstantive.[29] The epistemic and the ontic are merged together in the continuous evolution of knowledge through circularity of cause and effect between comprehension and cognition and their dynamic recreation.

This epistemological premise is instilled into the laws of life and thought throughout the socio-scientific domain.[30] They take up textual forms and are recorded, evolved and applied as the epistemic and ontic experience is regenerated continuously by cause and effect. Thereby institutions and rules are formulated to perpetuate the knowledge derived from the divine laws through socio-scientific actions. The interconnections between the *E* box (epistemology), the *DL* box (divine laws) and the *I* box (institutions) denote the interactive knowledge formation process taking place in the polity box.[31]

Unlike in the Gosplan or the Politbureau of the communist state,

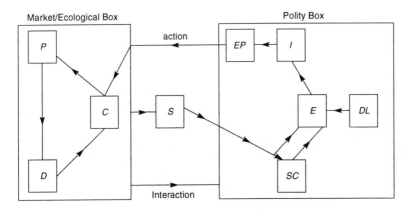

General ethico-economic equilibrium

Figure 6.1   The epistemic–ontic circular causation and continuity
model of unified reality: the world view of Islamic
political economy

wherein centralised decisions were made by bureaucrats with no cognisance of the markets and the grassroots of society at large, and unlike in the capitalist system, where all interactions become atomistic.
Interactions cannot then be explicitly manifested, the polity box cannot gain its knowledge while interacting with the market (ecological)
order. The reverse is the case with the interactive knowledge based
world view explained in Figure 6.1. In the case of political economy,
the market (ecological) box (Figure 6.1) comprises the consumption
function (*C*), the production function (*P*) and the distribution function
(*D*). Rule formation in polity based on the epistemological references
of all specific questions of life is made to act upon the market order.
That is, a set of polity-specific preferences are formed in the polity
box and are turned into actions that may impact on the moral–material
transformation of consumption, production and distribution. The net
result is delivery of the moral–material social good, *S* (common good).

The market order's response to the polity box is thus sensitised by
rule formation and its impact on the market's functions and choices.
Such a response is therefore a set of preferences formed outside polity
but in the midst of interactions between the sets of polity and market
preferences. Such reactions from the market order appear as checks,
balances, revisions and acceptance or rejection of the previous rules.
Post-evaluation thus ensues in the polity box of the past set of polity

preferences and their interactions with the market preferences. The polity and market systems are thus full of decentralised groups of decision makers. The prerequisite for such decision makers (*Sharees*) is their good understanding and close link with the rule-making methodology generated by the Islamic epistemological reference to *Shari'ah*. The decision makers are also required to possess high Islamic character and knowledge and be able to relate epistemological questions to the unicity precept (*Tawhid* and *Sunnah*).

When the sifting of the interactive preferences between polity and the market order (ecological order) reaches consensus, *SC*, an important juncture in the history of the continuous interactions, is attained.[32] Each interaction forms a bit of continuous knowledge; each integration forms social consensus. Subsequently fresh rounds of interaction–integration proceed and knowledge evolves. In this way, knowledge unifies all systems of thought and action through the process of interaction and integration. The actions formulate the epistemic; the responses formulate the ontic; the interactions form the epistemic–ontic; and the continuity of the process through the chain forms the epistemic-ontic circular causation and continuity model of unified reality, attained through the unification of knowledge.

In this system, since knowledge is both the input and output of all mental and cognitive systems, the equivalence between cause and effect, the epistemic and ontic, interactive–integrative preferences and the unification of knowledge based on the axiomatic and methodological uniqueness of the unicity precept, establish the universal principle of complementarity. Since knowledge is an affirmation of interactions through progression, and attains cognitive form, followed by new realms of knowledge, its cognitive forms must also be progressive. This dynamic, knowledge-induced cognitive process and the recreation of knowledge is denoted by the following functional chain:

$$E(\theta) \rightarrow (\theta_1) \rightarrow_{f1} (x_1) \rightarrow_{f2} (\theta_2) \rightarrow_{f3} (x_3) \rightarrow \ldots .$$

where $E(\theta)$ denotes the immutable epistemological premise of knowledge based on the unicity precept. This is an optimal stock, which is never realised or temporally manifest, but is functionally fundamental (foundational) in knowledge formation as flows (evolutionary epistemology). (θ_i) are flows of knowledge (evolutionary epistemologies) at the ith round of interactions, $i = 1, 2, \ldots$ (x_i) are the cognitive forms realised by the evolutionary epistemologies. The epistemic–ontic transformations between these variables are accomplished by the functional forms f_i. The values of evolutionary knowledge are assigned ordinally in polity on the basis of polity–market interactions. The knowledge-induced form of functions such as $f = f(x_1[\theta_1], x_2(\theta_2), \ldots x_n[\theta_n])$ can assume the most generalised systemic meaning in the socio-scientific order.

The polity box in Figure 6.1 shows that there is direct relationship between institutions, I (*Shura* in Islamic polity, but taken here in the strictly *Qur'anic* sense to mean embryonic and pervasive polity over the entire human domain), and the formulation of ethical policies, *EP*. These ethical policies interact with the market environment, as shown in Figure 6.1. In the market box the usual general equilibrium relationship is shown to exist: consumption, C, relates with production, P, and this with distribution, D. All these activities are influenced by ethical policies. This results in the generation of S, social product, which then sends feedback signals to the polity box: in the short run the institutions are influenced to revise their policies and the interactions continue; in the long-run social consensus, *SC*, is formed. This further influences the I and *EP* sets to generate a higher level of interactions between polity and the market/social system. General equilibrium in the market/society set is shown in terms of integration of the socio-economic variables. General equilibrium in the polity set is shown in terms of social consensus.

THE CASE OF THE MUSLIM COMMONWEALTH OF INDEPENDENT STATES

We will now examine how the Islamic politico-economic perspective of the *Shuratic* process can address development in the Muslim Commonwealth of Independent States. This particular case study is chosen because it involves all three ingredients of global change, namely the socialist old guard, the capitalist new guard, and Islam past and future. This examination of the Islamic politico-economic alternative is carried out in the context of the blueprint of privatisation now being launched under the auspices of Western development organisations, principally the IMF and the World Bank.

Borensztein, in a recent IMF paper on the privatisation drive in Eastern Europe,[33] points out that the cost of privatisation in the face of a 200–300 per cent inflationary run-off, and a 20 per cent decline in output in many sectors, calls for extensive reallocation of real and financial resources. This is bound to inflict huge private and social costs in the short run, which will in turn result in long-term dislocation for the economies concerned. The author points out that endogenous factors, such as the absence of capital markets and of administrative and human resource development, make structural transformation under privatisation immensely destabilising. According to the *IMF Survey*,

> The move from a centrally planned system to a market economy implies a structural change in production – a massive reallocation of resources. This change, according to Borensztein, 'is initially likely to result in an output decline', mainly because of the asymmetrical speed of response of those activities that are negatively and positively affected by the reform. 'Productive sectors,' Borensztein explains, 'that are not viable under market conditions quickly become financially strapped or face non-existent demand.' In contrast, productive sectors that should expand are reluctant to invest and thus tend to grow slowly, held back by adjustment costs and by uncertainty.[34]

The reality of immense adjustment costs applies equally to the Muslim CIS. They highlight the failure of the neoclassical perceptions behind the privatisation drive and of the underlying macroeconomic policies to take account of such disequilibria when prescribing an unsuitable Western model of change that will hardly ease the economic plight. Optimality and equilibrium, substitution and duality respecting to choices, sectors and economic goals, become abiding methodological prescriptions of the neoclassical unrealism.

Let us now take this analysis a step further and look at the social costs and dislocations caused by trade-offs under the neoclassical model of economic change in the Muslim CIS. Table 6.1 shows the extent of trade-off between unemployment, price level and output. Note that these are the aggregate variables that enter as inputs in the macroeconomic version of the social welfare function with neoclassical properties.[35] The severe decline in output, sharp increase in price level and general decline in employment are having a profound effect on social welfare. The deteriorating fiscal balance as a percentage of GDP (Table 6.2) implies that fiscal policies have been far from effective in correcting the socio-economic disequilibrium that has taken place. Furthermore, in the absence of adequate financial institutions and capital markets in the CIS, these countries have become subservient to the monetary policies of the Western bloc, especially its interest rate and exchange rate mechanisms.

Table 6.1   Socio-economic indicators in the Muslim CIS, 1990–91
(percentage change)

| | Real GDP | | Price level | | Employment | |
	1990	1991	1990	1991	1990	1991
Azerbaijan	−11.7	−0.7	7.8	87.3	–	–
Kazakhstan	−1.5	−9.6	4.0	84.0	–	–
Kyrghyzstan	4.0	−2.0	3.0	181.0	−0.4	−2.0
Tajikistan	−0.6	−8.7	4.0	103.0	3.0	0.4
Turkmenistan	1.5	−0.6	4.6	90.0	3.4	2.6
Uzbekistan	4.3	−0.9	3.1	82.2	2.8	0.4

Source: IMF staff estimates, quoted in *Economic Review: Common Issues and Interrepublic Relations in the Former USSR* (Washington DC: IMF, 1992).

Table 6.2   Fiscal policy indicators in the Muslim CIS (per cent of GDP)

| | Fiscal balance | |
	1991	1992
Azerbaijan	−5.2	–
Kazakhstan	−8.0	−3.2
Kyrghyzstan	3.3	−2.5
Tajikistan	3.4	−1.4
Turkmenistan	3.2	−8.0
Uzbekistan	−5.5	–

Source: As for Table 6.1.

The study by Borensztein, the evidence of massive trade-offs, and the methodological long-run prescription for optimality and equilibrium, methodological individualism, independence (non-interactivity), substitution and duality perspectives of neoclassical micro- and macroeconomic frameworks, all point to the destabilising nature of this approach. Yet at the point of long-run equilibrium, these prescriptive states are not reflected as the result of interactive processes in neoclassical methodology. The costs of adjustment are so large that long-run optimal equilibrium continues to recede, causing a quagmire of destabilisation. These debilities remain intact even in the Walrasian and Leontief type decomposition of production techniques, because of their reliance on neoclassically induced growth trajectories.[36]

The structure of Muslim CIS economies diversified between a predominantly agricultural and a heavily industrialised and resource base, points to a good degree of complementary possibilities between these sectors for inducing economic growth. The fervour of cooperative ventures has also been high, but the cooperative perspective in the Communist regime existed in the absence of markets and the presence of suppressed demand. Thus profit sharing among cooperative agents was never looked upon as an important economic activity.

Profit sharing under economic cooperation (*Mudarabah*) is a principal instrument of the Islamic political economy. Its objectives are to remove capitalism's socially divisive interest transactions and to ethicise the market system in the midst of interactive sequences of learning-by-doing processes engendered through the interactively established joint preferences of polity and market (ecology). The extensive nature of interactive decision making in this framework of profit sharing under economic cooperation subsumes in it questions of participation – social control of production, appropriate technology, consumption and production of social goods (common goods) and distribution of wealth, income and resources arising from menus of social goods.

The history of Islamic legacy and movement in the Muslim CIS is today found to rise up again in its expressions of grassroots pattern of self-reliance. This return to Pan-Islamic order aims at establishing the totality of political, social and economic life. In recent times such efforts have been coordinated by grassroots movements in Turkey, led by intellectuals, and by the Dar al-Arqam grassroots movement in Malaysia. The latter has established exemplary organisations encompassing social and economic activities in a communitarian setting.[37] The Middle Eastern countries, along with Iran and Pakistan, have been involved in the process of re-educating the Muslim CIS countries since their release from communist rule. The precept of communitarian life among all the Muslim peoples of the various artificially created by the communists Muslim CIS republics remains high. This is the idea of the *Millat* or *Shura*, collective decision making at the most decentralised levels of interest groups in the community. Such a politico-economic transformation can best be centred around the knowledge-forming experience employing Islamic Laws (*Shari'ah*) to all facets of life and to specific problems as they arise.

Communist rule proved a fiasco, and the capitalist transformation process is causing instability in the name of privatisation and price liberalisation. It is therefore important for the future Islamic transformation of the Muslim CIS that they return to the epistemological and organisational roots of Islamic political economy. The cost of bringing about Islamic change would be lower than the heavy costs incurred under communism and capitalism. This is so because an Islamic trans-formation means Islamicising (by epistemological reference) the exist-ing cooperative institutions, focusing on the sectorial interlinkages of the economies and their complementarities provided inter- and intra-CIS republics. The question of capital markets that will both protect the Islamicising Muslim CIS and engender effective profit sharing rather than interest-based transactions must appear as a most important issue for the CIS. This critical transformation will undoubtedly pose an ini-tial problem in the absence of an Islamic capital market today. But the matter is to be resolved in the context of a massive system of comple-mentary interlinkages in the Islamicising political economy of the Muslim CIS. Interlinkages would be required in such a transformation between the capital markets (monetary and financial sectors) and the real goods sector; between the various cultural sectors; in intercommunal trade and common socio-economic goals; and among the institutions of de-velopment and policy coordination. Effective interlinkages must exist between the institutions of the Muslim CIS and the Islamic Banks in the financial sector internationally, and with the Islamic Development Bank for economic cooperation with all Muslim countries. Such interlinkages are to be tied in through the knowledge-based process of sharing and learning-by-doing in the premisses of *Shari'ah* governing all transactions and developmental facets of an Islamicising political economy. Thus inter- and intra-CIS republic interactions as well as global interrelationships will reflect the most extensive kind of interlinkages and complementarity of the Islamic political economy. There must be a political will among the people to take up activism for grassroots democratic change.

Throughout all this the knowledge-centred, learning-by-doing pro-cess between the agents of change must prevail. This means extensive interaction between polity and the market order in line with the *Shari'ah* on all matters of political economy. As discussed earlier, this interac-tive process is called the *Shuratic* process and it takes place in and emanates from the polity *Shura*.[38] The understanding and application of *Shari'ah* to all facets of Islamic thought and life form the evolu-tionary epistemology of the Islamicising process. The *Shuratic* process is seen as equivalent to the epistemic–ontic circular causation and con-tinuity model of unified reality, exercising the broadest limits of the principle of universal complementarity, with its specific application now being to the Islamic political economy. There must be the political will for grassroots democratic change.

The transition from interest-based transactions to a profit-sharing system could follow one of two paths. There could be immediate replacement of all interest transactions by joint ventures, equity participation, foreign trade financing and profit sharing, as took place in Iran after the Islamic Revolution. Alternatively there could be a more gradual, phased-in transformation of this type, as took place in Pakistan. In both cases, according to the IMF, no particular instability will take place in the monetary sector.[39]

The difference between profit sharing and interest transactions is based on the capitalistic depriving nature of interest on the one hand, and the real nature of profit on the other. The difference between these values is the subjective cost (or understatement) of capital involuntarily forgone by the owner of capital. Since this cost as a surplus (or loss) is speculatively induced into the capitalist system, therefore, such a system with its economic relations, institutions, policies and individualistic preferences remains uncertain and unpredictive. This is the destabilising effect left by the rate of interest across the length and breadth of the capitalist order. Consequently, an undue subjective cost of capital and resource allocation brings about a resource leakage in the economy (usually in the form of withdrawal by way of saving), creating thus inefficient values of consumption and production. Through this inefficient consequence is engendered the depriving and inefficient nature of resource allocation. It is thus a neoclassical fallacy to claim that the rate of interest promotes allocative efficiency – the use of interest in the capitalist political economy is both inefficient and unjust.

Profit sharing is bereft of speculative elements and large surpluses, when this value is determined purely in a market system. Besides, the interactive polity–market preferences forming knowledge and social consensus in the *Shuratic* process ethicises the market order through the consequential influence of moral preferences in it.[40] Consequently, although not the classical normal profits because of the profit-sharing nature of the Islamic enterprises, surpluses in such ethicised markets cannot be large and must be fully distributive in the presence of participatory ownership. Hence, social justice (distributive justice) is attained along with maximal allocation of resources in a spending prone, profit-sharing economy.[41] The presence of profit sharing thus attains simultaneity between economic efficiency (material worth) and distributive justice (moral worth).

Profit sharing as a replacement for the capitalist interest for reasons of social justice and economic efficiency can be optimised in the presence of the Islamic epistemology of value, price and money. All of these are then institutionalised in the polity–market interactive process in its broadest sense. The central point to note in all of this is the endogenous nature of ethics in the moral–material simultaneity among all economic activities. Money too is an endogenous creation of this system, unlike the exogenously supplied money of the capitalist system or the labour theory of value affecting money – by means of valuation of precious metals in circulation that are produced by labour in the first place. The Marxist theory of value upholds the latter view.[42]

The endogenous theory of price, value and money in Islamic political economy upholds the epistemological stance that the intrinsic value of all goods lies in the felicity embodied in them by the primordial order of divine creation. Any good that does not promote felicity should not be consumed, produced or distributed in the Islamic political economy. The injunction in this regard is formed through the knowledge induction of the *Shuratic* process and not through moral coercion. It is because of the existence of this intrinsically endogenous felicity value, that deprivation, excesses and value subjectivity cannot constitute part of a theory of value and price. Rather, with the increased realisation of this intrinsic value of felicity in polity–market interactions, the abovementioned sources of 'dis-values' are reduced.

Let F denote felicity (well-being). The total value, $V_T(F)$, in market transactions is the sum of the value produced by social welfare, $V_S(F)$, and the value produced by economic welfare, $V_E(F)$. Both of these depend upon the endogenous premise of felicity, F. Thus $V_T(F) = V_S(F) + V_E(F)$. The principle of universal complementarity between economic efficiency and social justice implies that all of these values must increase together. Thus fundamentally, the knowledge for realising the felicity value must be enhanced in the *Shuratic* process.

F does not appear in capitalist and socialist theories. It is replaced by reductionism of the material order. Hence material essence, M, replaces F. Then $V_S(M)$ and $V_E(M)$ exist in a trade-off in the relation $V_T(M) = V_S(M) + V_E(M)$. In the capitalist order, $V_T(M)$ denotes exchange value associated with economic subjectivity. In the socialist order, $V_T(M)$ denotes use-value, say $V_T'(M)$.

Now $V_T(M[F]) - V_T(M) = \{V_S(M[F]) - V_S(M)\} + \{V_E(M[F]) - V_E(M)\} > 0$ because of the increasing returns to knowledge, $V_S(M[F]) > V_S(M)$. Here M denotes material essence (for example, labour power) and $M(P)$ denotes the material essence generated by the induction of moral values (F). Thus $M(F)$ denotes moral–material worth (for example, labour power generated in the presence of intrinsic felicity, as defined above). Then by complementarity between social and economic values in the Islamic order, $V_E(M[F]) > V_E(M)$, which is brought about by a significant increase in social value, carrying along with it economic value, as denoted by the simultaneity of moral–material worth, $M(F)$, in the above expressions. Hence, with this higher total value of goods in the Islamic order, deprivation, uncertainty, speculation and excess are reduced by inverting the relationship between value and 'disvalue'. Consequently, in Islamic political economy prices become relatively lower and more stable the higher the total value based on felicity and moral–material worth. It also means that profits (thereby profit rates) cannot be extraordinary surpluses. The economic arrangement and the nature of institutional and sectorial interlinkages and cooperative mechanism all cause such a regime to exist.

When interest rate is totally eliminated by this process of knowledge induction, then the quantity of money in the economy will be fully determined by the price of the goods. Hence money too is determined by the moral–material worth of economic transactions and is thus an endogenous aggregate. Money creation must then mean a flow of currency necessary to monetise the value of goods in circulation. Money is thereby not equivalent to the supply of promissory notes. This is the concept of the endogenous theory of money, which plays a distinct and central role in the Islamic political economy.[43]

The above theorising on value, price and money also points out that excess pricing is inherent in the capitalist and socialist economies. This arises from the effect of value difference on the prices through their inverse relationship. Hence there is inherent deprivation in these economies as well, for now the excess price (either as price of a good, interest rate, wage rate, or rent) is either taken by the capitalist or by labour in the socialist system. None of these is legitimated under the principle of fairness and equality necessary for eliminating deprivation, excesses, speculation and uncertainty and their adverse effects on the intrinsic felicity value derived from the enjoyment of goods primordially created, and thus absolutely owned only by divine providence.

CONCLUSION

The world view and methodology of the embryonic *Shuratic* process as a proper and more substantive characterisation of Islamic investigation into economic, social and political matters are distinct from the constrained economistic theorising of mainstream economics. Most notable in the latter category is the neoclassical school, which leans on other economic doctrines. The *Shuratic* element of Islamic political economy enriches its policy-theoretic content, unlike the interaction-free methodology of neoclassical economics. This is why, as we have shown analytically and factually with respect to Eastern European and Muslim CIS economic transformation, the neoclassical economic and macroeconomic approaches cannot explain the *process* of change, while providing optimal and equilibrium conditions of long-run expected adjustment without consideration given to the greater embedded social order.[44]

The Islamic political economy – as distinct from the neoclassical treatment of Islamic 'economics' – is embedded in a complex of inter-relationships that form socio-scientific reality in the midst of the principle of universal complementarity. The neoclassical treatment of Islamic economic matters poses a warning to Islamic scholars. In such a mould of thinking, no new contributions can be made respecting the substantively epistemological *praxis* of Islamic socio-scientific order.[45] The consequence will then be either a pitiful methodological nicety without meaningful content; or it will be a defeative scientific, empirical and institutional development in the framework of 'Islamic economics', a petrified scientific pursuit that is unable to address human predicaments, transform the *Ummah* in body and spirit, and construct a distinctive model of its own.[46] In this regard the *Qur'an* points out, 'Thus have We made of you an *Ummah* justly balanced, that ye might be witnesses over the nations' (S. II, vs. 143).

APPENDIX 6.1

Consider the following problems of individuation in the neoclassical social choice and welfare menu.

Let $U_i = U_i(X_1, X_2, \ldots, X_n)$ denote the utility function of ith consumer (agent) in n number of goods, X_j, $j = 1, 2 \ldots n$. Neoclassical methodology with utilitarianism allows for the following: $\Sigma_i U_i(X_1, X_2, \ldots, X_n)$ signifies individuation among decision makers, $i = 1, 2, \ldots, n$. Total utility, $U_i(X_1, X_2, \ldots, X_n) = \Sigma_j U_j(X_j)$, signifies individuation among goods, $j = 1, 2, \ldots, n$, for ith decision maker, $i = 1, 2, \ldots, m$. $\Sigma_i \Sigma_j U_i(X_j)$, signifies individuation among goods, j, and decision makers, i.

For the general case of individual commodity-specific utilitarian aggregation over utilities, we can write,

$i\backslash j$	1	2	$\ldots$	n
1	U_{11}	U_{12}	$\ldots$	U_{1n}
2	U_{21}	U_{22}	$\ldots$	$U_{2n}\ldots$
m	U_{m1}	U_{m2}	$\ldots$	U_{mn}

Here $U_{ij} = U_i(X_j)$; $i = 1, 2, \ldots, m$ as number of individuals; $j = 1, 2, \ldots, n$ as number of goods.

Now note the overall individuation among U_{ij}, $U_{ij'}$, $U_{i'j}$, for $i, i' = 1, 2, \ldots, m$; $j, j' = 1, 2, \ldots, n$.

But in the Islamic political economy we must have interactions and integration reflected in the following sets: (U_{ij}), $(U_{ij'})$: that is, $(U_{ij}) \cap (U_{ij'})$ must apply as the range of meaningful decision criteria. Likewise we have $(U_{ij}) \cap (U_{i'j})$. Hence these decision spaces give the interactive preferences $(\geqslant) = (\geqslant_M) \cap (\geqslant_P)$, where $(\geqslant_M)$ denotes pure market-determined preferences, $(\geqslant_P)$ denotes pure polity-determined preferences and $(\geqslant)$ denotes interactive preferences.

7 Integrating the Grassroots with Paradigms of Trade and Development: The Case of Malaysia

There are prominent grassroots movements today in Malaysia that are fired by a comprehensive Islamic approach to human and socio-economic development. They derive their model of socio-economic development from the Islamic concept of integrating the inner development of self with broad-based socio-economic development. Thus self-actualisation and knowledge formation find their expression in human and socio-economic development. Inner development as a self-actualisation process is referred to here as *Hablum Minallah*; the externalisation of this is referred to as *Hablum Minannas*.[1] The total developmental approach is the interaction and integration of these two activities. Hence the Malaysian grassroots movements hold an interactive–integrative world view of structural change.

In this chapter we will show that this world view is derived from the essence of knowledge formation that Islam treats as the unifying epistemology of its socio-scientific order. The same knowledge-centred world view can be applied to specific areas. One such study we will undertake here is that of applying the generic interactive–integrative knowledge-centred model to the approach of combining the trade and developmental theories together. Within this unifying model of total human welfare will be taken up the topic of social well-being at the grassroots. In this context, the interactive–integrative world view of unification of knowledge will be shown to underlie the necessary interlinkages between the rural and urban sectors, between trade and development, and among all these.

THE EMERGENCE OF THE GRASSROOTS MOVEMENT IN MALAYSIA[2]

The Islamic grassroots movement arose in Malaysia as an organised reaction against the Malaysian government's adherence to Western methods of development and Western culture, which were seen as having no bearing on the lives of ordinary Malays. Imported culture was seen as imprisoning Muslim minds and binding the Muslim people to dependency and misguided development paradigms that would do little to advance human development, social justice and ethical values. The movement saw in Islam a complete way of life for Malaysia, and as it spread from the rural to the urban sector it came to command substantial human and economic resources.

Because of the movement's unique integrative world view of *Hablum Minallah* (inner relations with God) and *Hablum Minannas* (outer relations to man and society through human relations with God), the grassroots followers organised themselves on two fronts. First, they educated themselves in Islam informally and formally in the school systems they had established. Second, they began to develop institutions that could mobilise and organise resources. Their economic enterprises now range from small-scale grocery shops to publishing houses, computer-assisted enterprises, clinics and agricultural research stations.[3]

The distributive system of the grassroots movement, called *Ma'ash*, pooled and distributed basic goods to all according to need. All members of the movement contributed to the pool, and in return their basic needs were met in the form of goods and a basic allowance. Thus through *Ma'ash* the grassroots movement intended to eradicate poverty among its members.

It is remarkable that the grassroots movement was able to carry out its aims without any external financial support. This independence from governmental and other external financial sources allowed it to be bold in its endeavours, and unlike most grassroots movements in developing countries it was pursuing both socio-economic and political change.[4] The philosophical and organisational capacities of the movement were presenting a challenge to the Malaysian government's orientation towards the Western approach to growth and development.

The integrated *Hablum Minallah–Hablum Minannas* world view of development and organisation was imparted by grassroots *Shuras*. These consultative assemblies encouraged discourse on all issues among all members. Discussions started at an informal level among members in organised groups. Formal presentation of their views took place at the regular meetings of the grand consultative assembly under the village heads, before passing on to the highest echelons. The consultative processes was open to both males and females, and recourse is made to

Ijma (consensus) or *Qiyas* (analogy made by the Islamically learned on the issues) in order to arrive at a ruling on the issues in question (*Ahkam* formation). Islamic textual references reigned supreme in these deliberations. In this way an interactive–integrative decision-making process was engendered by means of *Shari'ah* (Islamic law) and its application to particular problems. The latter approach opened up the process to enable further development of the rules of life and interpretation of the fundamental Islamic sources of knowledge (the *Qur'an*, *Sunnah*), and is known as *Ijtihad*.

Thus the organisational model of the grassroots movement followed a comprehensive Islamic approach to knowledge formation in all areas of life. It is also this approach that, by developing *Ahqams* (rules of life) from the embryonic levels, becomes the *modus operandi* of integrating the grassroots in the complex of socio-economic life. Individuals are empowered at all levels; they are given a sense of dignity and self-worth, and this enables them to contribute positively to community life. This in turn opens up scope for human development, and guarantees that individuals will contribute to the spirit of social cooperation. The entire process can be depicted as follows:

Goodness (*Islah*) ↔ charity (*Hasanah*) ↔ growth and well-being (*Falah*) ↔ enhancement (*Yue'id*) → continuity and movement to higher levels = *Hablum Minallah–Hablum Minannas*

Social life is known to start from the *a priori* conditions of human goodness that form purpose and cognitive abilities followed by the appreciation of the artefacts of life. Subsequently abundance and sustainability are maintained by sharing and preserving resources, rather than engaging in hedonic and wasteful activities. Abundance creates price stability and maintenance of real output. Human development in the midst of such material security produces the resources that are necessary for ownership, participation and greater well-being. Thus life becomes worth living, purposefully enjoyed and utilised. Its synergy is never exhausted in the midst of such cooperative scale of sharing, reproduction and enhancement. Unwarranted external intrusion is prevented by the spirit of self-reliance and zealous protection of the life so earned, and posterity is safeguarded by the continuity of this process of moral–material simultaneity and its recreation to higher levels. Every emergence and continuity of knowledge-based order to such higher levels causes the entire socio-scientific order to ascend to higher levels.

of excellence. This comprises the rational process of derivation, enhancement and continuity of the knowledge-based order in the plane of moral–material worth. This process endows the Islamic grassroots movement with its regimented dynamics.

Socio-economic rationality is now defined as the process of simulatively determining increasing levels of moral–material worth under the reproductive process that establishes reality and continuity of the knowledge-based order. Now if there are two possible states, A and B, to be attained either by two alternative approaches to the abovementioned *Hablum Minallah–Hablum Minannas* process or by a combination of this and other extraneous factors, choice between them would be explained as follows. The social choice function is determined by interactions between the two components, *Hablum Minallah* and *Hablum Minannas*. If one of these declines in measure, the other declines also. Each of these components is determined by its epistemological premise. But the nature of these variables is such that they interact among themselves to establish the two components simultaneously. In all cases, therefore, we find the process of interactions yielding simultaneity among possibilities to prevail in determining values for the social choice function. The higher the interaction, the higher the moral–material worth yielded by the corresponding social choice function. Thus the two alternatives, A and B, within the domain of *Hablum Minallah–Hablum Minannas* are evaluated accordingly. In this choice function it is now obvious that if, say, B is an extraneous choice, then the interaction will be null. Hence the social choice function will be zero. This is indeed the implication of the grassroots movement's drive for Islamic purity and its vehement opposition to the adoption of anti-Islamic elements in the development process in Malaysia.

In spite of its appeal to many in Malaysia, the Islamic grassroots movement remained an incremental one fixed on the strictness of its cause and the zealousness of its members to this cause. While this may at first appear to have placed a constraint on membership of the movement, it proved to its advantage in terms of its place in the Malaysian socio-economic and political scene. As Mohammad Sayuti Omar writes in his *Merdeka Kedua*, 'The era of overwhelming resurgence of Islam in our country will change the power, economic, social and political structure.'[5]

The Malaysian political magazine *ERA* has said of the Islamic grassroots movement: '[the movement] although not registered as a society, over the last twenty years has become a social grouping, a new subculture, and a very meaningful and important symptom in the social and Islamic development in Malaysia.'[6] There have also been government comments on the Islamic grassroots movement as, for example, Encik Shamsuddin bin Mohammad Dubi, deputy head secretary of the Ministry, reported.[7]

These various views on the Islamic grassroots movement point to a good understanding and dialogue between grassroots movements and the Malaysian establishment. This is yet another step towards the continuous, interactive–integrative knowledge-centred world view that lies at the roots of the *Hablum Minallah–Hablum Minannas* model for the greater benefit of Malaysia as a whole. We shall now examine this subject more objectively.

Unfortunately, when dialogue between the Malaysian Government and the grassroots movement called Daral-Arqam failed, the latter was banned in Malaysia. The Malaysian Government found unacceptable bigotry in the movement. This attitude was seen as anti-Islam and anti-development. Today Daral-Arqam, despite its earlier remarkable performance as an Islamic grassroots movement, does not exist in Malaysia.

THE MALAYSIAN PERSPECTIVE OF GROWTH AND DEVELOPMENT TO THE YEAR 2000[8]

The focus of the Malaysian New Economic Policy during the period 1969–90 was on social issues, the most important of which were the eradication of poverty, the provision of income to poor Malays (the Bumiputeras), the strengthening of asset ownership by the Bumiputeras, and human resource development. Liberal government spending, favourable lending terms and strong economic growth resulted in a commendable performance on the part of Malaysia in its bid to eradicate absolute poverty, which fell from 49.3 per cent in 1970 to 15 per cent by the end of 1990. In addition the average monthly income rose from M$75 in 1970 to M$421 in 1990 for the bottom 40 per cent of households in peninsular Malaysia, while the overall mainland average rose from M$264 to M$1163 during the same period. In the islands Sabah and Sarawak the average monthly income rose from M$76 in 1970 to M$421 in 1990.

With regard to asset ownership, equity holdings by Bumiputeras rose to 20.3 per cent, far short of the target of 30 per cent under the New Economic Plan. This contrasts significantly with the 44.9 per cent held by Chinese Malaysians. Much of the equity held by the Bumiputera

Malaysians was a result of government support, and just 8.2 per cent was due to direct Bumiputera ownership and investment. This slow development has made it difficult for the government of Malaysia to bring about what is to be known as the Bumiputera Commercial and Industrial Community.

On the side of employment, overall the employment of Bumiputeras was comparable to that of non-Bumiputeras, although out of line with the target figures. In the primary section in 1990, 71.2 per cent of total employment was accounted for by Bumiputeras (target 61.4 per cent) compared with 28.8 per cent for non-Bumiputeras (target 38.6 per cent). In the secondary sector the figures were Bumiputeras 48.0 per cent (target 51.9 per cent) and non-Bumiputeras 52 per cent (target 48.1 per cent), while in the service sector they were Bumiputeras 51.0 per cent (target 48.4 per cent) and non-Bumiputeras 49.0 per cent (target 51.6 per cent). The important point to note here is the significantly smaller share of manufacturing employment by Bumiputeras compared with that of non-Bumiputeras, showing that the structural shift in employment did not increase the productivity of the Bumiputeras significantly and they still held traditional jobs even after twenty years of the New Economic Plan.

The employment picture in manufacturing is linked to the skewed structure in this sector in favour of non-Bumiputeras. Manufacturing's share of gross domestic product increased from 13.9 per cent in 1970 to 27.0 per cent in 1990, whereas agriculture's share fell from 29.0 per cent to 18.7 per cent. The service sector's share increased from 36.2 per cent to 42.3 per cent during the same period. The share of manufacturing employment and the equity holding structure mentioned above make it clear that the economic welfare of Bumiputeras has not improved as much as it might, and the picture of absolute improvement hides the fact that growth in productivity and internal rentiership that will continue to benefit the privileged few in Malaysian society. Besides, a lack of relative productivity performance in this regard hides the cost that accrues to government in either mobilising greater amounts of public funds for ameliorating the underprivileged, or conversely in driving the Malaysian economy (with resulting adversity for the less skilful) toward significant privatisation.

The need to improve the plight of the Bumiputeras is all the more urgent when viewed against their population growth. The Bumiputeras made up 56.5 per cent of the population in 1985 but this had risen to 58.1 per cent by 1990, compared with a fall from 32.8 per cent to 31.4 per cent for Chinese Malays. The future performance of the

Malaysian economy, as envisaged in the New Development Plan, requires that the social and economic welfare of the Bumiputeras should be brought into line with that of others.

The New Development Plan envisages that Malaysia's gross domestic product will increase by 7.0 per cent by the year 2000. Of total GDP, manufacturing is targeted to contribute 38.7 per cent, services 45.4 per cent and agriculture 13.4 per cent. On the employment front it is predicted that 55.2 per cent of manufacturing jobs will be held by Bumiputeras as opposed to 30.7 per cent by Chinese; while in agriculture 75.8 per cent will held by Bumiputeras against 16.9 per cent by Chinese. Poverty is targeted to fall to 7.2 per cent for all of Malaysia: 5.3 per cent for peninsular Malaysia, 20.0 per cent for Sabah and 12.7 per cent for Sarawak. The plan will focus on reducing chronic poverty, bringing about a better distribution of income and wealth, and generating complementarity and sectorial interlinkages across the Malaysian economy.

The absence of sectorial interlinkages could be counted as one of the reasons, for the lower productivity of Bumiputeras. The challenge is to integrate the rural sector and the poor with the electronic goods sector, the textiles sector and the financial sector, as this will give an impetus to economic growth.

Here regionalisation and the Pacific Rim trading bloc have to be kept foremost in view. Intense competition from neighbouring countries in both manufacturing and commodities will force the Malaysian economy to adapt and exploit its comparative advantages in the production scene. Many of the traditional sectors, for example forestry and agriculture, will have to be replaced by new ventures. The dangers of intraregional competition are highlighted by the fact that the major export and import partner of most of the eastern Pacific Rim countries is Japan, whereas Japan's major export and import partner is the United States. Japan's domination of this region is imminent, and through its US trade and membership of the G7, Japan's dominance in the Pacific Rim will serve to enhance US dominance in the global trade scene.[9] The same picture would emerge if Australia were to join Japan in a shared hegemony of the Pacific Rim region in international trade. What Keynes called the 'animal spirit' for the acquisition of wealth fundamentally underlies the politico-economic change that is underway in the Pacific Rim countries.[10]

The inevitable sharpening of intraregional competition in the Pacific Rim will result in substantial adjustment costs being incurred by Malaysia, not simply in the form of firms closing and employment lost in the traditional sectors, but also in the form of massive government spending if the government is to meet the targets of the New Development Plan. If trade is to support the advance of the Malaysian economy, then the economy will inevitably become subject to the strictures of the world economy *vis-à-vis* the Pacific Rim.

Here one finds that the full onslaught of neoclassical models of economic efficiency, growth and marginalist substitution between alternatives are serving to negate global complementarity. Let us look at this topic more closely.

THE CONSEQUENCES OF GATT ON MALAYSIAN SOCIO-ECONOMIC REVIVAL

The conclusion of the seven-year Uruguay Round of talks and the replacement of GATT by the World Trade Organisation followed feverish activities by interest groups bent on maintaining their oligopolistic share of world trade. The emergence of the Pacific Rim trading bloc, the European Union, the North American Free Trade Agreement and Asia–Pacific Economic Co-operation are mechanisms to counter the fear of losing competitive advantage in trade and ownership of global resources by the United States and the Western Alliance.[11] The declining hegemony of the United States in global economic change, along with the relocation of multinational companies (something that is known as the deindustrialisation of the North)[12] and increasing economic instability in the industrialised economies, have brought about greater presence of the Bretton Woods institutions in favour of these countries.

The underlying philosophy guiding the economic activities in the North and in the world, in concert with the industrialised countries, is based on what has come to be known as macroeconomic coordination in these countries and the Bretton Woods institutions. It involves the adoption of fiscal, monetary and trade policies to promote privatisation and homogenise policies aimed at economic revival in the North which, it is claimed, will in turn generate a rise in national incomes that will favour trade flows from the developing countries in goods, services and capital. The world gross domestic product is seen to be influenced by the macroeconomic coordination in the North, which is held as a prerequisite for the export of goods, services and capital from the developing economies.

The Bretton Woods institutions act as instruments to promote such macroeconomic coordination. They were originally set up in the 1940s to assist the reconstruction of war-ravaged Europe. The developing countries entered the agenda much later on, when the West felt it necessary to expand its interests through worldwide institutional and market integration.[13] The result has been a series of conditionalities linked to aid for structural adjustment. In this approach, privatisation, price stability, population control, economic efficiency and growth are preconditions for structural adjustment funds to flow to net borrowers in the South. As a result government spending on the social sector and the attempt to bring about a fairer distribution of income and wealth have fallen victim to trade and economic growth. According to Alexander, the IMF 'is really a force in centralising economic power in the world rather than helping [people in developing countries] get more broad-based access to assets'.[14]

The consequences of this macroeconomic coordination are making themselves felt on all fronts – economic, social and political – in North–South relations. On the economic front, the opening up of Eastern Europe after the collapse of communism has led to development funds being diverted to the former Soviet bloc. This is manifest in the predominant presence of the IMF in these countries and the political move to extend membership of the North Atlantic Treaty Organisation to the Eastern Bloc countries. Malaysia was the first country to note this concern.[15] The possible replacement of the Russian rouble with the dollar following East–West integration, and the harmonisation of monetary policies in the European Monetary Union, could mean that just two competing currencies will govern the valuation of all currencies: that is, the US dollar and the proposed Euro. But at a later stage, on-going negotiations could lead to NAFTA integrating with the EU and with the Pacific Rim through Asia-Pacific Economic Co-operation (APEC). This could eventually lead to the existence of a single benchmark currency in the global economy – the US dollar. In this final state, the IMF SDR and the US dollar would attain parity and the use of the SDR would lose its importance in international transactions, loan capital and trade. The US dollar would emerge as the sole controlling currency in the world. Such are the uneasy consequences of globalisation through the neoclassical models of capitalism applied to trade and development.

Consequently, even in the event of deindustrialisation of the North through the relocation of multinational companies in productive regions such as the Pacific Rim, world liquidity would lie within the hegemonic grip of the United States. The result would be a perpetual flow of resources from all countries, particularly from the developing economies, to US dollar-denominated funds. Such is the picture of the new mercantilism and the world-system outlook on the theory of trade and growth dependency under the impact of global capitalism.[16]

How much longer must the developing economies wait to free themselves from neomercantilism and the Eurocentric development paradigms of the West?[17] It is said that the structural adjustment policies of the World Bank, which call for a reduction of government involvement in social restructuring for stablisation policies and price stability, could lead to devaluation on a massive scale in many developing countries. It is also said that the structural adjustment policies have caused economic and social hardship in the short run, but may work out better in the long run. But even the long-run changes under the rise of neomercantilism, Eurocentricity and US-led hegemony, turn out to ever increase the social costs to the developing countries, not to speak of the damage this will cause to the economic structure of the industrialised economies. The logic of global macroeconomic coordination thus fails.[18]

The rationale that macroeconomic coordination among the industrialised economies would aid global economic recovery was suspect from the very beginning. When this idea was taken up by the Bretton Woods institutions, the aim was to formulate a unified institutional approach to economic regulation across the world, so that price stability could be maintained for primary commodities and enhanced income levels in the industrialised countries would enable goods to be purchased from the developing countries, albeit at very low prices. This fuelled the continuation of the industrial revolution and became a methodologically accepted fact in linear models of economic growth, such as the Harrod–Domar model and the Rostowian models. With international Keynesianism was born the International Monetary Fund, with its mandate to regulate the external-sector balances of developing countries. In the sweep of economic history since the Second World War, first the current account balances and then the debt situation of developing countries worsened.[19] Hence there is no evidence that macroeconomic coordination, as perpetuated by the West, has brought about economic recovery in the developing countries.

Furthermore, for the industrialised countries the degree of internal instability caused by their institutions and policies has always been uncertain. The hopes of the full employment that would be achieved by national and international application of the Keynesian general equilibrium paradigm or by the optimality and equilibrium concepts of neoclassical growth models crashed under the impact of repeated short-run business cycles. This also highlights the impossibility of attaining full employment except when resource allocation is driven by the conditions of war.[20] The short-run nature of economic recovery from deep recessionary periods in the industrialised economies is proving to be adversely affected by uncertain expectations in investment, consumption, interest rate and price level in the face of high demands for capitalistic surpluses. Such surpluses are caused by excess demand by households and businesses, fanned by neoclassical preferences based on insatiable demand. Thus the fiscal, monetary and stabilisation policies of the industrialised economies are continuously generating speculation and random preferences that do not allow for equilibrium, despite economic models based on predetermined notions of equilibrium. Any kind of macroeconomic coordination based on such models, perceptions, institutions and policy instruments will be ineffective, both for the industrialised countries and for the developing ones in their long and uncertain wait for fulfilment of the neoclassical, Keynesian and monetarist promises.[21] Indeed many in the West consider that the recent US recession was the result of the structural debility of the economy caused by economic stagnation, productivity decline and low demand for both consumption and investment goods.[22]

The other side of the coin is the picture presented by the IMF special facilities under GATT, aimed at providing relief for adjustment costs under the prescription of phasing out export subsidies and tariff barriers while protecting infant industries. In the long-run perspective of the post-GATT evolution of events in the area of trade and development, borrowing from the IMF special facilities will predominantly mean borrowing US funds. The result will be monetisation of the productivity gains of developing countries in the Pacific Rim and East and South-East Asia in terms of the monetary policies of the United States and their consequences on interest rates, exchange rates, macroeconomic policy coordination, allocation of development funds, balance-of-payments disequilibria and the drive for global privatisation – the old Brady–Baker Plan.[23] Growth will thus become entrenched in a spiral of subservience to policies guiding loanable funds denominated in the US dollar.

Malaysian Prime Minister Mohammad Seri Mahathir was quick to recognise the disabling consequences that might flow from the formation of Asia–Pacific Economic Co-operation (APEC), post-Pacific Rim and post-GATT. The Most Favoured Nations (MFN) Clause of GATT indeed prescribes loanable funds denominated in US dollars, for the expansion of trading blocs under the hegemony of the US must mean guarantee of her trading rights with GATT (now World Trade

Organisation) members. Thereby American investors would have the same right to invest in Malaysia as any country that Malaysia might favour instead. The MFN here would be most strictly followed in the services sector: international trade in services, including financial services, telecommunications, transport, audio-visual, tourism, professional and expatriate services. US products will become increasingly competitive with the rise of the Pacific Rim countries, and as a result the United States will become increasingly service oriented and perhaps the hegemon of global finance.[24] Consequently the application of MFN post-GATT has greatly strengthened the US-led North and the institutions that manage globalisation on behalf of the North.

The foregoing economic changes will be mirrored in the social and political worlds. Control of world resources through financial means and the rise of an integrated North, subsequently engulfing the other parts of the global order in trade, also means control of real resources. It is not difficult to see that the continuing economic bondage of the developing countries is a way of maintaining the military dominance of the West. The emerging grassroots movements in the developing countries, especially Islamic movements, will be targeted through the process of economic hegemony. The result could then be either bipolarisation of the world between the Islamic grassroots political unrest and the collective Western onslaught on it, or a dismal oppression of the Islamic grassroots nationally and globally at the expense of lasting peace made impossible by capitalising the globalising order.[25]

The hegemony and intellectual poverty of the neoclassical framework of global capitalism has had two debilitating consequences in the Muslim world (*Ummah*). First, Muslim thoughts and activities have fallen into the grip of Western markets and self-interest. Second, the sweeping of Muslim countries into the capitalist globalisation process has empowered the West all the more but reduced the power of Muslim countries to govern their own internal matters and hindered the drive for global Islamic solidarity.

Thus the political agenda for change in the Islamic world order must be based on Islam and not on the philosophy presented by the Hegelian school and by Fukuyama in his thesis on democratic liberalism.[26] Nor is there any place in the Islamic world view for the divisive cultural pluralism advocated by Mazrui.[27]

Returning to the social repercussions of global capitalism, the harmonisation of technological change across countries will mean the permanent existence of poverty and inequality. For technological change in the midst of global capitalism must mean continuous substitution of the old by new alternatives. A sense of short to long-run alienation, social/transaction cost and skewness of distribution of wealth and incomes will mark the underlying marginalist substitution process. Even human resource development as an instrument to generate technological change will serve the perspectives of economic efficiency and growth that arise from trade and development. Technological change in this marginalist substitution process will mean a perpetual treatment of centre-periphery configuration of world economic regions. Without this persisting de-equalising relationship, technological change in the capitalistic order cannot continue.

The forms of global changes arising from the deliberate goal of the predominating capitalistic order after the age of socialism/communism will adversely affect in specific ways the national policy perspectives of the Malaysian economy, if they are swept away and integrated with the Western hegemonic tempo of change.[28] The most important area to evaluate in this regard is the long-term ability of the Malaysian economy to sustain both economic growth and its socio-economic goals of poverty alleviation and income and wealth distribution, while maintaining its strength as a trading nation.

Acceptance of the neoclassical model of trade and economic growth in the interest of global transformation means acceptance of the methodological individualism, substitution and social/transaction costs of the transformation process. Here a dominance model has to prevail by virtue of methodological and institutional necessity, but the much needed interlinkages among sectors, institutions and interest groups at all levels of society from the grassroots upwards cannot prevail where substitution, dominance and methodological individualism remain intrinsic features, and it is this that marks the entire trade and development paradigms of neoclassicism. We will present this viewpoint later.

To come back to the effect of the Western models on Malaysia's socio-economic future, we invoke here the picture presented by the substantial decline in employment, share of gross domestic product and productivity in the Malaysian agricultural sector to the year 2000. The share of exports is expected to be highest for the manufacturing sector (81 per cent) and a mere 6 per cent for the agricultural sector. Balances on the current account as a percentage of GNP are expected to remain healthy. Finally, poverty is expected to decline to 7.2 per cent for all of Malaysia.

An implication of these targets is that much of the alleviation of poverty will depend on government involvement in the social sector. Transfer dependency will increase and consequently productivity will remain low, being categorised by the contribution of marginalised groups. Much of the value added will then be contributed by the rentier class favouring the policies on international trade and national economic growth. The focus of the New Development Plan on privatisation as the engine of growth will be the cause of such skewed development. Grassroots empowerment, fairer distribution and the promotion of sectorial and social interlinkages cannot be realised within the paradigm of international trade and economic growth that Malaysia will be adopting within the Pacific Rim *vis-à-vis* the world economy. Yet they are the very conditions that Malaysia most cherishes. As mentioned in *The Second Outline of Perspective Plan, 1991–2000*: 'The NDP will continue with the efforts to correct imbalances to create a more just, united, peaceful and prosperous society. To this end, more effective efforts will be made to reduce poverty, irrespective of race, as well as to restructure society so as to achieve an equitable distribution in the context of a healthy and sustained economic growth.'

While it would be possible for a benevolent Malaysian government to channel its resources away from national growth and external trade towards social expenditure, yet the contribution of such spending towards integrating the grassroots with the hub of socio-economic activity in the nation will exist as a separate issue from that of economic efficiency, growth and privatisation. In the neoclassical model of international trade (efficiency goal) and economic growth, the social spending so undertaken by a benevolent government will appear as a marginalist substitution goal against the goal of economic efficiency.[29] There remains then every fear that such developmental substitutions in the presence of ethically neutral market consequentialism can ultimately marginalise the approach of integrating the grassroots with trade and development regimes. We shall take up this issue below.

THE ROLE OF ISLAMIC GRASSROOTS MOVEMENTS IN MALAYSIAN DEVELOPMENT

Although the Islamic grassroots movement called Daral-Arqam became defunct, other Islamic grassroots movements exist today in Malaysia. Amanah Aktiar and Islamic NGOs, for example, have been functioning well under the watchful eyes of the Malaysian Government. We will argue that there exists good scope for cooperation between Government and Islamic grassroots movements. The latter have much to contribute in Malaysian development.

From our arguments above, it appears that the criticism by the Islamic grassroots of Malaysia's imitation of Western paradigms holds substantial weight. Yet the government's moral obligation to provide social welfare along with economic development, as laid down in the New Development Plan, provides an important opportunity for the Islamic grassroots to act in tandem with the Malaysian superstructure in the interest of a constructive politico-economic future. Its role, on the one hand, must be to forward the Islamic world view of development within the context of the South-East Asian region. On the other hand, this effort cannot be limited to the regional scene, but rather should be aimed at a global Islamic movement for structural change with Malaysia at the pivot.

The *Hablum Minallah–Hablum Minannas* approach to socio-economic development means that the grassroots movement would serve as a link between the microeconomic domain of Malaysian society and the macroeconomic superstructure of the Malaysian government. This micro–macro interface, being a singularly important aspect of Islamic political economy, would bring about the methodology and institutional developments toward establishing interlinkages, starting with ethical needs, preferences, knowledge development, participation and human development. All these should first be at the level of microenterprises and then proceed onward to their logical links with economy-wide sectoral developments.[30] In this context, growth centred on the manufacturing sector would cease to be an externally imposed planning exercise. It would be initiated, formalised, grounded and realised according to the pattern of change desired by those participating. The urban and rural sectors would thus be brought together; the manufacturing and agricultural sectors would be interlinked; consumers, producers, financial and marketing agencies, development planners and institutions would interact in line with their shared views on specific national development issues. Finally, the national government would come to learn from and share information with the grassroots and other microenterprises on the desired, not imposed, pattern of structural change.

This approach of grassroots, microenterprises-led economic change and micro–macro interface in determining the direction and tempo of development is the interactive–integrative knowledge-centred world view presented by the Islamic *Hablum Minallah–Hablum Minannas* model. At the same time, this model of structural change is a responsibility-oriented approach, as participation at the grassroots and all other levels of decision making must be knowledge based and not reactionary. Indeed knowledge itself is the cause and effect of responsible and purposeful participation. The Islamic grassroots movement holds a key to change because of its position as a microenterprise movement promoting the interactive–integrative world view. Thus the onus rests on the grassroots movement to assume the following two responsibilities: first, to pull together its own governmental and other institutional participants to handle specific issues related to national development goals; second, to externalise the process of interaction–integration for the common good through the same formula of knowledge-based change in an integrated regional perspective. It is an asset that has been presently built up globally, so that the association can then be relied upon to instil and launch similar interactive–integrative developmental processes in a regional framework. The Islamic grassroots cannot, however, to do it alone. It can do it only in cooperation with other institutions, of which the most important are national governments. This is an externalising process of participatory action on issues of development for the common good.

When the role of the movement is so understood, specific areas of immediate importance for development can be pointed out. First is the role that the grassroots movement can play in poverty alleviation through microenterprise decision making and integration. This interactive–integrative micro decision making is the *Shuratic* process described throughout this book. Second, the movement should coordinate its efforts with the Malaysian government in the areas of poverty alleviation, income and wealth distribution and empowerment of the grassroots. Third, the movement should coordinate its micro–macro interface with the government to spread the interactive–integrative world view of development interregionally among Islamic countries. The important countries in this regard are Indonesia, Brunei, Bangladesh and Pakistan, which together with Malaysian make up SEACO (South East Asian Co-operation). The movement should also note the praiseworthy ideas advanced by Prime Minister Mohammad Mahathir with regard to SEACO, and his stand against US hegemony at the APEC meeting in Seattle.[31]

These common virtues should establish the platform for continuous, vigorous and purposeful dialogue between the Islamic grassroots movement and the Malaysian institutional superstructure, with the ultimate goal of realising the common good. Governments, on the other hand, can be effective channels for advancing, organising and implementing the grassroots-oriented world view of change in the regionally intralinked trading bloc. The momentum gained from this can then be expanded across the Muslim world. Indeed the future Islamic Common Market must present this unique world view. It is a world view that remains distinct from the model of global capitalism and socialiam/communism. It proves the *modus operandi* of the interactive–integrative world view now externalised to the new paradigm combining trade and development theories, in which the grassroots get integrated by cause and effect. (In the section below we will present a methodological outlook on the knowledge-based, interactive–integrative model of trade and development with the grassroots at the centre.)

The end result will be that development will become representative, fully participatory and grounded in the national will, and it will reflect the ethical and material focus of common preferences. Planning will not be an exercise that is carried out against the extraneously wills of, independent interest groups and individualistic agents, as in the neo-classical model of de-equalising global capitalism. The immediate effect of the grassroots approach to trade and development will be global complementarity, not the substitutional trade-offs of neoclassical thought. Poverty alleviation will generate the cause and effect by the complementarity interlinking the agricultural and manufacturing sectors. Technological change will come about through the application of available capital to skills. A graduated basic needs approach to development, categorised by its stages of manufacturing linkages, will be pursued. The consumption, production and distributional functions must then logically accord with such a balanced design of development and economic growth.

The strength of the national economy in the external sector will then be derived from the dynamically shifting comparative advantages arising from developmental regimes of graduated basic needs baskets of tradables with their appropriate manufacturing linkages. The debt burden will be reduced, while the trade balance and the balance of payments will represent the real value of value added. The generic structure of production will reflect interlinkages in value added intersectorally. Employment creation and income, by virtue of their intrinsic links with microenterprises and complementarity between the agricultural and manufacturing sectors, will reflect real productivity growth. Consequently, while a graduated basic needs approach to development will promote employment and productivity, it will also generate real economic growth and external sector equilibrium. The important point to note here is not that there will not be differentiated variations in the structure of production between the agricultural and manufacturing sectors, but that all such variations will be the result of cause and effect of sectoral interlinkages invoked by extensive complementarity and not by any vestige of neoclassical marginal substitution. All investments, nationally and internationally in these sectoral directions, become catalysts of the graduated basic needs approach to development with the kinds of interactive–integrative development medium in place. Thus, while there is all-round interaction–integration in the internally consistent process of development, this is also extended by cause and effect to the external process of international trade. The micro-genesis of the grassroots at the developmental level is now externalised to the level of micro–macro interfaced policies guiding international trade and development viewed as a combined approach.

Finally, externalisation of the grassroots-oriented trade and development process, first to the Islamic countries in the region, and then by leadership and dialogue to the rest of the Muslim world, will provide a platform for authentic global Islamicisation of trade and development. It will lead to the formation of an Islamic Common Market, which will operate according to a world view that is distinct from the one represented by the globalisation of trade under the capitalist system of markets and politico-economic relations. For Malaysia, this formula of structural change holds out the prospect of future Islamic leadership in the modern world. It would also allow its fear of delinked development and trade under post-GATT global capitalism.

It is therefore suggested here that serious dialogue should take place between the Islamic grassroots movement, the Malaysian government, the educationalists and all relevant institutions to formulate a participatory economic planning process in Malaysia. The aim of such a dialogue would be to evolve a comprehensive micro–macro interface in development planning that could integrate grassroots decision making and generate empowerment as an endogenous (cause and effect) process of developmental change. Subsequently Malaysia should sponsor such an interactive–integrative, knowledge-centred model of grassroots integration in the global scene through the Islamic Development Bank and the Organisation for Islamic Conferences. Knowledge-centred responsibility, earnestness and Islamic solidarity must prevail in this endeavour, rather than the political clichés of some member states.[32]

METHODOLOGICAL APPROACH TO GRASSROOTS INTEGRATION[33]

While some important institutional developments have occurred in world trade, such as the European Union, the conclusion of the Uruguay Round of trade liberalisation talks in GATT, the rise of the Pacific Rim as a significant trading bloc, the establishment of the North American Free Trade Agreement as the largest free trade deal in the world, and the advance of Asian Pacific Economic Co-operation, other trading blocs are still trying to coordinate their policies in the face of global transformation.

Among the latter are the continuing deliberations on the formation of a trading bloc of Islamic countries, leading to an Islamic Common Market (ICM) under the auspices of the Organisation of Islamic Conferences (OIC) and its subregional nation states. This call for an ICM is of course not a new one, for the OIC took it up in its Dakar Resolution. Efforts to bring about economic cooperation through development, trade and financial instruments, such as foreign trade financing, joint ventures, cofinancing and equity participation, have been made for some time now by the Islamic Development Bank and its member Islamic states.

However, what is new and necessary in this process is the inclusion of poverty alleviation in the deliberations. First, how will these developments affect the multitude of poor people, who at one point were estimated to number a hefty three billion, not to mention the much more numerous relative poor? Second, how can the question of the poor be integrated with trade policies, programmes and institutional changes?

In the following subsections we will discuss the important question of fusing poverty alleviation with world trade. For if the goal of poverty alleviation is consistently taken up within the complex of world trade, then the powerful impetus of the latter is bound to help alleviate poverty. Conversely, if matters of trade are kept separate from poverty alleviation – conceptually, institutionally and on the policy front – then poverty will remain forever.

Post-GATT Structural Adjustment

We can now take up the topic of structural adjustment with that of conditionality, flow of the external financial resources and trade policies. It has been well established in critical studies that structural adjustment has focused on the goal of economic efficiency. The argument presented is that if market forces, privatisation, price stability, economic growth and capital formation can be generated, then the ensuing growth will improve the conditions of the poor. This is the well-known neoclassical idea of distribution with growth, or the much criticised trickle-down effect. The problem is that the forces generated in market exchange remain independent of the forces generated in a redistributive system. Therefore the social goal of poverty alleviation through government spending is in conflict with the goal of economic efficiency.

The existence of trade-off is pervasive in the conceptualisation of trade and development ideas as well. Poverty alleviation is development centred; trade is growth centred. Market forces are economic in nature and generate conflicts between these goals. Thus in the paradigm of international trade promoted by the IMF, GATT and the various trading blocs, poverty alleviation has not been taken up. Neither has the possible role of trade been included in World Bank poverty alleviation programmes. Yet the World Bank structural adjustment programme complements and is complemented by IMF conditionalities governing loans, financial flows, control of debts/deficits, balance-of-payments disequilibrium and export orientation.

In the market milieu that we have referred to as the substituting institution of social order, the trade policies underlying the IMF conditionalities would strengthen World Bank structural adjustments in the direction of economic growth, efficiency, and capital accumulation in member countries. Likewise the structural adjustment policies could not help but reinforce the IMF growth targets and conditionalities.

Instead we find that the policies and socio-economic changes resulting from market forces reinforced by the World Bank and IMF approaches have crippled the poor. Among such market consequences are the plummeting world prices of commodities and primary goods, protectionism, and lost export revenues by developing countries and their consequent inability to pay off external debts.

A ratchet effect between market forces and social forces is thus perpetuated under the IMF–World Bank approach to trade and development. The poor have therefore become marginalised from world trade and development. To break this deadlock and integrate poverty alleviation and world trade, a distinctly new approach is necessary. This was recognised at an IMF seminar, where it was pointed out that the IMF's traditional focus on economic growth had caused a neoclassical substitution approach to poverty alleviation.[34] It has also been found that, during the worst years of external sector imbalances, IMF special funds for developing countries were scarcely available.[35]

A General Islamic Approach to the Integrated Issue of Trade and Development

The alternative approach proposed here is what was called above the Islamic paradigm of trade and development with the focus on poverty alleviation. We will first examine the concept and then the policies and programmes of this paradigm.

On the conceptual plane, the Islamic trade and development paradigm involves *simultaneous* realisation of social justice, fair distribution and economic growth. This goal is explained first by means of theorising the resource allocation and resource mobilisation concepts in an extensive nexus of society-economy politicised interactions amongst all the possible agents, sectors and other echelons of decision makers. Second, the *modus operandi* of such extensive interactions is realised by means of consensual orientations among these decision makers on the basis of Islamic Law (*Shari'ah*) governing the underlying issues and problems. The development of rules from the premise of Islamic Law on the issues at hand proceeds by recourse to participatory investigation (*Ijtihadi*) based on the *Qur'an* and *Sunnah* (traditions of the Prophet Muhammad).

The poverty-centred approach to trade and development involves the generation of grassroots enterprises and a gradually evolving basic needs approach to development. Within this tempo of development, the direction of change adapts to the available, and subsequently, to the uplifted levels of human development, knowledge formation, participation, skills, entitlement and grassroots politicalisation. In this process of change, intellectuals, educationalists and the grassroots join forces to work towards the realisation of technological change, goods and resources in the direction of realising socio-economic complementarity and diversification of possibilities.

The development, trade and financial instruments that bring about such grassroots transformation are human resource development, financial and material cooperation in joint ventures, cofinancing, equity participation, interest-free loans, distribution of the Islamic wealth tax (*Zakah*) to the needy, and the trading of goods produced cooperatively by the grassroots and others. The microenterprises thus launch a new form of market-based medium of producing and trading the specifically basic needs goods of such grassroots enterprises.[36]

The incentives to bring into operation such instruments of grassroots development are the very ones held out by the human-centred approach to sustainable developments: price stability, increased real growth per capita, expansion of the capital, labour and resource bases, and balanced non-inflationary growth that arrests external indebtedness and increases self-reliance. These can be seen as both national and international targets.

Thus through internal (national) and external (international) processes poverty alleviation is included in the new paradigm of complementarity, replacing the conventional paradigm of substitution or separation (independence) between trade and development. In this perspective of global change, the poor are seen to be integrated with a new form of market system and ethical market consequentialism. These are now seen to emerge as social contracts based on the consumption, production, effective exchange and distribution, entitlement, preferences and endogenous technological change, all of which are interactively generated and integrated at the micro- and macro-levels of socio-economic activities. In this framework of structural transformation, grassroots interests are naturally focused upon in global development policies, programmes and institutions. Such then is the Islamic prescription for a poverty-centred complementary approach between trade and development.

We now turn to the second part of the discussion, namely the formalisation of a general equilibrium model of trade and development that integrates the central question of the grassroots.

INCORPORATING THE GRASSROOTS IN AN INTERACTIVE–INTEGRATIVE MODEL OF TRADE AND DEVELOPMENT

The following variables are included in a general equilibrium model unifying trade and development: public expenditure, the taxation structure, productivity measurement in a dual/mixed economy, market integration in the global capitalist system, and grassroots participation. This model is substantively different from the neoclassical model and its latterday prototypes, which will not be discussed here as it is assumed they are already familiar to the reader (for example, the Walrasian general equilibrium model; non-tatonement (prices do not equilibrate) models of punctuated equilibrium; social choice and public choice types of general equilibrium, and so on).[37]

The Knowledge-Centred Model: A Non-Technical Introduction

The interactive–integrative order assumes the existence of a continuous generation of knowledge that remains inherent in all systems. It is discovered through the exercise of social interrelationships and investigated by means of discursion. The end result of this is consensus formation within a process that depends on issue-specific interactions. Knowledge is thus the result of realising ethical potential by means of interactions over a set of endogenised preferences that keep on evolving in the system through interactions between the textual references of law, order and world view on the one hand, and the market system on the other. The textual reference *Shari'ah* acts as an endogenous force in this process. Post-evaluation of the process of change with respect to specific issues and systems (also agents) is thus carried out by the interactions between preferences of a given polity (institutions, government) and the market order (general body). The resultant preferences thus become endogenous in type. Exogenous preferences as datum, as the neoclassical economists would use to realise optimality and stable equilibrium, cease to exist.[38] Knowledge is ordinalised in our system of the realisation of endogenised preferences either by consensus or by majority rule, given the text of reference that unifies polity with the general body. Such integration by unification via the process of polity–market interactions is the essence of interaction–integration in this knowledge-centred order. The unifying textual reference across issues, thoughts, systems and agents is the unifying epistemology of the knowledge-centred order.[39]

Within this context of the interactive model is subsumed the context of development as the process of endogenous preference formation and its cause and effect on the entire gamut of socio-economic and policy variables. All of these are endogenously affected by the primacy of the knowledge model, with the substantive condition, however, that the knowledge values are evolved and are functionally ordinalised by series of regenerative cause–effect sequences. In the language of philosophy of science, this is the epistemic–ontic circular causation and continuity model of unified reality that pervades the development process, now seen as an entire gamut of systemic interrelationship.[40]

Within this knowledge-centred world view of the interactive–integrative order we conceptualise the following set of relationships. First, the grassroots has a production function which, say, is land and labour intensive. Land and labour are abundantly available to be knowledge-induced (as defined in terms of interactions). Thus an appropriate technology here suggests that secondary lines of production of basic needs with a continuously advancing basic needs menu of production would be pursued.[41] Labour is not required to adapt to technical change. Instead the available skills are used to generate appropriate technology and production, which in turn generate higher levels of goods. We thus have a graduated basic needs orientation to development in terms of technological adaptation to skills, excess capacity for interactions, and hence to interactions creating knowledge and being led by knowledge in turn.

The urban sector is seen to be equally induced and to have latent possibility for knowledge induction. Yet a dominant role of the urban sector on the rural sector is negated by the presence of a basic needs approach to development, as mentioned earlier. The incentive on the part of the urban sector to adopt a graduated basic needs strategy of development is triggered by the consumer preferences to buy such goods and the cost-effectiveness (private plus social costs) in producing and marketing a wide mix of basic needs in the primary, commodities, manufacturing and services outlets.

On the side of income distribution, the interactive–integrative model, through appropriate technology (as defined above) and by the nature of goods produced, causes the urban and rural sectors to buy the goods of each other. The ensuing creation of wealth through productive engagement of the urban and rural sector endogenously determines the nature of organisation, empowerment and participation at the grassroots with cooperation between itself and the urban sector.

The dualistic nature of a two-sector model of economic growth is thus rendered unacceptable in this interactive economy.[42] For otherwise, a substituting regime of competition and displacement, alienation and methodological individualism, would be generated as in the neoclassical type of dual economy. The very incentive to avoid such neoclassical resource allocation is that the complementarity between various productive activities in a graduated basic needs regime of development necessitates economic cooperation and coordination. The result is price formation in interlinked markets for such products.

We now have an institutional framework of action for initiating paradigm of ethico-economic change. This is a cooperative mechanism based on epistemological precepts that unify through interactions and then generate integration out of them. An example here is of the formal and informal education system that creates such responsibility, appreciation and know-how.

Public Expenditure and Tax Structure in the Knowledge-Centred Model

The issue of public expenditure now is subsumed in the nature of distribution that takes place between the rural and urban sectors within a market driven tempo of change but with knowledge-induction being embedded in such market transformation via enlightened interactions and integration. Governments play marginal but specific role in social spending. They reduce to role players in a diminishing scale of social spending as the economy gets progressively endogenised in the ethical polity–market interactive menu of change.

Thus the tax structure of such an ethicising economy is marginalised to the maintenance cost of an effective polity that is necessary for bringing about the knowledge-based developmental process and providing the necessary information flow required for this. Other functions are those of providing education and defence, maintaining law and order, and dealing with external sector matters. But the government's role in subsidising private sector consumers and investors is increasingly marginalised as the ethicising market takes effect. On the other hand, a negation of the latter type of transformation is shown by the increasing role of government expenditure, the ensuing debts (deficits), lower productivity and a dependency syndrome of both the rural and urban sectors on government expenditure.[43] The increase in social costs compounds with the escalating private costs of production. Prices increase as a result, and the long-run evolution of socio-economic conditions accentuates this de-equalising process.

The negation of an over-reliance on government spending is the result of knowledge-induced consequence of assuming responsibility for ethicising change through ethical polity–market interactions. This brings about the relevance of rural–urban sector participation in cooperative productive activities. It is just a special case of the type of integration that takes place between polity and markets and among various agents in the knowledge-centred order.

Mixed Economy and Dual Economy in the Knowledge-Centred Model

Increasing reliance on an ethicised market and decreasing reliance on government spending also reduces the importance of government in a mixed economy. While the government must remain in place, its functions are restricted to defence, security, education and the promotion of knowledge.[44]

While we have also negated the existence of dual economy in a rural–urban setting through the preconditions of cause–effect of cooperative joint ventures between the two, so also the nature of government involvement in economic development is marginalised. Now a general tax revenue cannot be ethically used to venture out in government-sponsored projects. Because of the regressive results that such public involvement often generates, solely government owned projects cause unjust use of public funds. Likewise the formation of capital, human resource development, pricing for profits, generation of national output, creation of wealth, organisation and empowered participation now emerge from the interactive–integrative process. All these can be undertaken cooperatively by government playing the institutional role of guidance for change and the agents whose preferences are progressively endogenised in the market venue (that is, the ethical transportation of consumption, production and distribution).[45]

FORMALISATION OF THE KNOWLEDGE-CENTRED GENERAL EQUILIBRIUM MODEL

Let θ_i denote ordinalised knowledge parameters at the ith round of polity–market (rural–urban) interaction, $i \in N$ (natural number system), $\theta_i \in N$ (or more generally, the real line $\mathbb{R}$). θ_i is generated by a recursive relationship, which for a simple Markovian process may be taken as $\theta_{i+1} = a.\, \theta_i + u$, u being a random variable, and a a constant indicating the linearity of the knowledge formation process as interactions (i) proceed.[46]

Furthermore θ_i is formed by the endogenising preferences of the rural and urban sectors. That is, the set of endogenising preferences is denoted by $\mathcal{P} = ([\geqslant_M] \cap [\geqslant_P][\theta_i] \neq \Phi)$, where the preferences shown here are first individually formed in polity, P, that is $(\geqslant_P)$, and market, M, that is $(\geqslant_M)$. They are then transformed by interactive preferences to generate either social consensus or majority agreement.[47] This is indicated by the simultaneous causation of $\cap$ and (θ_i) as interactions proceed for $i = 1, 2, \ldots$ The dynamic nature of knowledge formation always makes $\leqslant$ evolve to higher levels of new interactions. What is true of polity–market interactions in terms of positive knowledge formation is also symmetrically true of interlinkages between with the urban (U) and rural (R) sectors.

Production and Investment

The aggregate production function of the rural–urban interactive type is of the form $Q_{UR} = (Q_R[\leqslant] \cap Q_U[\leqslant])$. Throughout, U stands for urban and R stands for rural. The preferences are defined as above for these sectors.

Consequently capital stock and quantity of labour follow such similar kinds of relations. In this respect, capital formation is explained by $I_{UR} = b \cdot (dQ_{UR}/d\theta_i)$. This shows that the direction of capital investment follows the direction of knowledge formation, which in turn endogenously induces output.

Note here that $dI_{UR} = b \cdot (d/d\theta_i)(dQ_{UR}/d\theta_i) > 0$, for the knowledge set, (θ_i), is continuously changing and establishes monotonicity with the values of all variables. On the other hand it is known that $dI_{UR}/dr < 0$, where r denotes the rate of interest. Hence the presence of interest, both as an institutional financial and policy variable and as a market variable, centrally opposes the interactive–integrative formation process and all the rationale that this process of change involves. The implication is then immediate: the cooperative process between the rural and urban sector is at once negated by the existence of the interest rate mechanism, and simultaneously so in a capitalist system. Yet the existence and profound presence of markets in conjunction with institutionalism, which is a permanent sign of a limited mixed economy, also negates the socialist and communist order in all shapes and forms. All these systems are here supplanted by the knowledge-centred regime.

Labour and Human Resources

The investment relation mentioned above is furthermore related to knowledge-induced change affecting the mobilisation of labour. Note that,

$$I_{UR} = b \cdot dQ_{UR}/d\theta_i = b(\sum_{j=1}^{n} [\partial Q_{UR}/\partial x_j][dx_j/d\theta_i] + (\partial Q_{UR}/\partial L][dL/\theta_i])$$

where x_j denotes the various resources of production, excluding labour, and all are knowledge induced. L denotes human resources as the service of labour, which is centrally induced by knowledge.

Since $dI_{UR}/d\theta_i > 0$, therefore each of the relations, such as $d^2x_j/d\theta_i^2 > 0$, $d^2L/d\theta_i^2 > 0$, $i \in \mathbb{N}$, held. Thus the underlying relations imply that wages would be paid for effort in knowledge-induced activity, since these will be the ones promoted. Returns on resources would similarly be compensations in knowledge-based activity. In this way an equally knowledge-induced resource-labour augmenting technological change is generated.[48] Thus wages and returns to resources reflect the real productivity of factor use augmented by knowledge (a specific case of endogenous technological change). Note that such a relation between productivity and returns on resource use is quite contrary to the neoclassical one. The underlying reason is the simultaneous action between knowledge induction and the creation of knowledge-induced factors of production.

In such a knowledge-induced relationship, changes in the wage–rental ratio, w/r, in, say, the derived labour demand function, become interlinked; labour and capital are complementary factors: the wage rate, w, will not change unless knowledge-induced capital augmentation drives productivity of capital, r, forward. The nature of this interlinkage is due to knowledge induction in the specially endogenous sense of interactive decision making and organisation we have invoked here.

Negation of Neoclassical Notions of Resource Allocation

The knowledge-sensitivity of the above model negates all notion of the neoclassical stable, optimal, exogenously predetermined resource allocation points in any of the following: the optimal production possibility frontier, production isoquants, and the wage–rental relationship. The fundamental reason for this is that any such neoclassical allocation point must be continuously perturbed by knowledge sensitivity in the vicinity of the allocation points. Thus product and factor prices cannot be determined by the neoclassical of price–income line or iso-cost line. Instead prices are formed by continuously adaptive methods, intensified by the nature of goods and factors, that are continuously induced by knowledge in unending sequences of knowledge formation and their induction by cause and effect.

Price stability now means attainment of a certain 'limiting' price level corresponding to an attained level of knowledge induction of output. Correspondingly, such prices reflect the real value of productivity as induced by knowledge. To prove this claim we proceed as follows. Note that

$$(d/d\theta)(p_1/p_2 - w/r)(\theta_i) = ([1/p_2][dp_1/d\theta_i] - [p_1/p_2^2][dp_2/d\theta_i])$$

$$- ([1/r][dw/d\theta_i] - [w/r^2][dr/d\theta_i]) = ([1/p_2][dp_1/d\theta_i]$$

$$- [1/r][dw/d\theta_i]) - ([p_1/p_2^2][dp_2/d\theta_i] - [w/r^2][dr/d\theta_i]) = 0$$

must hold along the path of evolution of θ_i if prices and factor payments are to represent real productivity. For this to be true, two conditions must be satisfied.

First, if (θ_i) becomes constant locally, then $(p_1/p_2) = c + (w/r)$, c being a constant. This proves our claims as mentioned above. Second, it can be shown by rearranging the above expression that both of the following must hold simultaneously: $dw/dr = \alpha \cdot w/r$, and $dp_1/dp_2 = \beta \cdot p_1/p_2$, where α and β are positive constants. Thus the price of goods and factors change in the same direction. This implies global complementarity between goods and factors of production. p_1 and p_2 can change in the same direction only because the goods are complementary. Consequently the factors used, whose prices are r and w, must also be complementary in the production processes of the rural and urban sectors. This complementarity is global but can only be so if prices and factor productivities are monotonically interrelated.

Finally, marginalism loses its meaning in this system because global complementarity exists rather than gross or partial substitution. This is the essence of interlinkages, economic cooperation and knowledge-induction in the institutions and resource allocation between the urban and rural sectors.

International Trade in the Knowledge-Centred Model

Finally, international trade can now be integrated with the development model based on knowledge induction. The matter is too complex a one to be treated extensively here. However, in general the principle of interlinkages, complementarity and institutional organisation is extended to the production function (developmental) by including tradables, denoted by Q_T in the production function Q_{UR}, and by endogenising preferences through increasing interactions involving appropriate international institutions and regionally interlinked markets for the tradables.

Now the principle of complementarity, interlinkages and cooperation in the trade model with developmental focus, when applied to issues of terms of trade, exchange rate determination, debts and direction/diversion of trade flows, would mean formulation of developmental plans in regional context based on the knowledge-based model. The incentive to undertake such a coordinated approach is the possibility of balanced growth, as manifested in productivity growth, structural transformation, price stability and real income growth. Revenue losses by trade diversion in such a case would be extensively compensated by a sharing of developmental funds that such diversion would generate by means of, say, the instrument of foreign trade financing.[49]

The larger the trading market in the interlinked regions, the more effective the coordination efforts. As a consequence, population growth, when induced by the knowledge induction process, will act as a catalyst for trade and developmental change, rather than debilitate it. The presence of a knowledge-based order between the rural and urban sectors provides the impetus for grassroots organisation. Thereby households assume the responsible choice to bear additional children or not. Population growth and family planning become a matter of individual preference rather than government policy, costly as this implementation has proven to be to least developing countries. The age-old debate about reducing the birth rate in order to promote economic growth remains inconclusive, and a politically motivated prescription advanced by the industrialised countries for the developing ones.[50]

A Simple Knowledge-Centred International Trade Model

A simple model of trade and development with interactions would be the input–output model with dynamic coefficients induced by ordinalised knowledge values. Within such an input–output model, the whole gamut of capital formation and allocation of intersectoral (interregional) flows of goods, services and labour would be undertaken in a manner similar to that above.[51]

Consider equations where, for simplicity, the input–output technological coefficients are assumed to be linear functions of the basic knowledge parameters (thus not explicitly shown):

$$Q_k = \sum_{l=1}^{n} (a_{kl} Q_l) + F_k$$

across regions/industries, where $k, l = 1, 2, \ldots, n$, and F_k denotes final demand.

$$dQ_k/da_{kl} = \sum_{l=1}^{n} (Q_l + a_{kl}\, dQ_l/da_{kl}) + dF_k/da_{kl} = Q + (dF/da_{kl})$$

$$+ \sum_{l=1}^{n} a_{kl}(dQ_l/da_{kl})$$

$$a_{kl} = Q_{kl}/Q_l = (Q_{kl}[Q_{UR} \cap Q_T]/Q_l[Q_{UR} \cap Q_T])(\theta_i),\ \theta_{i+1}$$

$$= a\theta_i + u,\ i \in \mathbb{N}$$

The dynamic input–output coefficients can now be defined as follows: $a_{kl}(\Theta_i) = (Q_{kl}[Q_{UR}]/Q_l[Q_{UR}] \cdot Q_{kl}[Q_T]/Q_l[Q_T])(\Theta_i) = (a_{kl}[UR] \cdot a_{kl}[T])(\Theta_i)$, where $a_{kl}(UR)(\Theta_i)$ denotes internalisation of grassroots development, and $a_{kl}(T)(\Theta_i)$ denotes externalisation of grassroots development. We can now write

$$I_k = b \cdot (dQ_k/da_{k1}) = b(Q + 1/a_{k1}[T] \cdot dF/da_{k1}[UR] +$$

$$\sum_{l=1}^{n} a_{k1}[UR] \cdot dQ_1/da_{k1}[UR]) = b(Q + 1/a_{k1}[UR] \cdot dF/da_{k1}[T] +$$

$$\sum_{l=1}^{n} a_{k1}[T] \cdot dQ_1/da_{k1}[T]); k, 1 = 1, 2, \ldots, n$$

This equation implies that development (*UR*) and international trade (*T*) establish mutually enhancing interactive–integrative investment menus by cause and effect.

Here each (θ_i) is shown to be generated iteratively through interactions $\mathcal{P}'$. (a_{k1}) coefficients are consequently induced by (θ_i) values. We can therefore, determine a_{k1} via the route of (θ_i), first determining Q_1 and Q_{k1} as shown above, followed by determination of (a_{k1}), which then reiterates the value of new Q_k, and so on. This is the essence of cause and effect in the knowledge-centred model. It at once endogenises the entire set of variables, starting from the knowledge values. Such models are better handled by simulation techniques. It is also a specific case of the universally applicable model referred to here as the epistemic–ontic circular causation and continuity model of unified reality.

The Human Factor in the Knowledge-Centred Model

Whatever the technical orientation of the above exercises to integrate the grassroots with the complex of trade and development models, the primary focus will always be the human factor. This will involve, most importantly, institutional developments, interactions with market venue and the interactive relations to bring about a rational perspective of development and change. Such is the process that essentially determines the cause and effect function of the knowledge-centred world view.

We will prove this point about the human factor by showing that it cannot be replaced by any other resource in the knowledge-centred order. We will thus show that the human factor leads to the realisation of the principle of global complementarity among all resources. Hence we shall investigate the following problem of choice in the knowledge-centred model of trade and development.

The trade–development, interactive–integrative preference formation is given by $\mathcal{P}' = \{([\succeq_P] \cap [\succeq_M] \cap [\succeq_T])(\theta_i) \neq \Phi\}$, which then qualifies the total output, $Q'_{UR} = (Q_{UR} \cap Q_T)$. All other resulting economic relations are accordingly defined, as mentioned above, with the trade variable, along with its interactive preference formation.

Now for two alternatives, A and B, confronting the national economy in respect to trade and development with grassroots focus, the choice in the knowledge-centred order is given by an evolutionary regime of change, not by a static one. This is due to the evolutionary nature of unification epistemology in the system that continuously dynamises the system with endogenous preferences. Thus the only possibility under such evolution is for $\mathcal{P}'(A)(\theta_i) \rightarrow \mathcal{P}'(B)(\theta_{i+1})$, via the route of knowledge simulation affecting (θ_i). Consequently, whenever there is an input of knowledge in the resource allocation process, such an allocation shows up with a real possibility. New possibilities can arise by a subsequent knowledge input.

Now assuming that the above knowledge evolution results in a higher measure of knowledge, then with $([\geqslant_P] \cap [\geqslant_M]) = (\geqslant_D)$, D denoting the developmental component of total preference endogeneity, the associated knowledge-induced measures of the alternatives can be written as follows:[52]

$$\text{Measure } ([\geqslant_D] \cap [\geqslant_T])(B) > \text{Measure } ([\geqslant_D] \cap [\geqslant_T])(A)$$

This implies that an increase in the core of either of the developmental subsets will expand the core of the other developmental subset. Furthermore, these together will increase the core of action of the trade set on the other sets of preferences. The effect of this knowledge-induced endogeneity is subsequently transmitted to all the socio-economic and policy variables by cause and effect. Hence complete complementarity exists between the development and trade activities, carrying with it the embedded regional focus on rural–urban sector interlinkages.

Contrasting the Knowledge-Centred Order with Neoclassicism

The above kind of simultaneity of action via the principle of global complementarity cannot be found in the neoclassical framework. For polity and markets, trade and development, growth and distribution all exist in marginalist trade-off (or substitution). The exogenous preference preconditions of optimality, stability, independence and competition between the above targets, now cause $(\geqslant_D) \cap (\geqslant_T) = \Phi$. By the same generalisation, $(\geqslant_P) \cap (\geqslant_M) = \Phi$. This is also applicable to rural–urban conflict.

Furthermore, since knowledge is either exogenously set or is parametrically introduced into the neoclassical growth model, social choices for alternative trade-offs between $(\geqslant_P)$ and $(\geqslant_M)$ are possible.

Neoclassicism now invokes a utilitarian philosophy guiding the principle of greatest happiness (defined as material acquisition) for the greatest number.[53] The result is market consequentialism based on consumerism. The production and distribution functions then follow suit. The effect of this market consequentialism is to wipe out the relevance of ethical considerations in social choice theory. For the same reason, public choice theory has also been shown to be a purely neoclassical formulation of individuated, self-seeking, competing political/institutional behaviour.[54] Subsequently national output, capital formation, the social welfare function based on price stability and unemployment, and so on are all optimised in the neoclassical order by moving towards greater economic efficiency at the expense of distributive equity.

In the IMF–World Bank prescriptions for trade and development, which are seen as independent criteria under their conditionality and structural adjustment formulae, respectively, the emphasis has always been on economic efficiency according to the neoclassical framework. Other variations of neoclassicism, such as international Keynesianism and monetarism, have yielded the same impoverishing results.

Such substitutional trade-offs between trade and development, and economic efficiency and distributive equity, are a permanent feature of the neoclassical model, with or without technical change. Technological induction in the neoclassical model of growth is merely an exogenous artefact, inducing exogenous preferences and perpetuating the marginalist substitution between productive factors. As the production possibility surface points out, movement from one production possibility to another is a long-run phenomenon. Hence such trade-offs incur long-run transaction costs, which eventually cause social and economic disruptions that neoclassical economics is not capable of explaining within a given shift in the production possibility surface.

CONCLUSION

Both the Islamic grassroots movement and the Malaysian government have much to gain from the interactive–integrative knowledge-centred model of trade and development. It is the only kind of world view that will enable a study of the grassroots in the entire gamut of methodology, institutions and policies of trade and development with the additional potential to deliver a distinctive Islamic model of structural transformation. Collaborative action between the Islamic grassroots movement and the Malaysian government, it is proposed here, is the only just approach to trade and development. Because they lack this fundamental and distinct world view, it has been argued, the Pacific Rim alliance, the European Union, the North American Free Trade Agreement and GATT have served to intensify global capitalism of the neoclassical type. Hence this chapter has emphasised the importance of the interactive–integrative model of the Islamic grassroots movement generalised over the Malaysian politico-economic superstructure and the Muslim world. The process underlying this world view was termed the *Shuratic* process.

This *Shuratic* process, by virtue of its pervasiveness at all levels and in all forms of decision making in the Islamic framework, is to be promoted by an earnest, responsible and rational approach to Islamic solidarity within Malaysia, and through the Malaysian government's initiatives in the Islamic world. A model of development planning and micro–macro coordination has been proffered here to present the rationale of the underlying interactive–integrative model based on the *Shuratic* process for the Muslim nations and the Muslim world during post-GATT times and against the rise of global capitalism. This new paradigm is shown to be the answer of Islamic change for the common good.

This chapter has presented a formal analytical model of trade, development and structural change that carries with it the cause and effect of interactions and integration between the grassroots and all other echelons of decision making. It assumes its rational approach within a complex of science, economics, society and technical analysis, wherein polity–market interrelationships are shown to simulate endogenous preferences as carriers of knowledge-induced perspectives. Markets become an ethicising core of immense value, while institutions, governments and regional developmental organisations serve to guide, inform, educate and defend the institutions of goodness and truth that unify knowledge and people at all levels. Indeed these are the fundamental goals of *Shari'ah*. Beyond these basic functions, the role of government in development is minimal, as evolutionary, endogenised preferences constantly transform markets and polity in line with *Shari'ah* laws.

8 The Concept of Money in Islam

Two questions have to be asked in relation to money in Islam. First, in what sense is money used as a store of value and a medium of exchange? Second, what is the nature of stability of monetary aggregates in the Islamic economy in order to establish money as a standard to value assets? In this brief exposition we will simply introduce the salient concept of money in Islam while answering these questions. Detailed development of the idea of money in Islamic economy in comparative perspectives can be found elsewhere.[1]

EXOGENOUS MONEY IN THE KEYNESIAN AND RATIONAL EXPECTATIONS SYSTEMS

In received monetary theory, the stock of money is seen to be exogenously supplied, as in the Keynesian system, or it is targeted to the number of real transactions in the goods/services market through the money multiplier expressed as a function of the speed of circulation of the quantity of money, as in the quantity theory of money.[2]

In the pure treatment of monetary aggregates as exogenous stocks, the demand for and supply of money are predominantly determined by the rate of interest and national income. Furthermore the rate of interest affects national income in this system. In this demand–supply relationship, the presence of the interest rate, particularly in the speculative and precautionary components of money demand, destabilises monetary sector equilibrium. This is so because the rate of interest is governed by expectations. Consequently a field of interest-induced randomness surrounding the expected equilibrium point perpetually generates an endless cycle of excess demand and excess supply of money. These excess demand–supply situations cannot be eliminated by recourse to a cobweb-type lagged adaptation model or a rational expectations formalisation. The reason for this is that there is no specific incentive in the speculative demand component to establish an adaptive cobweb equilibrium when consumer preferences predominate. Exchange rate randomness further compounds the uncertainty.

Likewise, since the anticipated money supply causes an increase in the price level under rational expectations, real output remains neutral of the increase in both money supply and price level. Consequently, stabilisation of interest rate fluctuations is not seen to be a policy focus in the anticipated money and adaptive price lends under the rational expectations hypothesis (REH).

Conversely an 'unanticipated' money supply according to REH causes price increases of the demand-push type. Any excess demand situation in such a case is arrested in the short run. Inflationary pressures subsequently die down. The process of monetary equilibrium here is similar to the Keynesian demand-push phenomenon. Consequently monetary policy becomes neutral in the attainment of full-employment level of income. Thus monetary sector equilibrium makes little sense in attaining full-employment target of output in this case.

The offshoot of the above discussions is that the exogenous supply in the presence of a speculative and precautionary component of the demand for money causes unresolving random fields around expected monetary equilibria. Monetary disequilibrium thus perpetuates in the presence of interest rate fluctuations. Such a randomness causes the exchange value of money to be influenced by fluctuations in the rate of interest, and does not reflect either the properties of store of value in money or stable valuation of assets. The resulting monetary aggregates thus fail to satisfy the essential conditions of stability, exchange, valuation and convertibility of the monetary *numeraire*.[3]

A SIMPLE FORMALISATION OF RANDOM MONEY, PRICE AND INTEREST RATE FLUCTUATIONS

A simple formalisation proves the above results, as follows. Let $M_s = M_s(Y, i)$ denote the supply function of money in nominal income, Y and nominal interest rate, i. Let the demand for money be denoted by M_d, $M_d = M_{d1}(Y) + M_{d2}(Y, i) + M_{d3}(i)$, with, M_{d1} as transaction demand, M_{d2} as precautionary demand and M_{d3} as speculative demand. Real income, y, is given by $y = Y/P$, P being the price level, such that $y = Y/P = (Y_0/P_0)\exp(g_Y - g_P) \cdot t$. In log-linear form this expression is written as $\log y = \log(Y_0/P_0)\exp(g_Y - g_P) \cdot t$.

When Y increases at the same rate as money supply, M_s, in order to establish long-run, full-employment output g_P must be proportional to the growth rate of the money supply. Thereby such movements will neutralise the effect of M_s or P on y.

In all other cases, using the monetary sector equation provides the following result: $M_s/P = M_d/P$ for monetary sector equilibrium in real monetary form. That is,

$$M_s(y, r) = M_{d1}(y) + M_{d2}(y, r) + M_{d3}(r)$$

where r denotes the real rate of interest and is a random variable, as explained earlier.

Now if $M_s = M_s^0$, exogenously supplied monetary aggregate, and if linearity of the money demand function is assumed, then

$$1_0 + 1_1 y + 1_2 r = M_s^0$$

That is,

$$1_0 + 1_1(Y_0/P_0)\exp(g_Y - g_P) \cdot t + 1_2 r = M_s^0$$

We rewrite this as

$$\exp(g_Y - g_P) \cdot t = (A - 1_2' r)$$

or

$$g_Y - g_P = (1/t)\log(A - 1_2' r)$$

where

$$A = (M_{s0} - 1_0)/(1_1[Y_0/P_0]); \quad 1_2' = 1_2 P_0/1_1 Y_0$$

Now as long as r remains random, along with i, either in stochastic or conditional expectation forms, g_Y and g_P will vary randomly with r and i. As t tends to infinity, $g_Y = g_P$, causing neutrality in the relationship between money supply, price level and output. Figure 8.1 demonstrates the above case.

MONETARY INDETERMINATENESS IN THE QUANTITY THEORY OF MONEY AND PRICES

In the quantity theory of money it is difficult to determine the causal direction of the relationship between prices and quantity of money. If

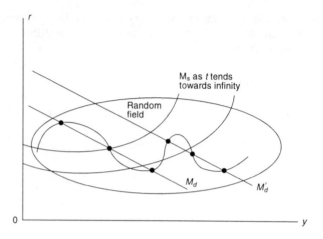

Figure 8.1   Randomness of monetary sector equilibrium

it is the money supply that increases prices, then the only way that (M/P) can remain constant in the quantity equation $MV = PT$, where V is the velocity of money circulation and T is number of money transactions, is for (T/V) to be constant. This implies that there is a one-to-one relationship between the real goods sector and the monetary sector, through the one-to-one relationship between V and T. Now the equilibrium level of output exists but is non-sustainable, as any speculation in the financial markets will disturb the constancy of (T/V). This will generate the same kind of randomness between M_s, P and r (and thereby i), as explained earlier.

If the direction of causality is from P to M, then any expectation of a movement in P will have the same effect on the extreme randomness of M, as explained above for the case of rational expectations. In such a case, V will probably increase but T will remain low. Thus (T/V) will decline, causing (M/P) to decline also, as expected. Such a consequence would reduce real output.

These results show that the function of money as a store of value is only partly effective in the presence of inflationary price movements. On the other hand the presence of r in the quantity equation causes extreme randomness. The same is true of i. Now $M(i) = (T/V)P(i)$, with $i = r + (1/P)(dP/dt)$. Furthermore

$$dM/di = (T/V)dP/di = (T/V)(1/P)(dP/dt)/(1/P)(di/dt)$$

That is, $dM/dt = (PT/V)(i - r)$, a positive value. Finally, $dM/dt = (Y/V)(i - r)$, where $Y = PT$.

Hence the quantity of money is fully influenced by random variations in the rate of interest. This destabilises the monetary equilibrium from the side of both price movements and the quantity of money. This result extends the Friedmanian observation on the constancy of (T/V) in the quantity equation.[4] The randomness of monetary equilibrium as a result of interest rate variations was shown in Figure 8.1.

THE NATURE OF MONEY IN ISLAMIC POLITICAL ECONOMY

In the Islamic framework the rate of interest is replaced by the profit rate, which again is a suitable aggregation of firm/project-specific profit-sharing ratios taken up at the economy-wide level.[5] Consequently the demand for money is determined by the rate of profit, which again is determined in the real sector under pure market transactions and market forces. Since these rates of profit, and generically the profit-sharing ratios, are determined in the real goods/services sector, they are essentially returns on flows of monetary investments. Therefore the resource flows that link the real sector to the monetary sector as aggregates of the Islamic economy are given by the equation

$$M_s(r^*) = I(r^*) + e(S)$$

where $I(r^*)$ denotes the investment function in terms of the rate of return (rate of profit), r^*. $e(S)$ denotes a residual savings function in the form of the liquidity required to pay off outstanding debts. But as r^* increases, $e(S)$ tends towards zero by the force of the increasing investment propensity in Islamic political economy.

In Figure 8.1, the random field is shown either by shifting money supply, M_s-curves, and/or money demand, M_d curves. Thus monetary equilibria in this field responding to interest rate variation and instability caused by fiscal and monetary policies, remain random. Only when t tends towards infinity can there be a long-run, full-employment rate of real output.

This linkage between the monetary and real goods/services sectors through the investment function in terms of the rate of profit endogenises money in Islamic political economy. Note that r^* is endogenously determined. Hence $M_s(r^*)$ must be endogenously determined as well. The stability of r^* equilibrating to a near-normal profit rate in the

Islamic economy[6] imparts stability to the investment function along an expected trend in the rate of return. Consequently money demand (now equal to investment demand) is always equated to money supply *ex post*, not *ex ante*. The quantity of money thus always equals the value of transactions in terms of investment.

The transformation of money into an endogenous form in the Islamic political economy becomes the cause and effect of the relationship between the monetary sector and the real goods/services sector. Money as an exogenous aggregate is thus abandoned in the Islamic conception of money. Consequently money ceases to have an exchange value, for the price of money as an endogenous aggregate is simply a function of r^*, which is generated in the real sector. Thus endogenous money functions as a store of value; it is stable and convertible. Also money ceases to have an exchange value, because any exchange that imparts value to transactions is determined in the real goods sector and is imparted into the system by r^*.

The equilibrium between the monetary and real goods/services sectors in the Islamic economy are illustrated in Figure 8.2.

SOME COMPARATIVE MONETARY PERSPECTIVES AND THEIR RELEVANCE TO ISLAMIC POLITICAL ECONOMY

Most of the recent works in the area of money and Islamic banking have ignored the nature of money in Islam. Consequently the Islamic banking sector has come to accept money and goods transactions mechanically while dealing with the various Islamic financing instruments for projects and loans. As a result Islamic banks have failed to contribute to the necessary structural transformation of Muslim countries, even though it has been forty years since the first Islamic bank was established (in Pakistan). Many of their operations have been subsumed by interest-rate-based transactions, and when Islamic financing instruments have been tried – in a forced manner unrelated to Islamic politico-economic transformation – they have proved ineffective. Thus the profits of Islamic banks have been private in nature. Social profitability has been either ignored or has proved unrealisable by Islamic banks being placed as unfitting financial institutions within global interest-based financial markets.

The above observations are based on the experience of Islamic banks since the founding of the first one in Pakistan in the 1950s (which later suffered a demise) and the more recent cases of the Nasser Social

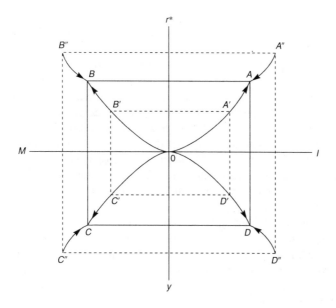

Figure 8.2 Development of monetary equilibrium in the Islamic endogenous theory of money

Bank of Egypt, the Dubai Islamic Bank, Faisal Dar al-Mal al-Islami in Geneva and the Faisal Islamic Bank in Sudan. In each of these cases, rich or pious depositors with village or tribal connections were able to muster sufficient deposits to start up the banks. But these and other Islamic banks ran into liquidity problems because they only undertook limited kinds of financing, such as lending at zero interest as a principal *Shari'ah* requirement, trade financing and later on profit sharing.[7]

In Figure 8.2 the r^*–I quadrant shows points on the trajectories here to be positively related to those in r^*–M quadrant, M–y quadrant and y–I quadrant. This means that the rate of return, r^*, increases as a result of increased investment, I, as does the quantity of money, M. Subsequently real output increases, since money is now mobilised through investment in the real sector, while the direct relationship of r^* to price, p, causes r^*/p to remain stable. Hence sustained inflationary pressure is ruled out. Consequently real output, y, increases. Finally, by cause and effect, increasing y causes investment to increase. The points A, A', A'', B, B', B'', C, C', C'', D, D' and D'' are thus related one-to-one. The convergence at points A, B, C and D means that, since over a certain range of interactions in the Islamic political economy

r^* must tend towards near normal profit rates, there must be temporary convergence towards A. This triggers convergence to B, C and D as well. The direction of the arrows indicates the equilibrating process.

In the face of low global equity capital during recessionary times, real profit shares were unattractive compared with the high interest rates that were being offered to depositors. These savings were not mobilised into productive investments during the protracted recession of the 1980s. In the midst of this global disorder, profit sharing, which should have been one of the strongest features of Islamic banks, proved to be completely ineffective in sectoral development. The pressure to generate capital by Islamic banks thus fell upon the financial instruments of administrative charges on loans and mark-ups (*Murabaha*) in trade financing.

The mark-ups were totally devoid of the otherwise much emphasised market transactions for productive valuation, sectoral interlinkages and appropriateness of goods to be developed and traded, all of which are necessary to establish risk-diversification and social complementarity with economic growth.[8] Thus we return to the old argument that money and bullion do not form the wealth of the nation, as thought by the mercantilists. The wealth of a nation rests upon its productive activity. The physiocrats thought of this productivity in terms of agricultural activity, the classical economic school in terms of manufacturing.

In the Muslim countries today, this argument would suggest the need for good sectoral interlinkages in the investment portfolios of Islamic banks. However, the findings in Tables 8.1 and 8.2 show a weakness here.[9]

Table 8.1 shows the combined investment portfolio of Islamic banks in 1988. Short-term investments, to which must be added other short-term instruments such as current accounts, saving accounts and *Murabaha*, had the highest ratio in the bank portfolio. Medium and long-term investments, particularly of the profit-sharing type (*Mudarabah* and *Musharakah*), had distantly low ratios. Social funds and *Zakah* funds were minimal. Real estate investments were second in volume. Interbank participation among Islamic banks was almost non-existent.

Table 8.2 shows the sectoral allocation of investment funds. With the exception of the Sudanese Islamic Bank, all the Islamic banks listed directed their investments into industry and trade, with a minimal share going to agriculture, food, industry and the service sector. It is sad that even the Bangladesh Islamic Bank overly emphasised manufacturing and trade, because in a poor, rural economy such as Bangladesh the agricultural sector should have received special attention. In 1984, 73.07

Table 8.1   Investment portfolio of Islamic banks: aggregate balance
sheets, 1988

	US $ (million)
Short-term investment	4909.8
Medium-term investment	453.1
Long-term investment	141.4
Real estate investment	1498.2
Social spending	64.2
Zakah funds	3.1
Current accounts	1044.3
Credit accounts	114.7
Savings accounts	6811.1
Total shareholders' equity	427.3
Participation in other Banks and companies (Kuwait Finance House, Faisal Islamic Bank of Egypt, Nasser Social Bank, Dubai Islamic Bank and International Islamic Bank; zero for all others)	113.2

*Source: The Aggregate Balance Sheet of the International Association of Islamic
Banks, 1988* (Cairo: International Association of Islamic Banks).

per cent of the resources of the Bangladesh Islamic Bank were directed
into trade, while 26.10 per cent went to the manufacturing sector and
only 0.83 per cent to agriculture. Yet *Mudarabah* and *Musharakah*
accounted for the highest proportion of the finances of the following
Islamic banks in 1984: Qatar Islamic Bank, 97.7 per cent; Jordan Islamic
Bank, 72.0 per cent; Bangladesh Islamic Bank, 65.3 per cent; Sudanese
Islamic Bank, 53.6 per cent.

How can we reconcile these statistics with social duty? As pointed
out earlier, the Islamic banks were launched by rich supporters, whose
principal objective was to safe-guard their deposits, irrespective of
sectoral distribution. This point is also supported by the very high profit
rates declared by the Kuwait Islamic Bank (186.96 per cent in 1980,
104.36 per cent in 1983) and the Jordan Islamic Bank (10.56 per cent
in 1981, 20.25 per cent in 1982). Yet in most cases the profit rates
had declined dramatically by 1983 (2.07 per cent for the Islamic Bank
International, Denmark; 8.69 per cent for the Islamic Bank International, Cairo).[10] Clearly then, neither the social perspectives that
should be foremost for Islamic banks nor sustainable profits could be

Table 8.2   Sectoral investment allocation by Islamic Banks, 1988
(percentage of total financing)

	%
Faisal Islamic Bank of Egypt	
Industry	30.6
Trade	30.4
Agriculture	3.0
Other sectors	36.0
Total	100.0
Dubai Islamic Bank	
Trade	90.6
Service and family	7.6
Other sectors	1.8
Total	100.0
Sudanese Islamic Bank	
Agriculture	34.0
Industry	23.5
Trade	10.8
Transportation	10.0
Other sectors	21.7
Total	100.0
Faisal Finance Institution Inc, Turkey	
Metal Industry	26.3
Chemical and petrol	17.8
Clothing	16.7
Food	7.9
Tools	5.7
Paper, printing	5.3
Agriculture	16.9
Contracting	3.4
Total	100.0

Source: As for Table 8.1.

realised in the midst of growing uncertainty in the global financial markets, as these banks were susceptible to such external market and institutional forces.

The failure of Islamic banks to engender social change according to the goals of *Shari'ah* was also due to the subservience of the banks to the kings, sheiks, dictators or political demagogues of some Muslim countries. Saudi Arabia has never allowed Islamic banks to operate within its boundaries. The Dar al-Mal al-Islami was founded by Prince Mohammad Faisal in opposition to the Islamic Development Bank, which is a non-commercial, Islamic, development financing institution. The absence of sustained and well-defined directions of Islamicising the financial institutions of Islamic countries, except in the case of Iran, has left the issue of developing an Islamic capital market outside the national development plans and left it to the Islamic development and economic cooperation resolutions of the Organisation of Islamic Conferences.

Much of the economic and financial cooperation provided by the Standing Committee for Economic and Commercial Cooperation (COMCEC) of the Organisation of Islamic Conferences is limited to bringing about economic integration in global competition. Although this goal by itself is not being critiqued here, it is important to note that this globalisation focus is being carried on within the framework of Islamic countries taken altogether in view of their diverse economic and political interests, rather than on a rational prescription of Islamic change that would move Islamic countries towards integration and harmonisation under Islamically directed development planning, development cooperation and self-reliance. Note the objectives and basic principles of the Strategy to Strengthen Economic Cooperation Among OIC Member states: OIC Economic Cooperation:

1. will aim at establishing a more integrated OIC community, in line with the recent developments concerning the formation of large economic blocs as one of the means to ensure fuller participation in the globalisation process. . . .

4. will pursue the objective of increased economic integration in such a way as to support the basic aspirations of the OIC community for a larger share in world economic activity and a more equitable division of labour vis-a-vis the rest of the world. Towards such an end, the OIC member countries would coordinate their positions, without prejudice to their national and regional interests as sovereign states, in order to fully participate in the global negotiations and in the decision-making process that aim at helping improve the world monetary, financial and trading systems.

While, again, it is not these goals that are being critiqued here, the experience of Islamic banks and of the Islamic Development Bank as financial and developmental institutions, respectively, shows that the integration effort by Muslim countries is no different from the worldwide integration process towards global capitalism. Besides, the competitive external environment is likely to remain extremely adverse to the Muslim world. This will make Islamic countries compete with rather than complement each other in other markets. The Islamic essence of social change in Muslim countries therefore cannot be realised under the prevailing conditions. The monetary and financial integration referred to above in the COMCEC statement cannot be seen as evolving from the nature of transactions and the economic and social neutrality of Islamic financial institutions in Islamic transformation. Consequently, any such monetary and financial institution must mean the globalisation of Islamic banks in the general capitalist order. No particular meaning of the common good can come about from such other transformation. Such structural debilities and assimilation contradict the realisation of COMCEC modalities and mechanisms.[11]

Considering the aspirations of Member States, maximum use should be made of the existing programmes within the OIC and priority should be given to the identification of mutually beneficial new feasible projects and schemes involving the private sector and including joint ventures. These would contribute to the cooperation process, produce greater impact and yield higher benefits within the short and medium term and would offer prospects for identifiable action in the future.

The need for Islamic monetary and financial systems to bring about structural change in Islamic countries in the true name of Islamicisation is not simply an economic issue. It must be part and parcel of a political and social transformation process that adheres to Islamic principles of life, knowledge and organisation. This comprehensive embodiment of Islamic transformation within which we take up the monetary and financial systems with a special concept for money, brings about the true relevance of money in the Islamic political economy – a part of the Islamic world view wherein economic, political and social forces interact through the participation of members in accordance with Islamic principles. The treatment of Islamic banks in the context of Islamic political economy guided by its institution–market oriented interactive decision–making process, called the *Shuratic* process for the case of Islamic political economy, becomes all the more relevant because this gives rise to joint institutional and market ventures resulting in productivities and returns, which presently the Islamic banks badly lack. The incorporation of the interactive process in the Islamic banks would also be an endogenous process of decision making, like money aggregates are, and this would improve the efficiency of these banks.

In this context, the endogenous nature of money in Islam brings out the deterministic nature of the relationship between the quantity of money in exchange in accordance with the real goods and services that are being exchanged. The speculative and expectational nature of agent-specific preferences is thus removed from such a concept of money.

The transactional value of money demand is then determined not by the relative value of rates of return (on joint ventures) to interest rate (i), so as to ascertain the economic and social profitability of projects. Rather, the value of money in circulation is measured by the relative between the rate of return on projects (expected or realised) and the aggregate price level (p). This is also the real return on the projects. Since the rate (r) arises strictly from market exchange, $r* = r/p$ is always sustained. In this way, any inflationary effect is automatically built into the transactional value of money. This would increase r and p together. Hence $r*$ would remain stable. As discussed earlier, it is the stable and steady transactional value of money, in terms of the price level, or equivalently in terms of the profit rate, that must guide the Islamic monetary and financial policies of the OIC countries.

Islamic financial institutions embedded in the interest-ridden global system should diversify their financial sources between capital-rich depositors and the grassroots. The portfolio of investments should be in sectorally interlinked projects that will simultaneously generate economic efficiency and social justice (economic distribution). This would encourage increasing grassroots participation in both investment and decision making, as property rights are progressively formed at these levels and human resource development augments the process. Simultaneously attaining economic efficiency and distributive equity would lead to extensive interactions in the economy among possibilities and decision makers. This approach would help to prioritise projects. These are indeed the requirements for structural change, now taken up in the Islamic sense of endogeneity of interactions, integration and self-reliant politico-economic developments. The monetary question is thus seen to be intrinsically influenced by the institutional preferences ethically interacting with market forces and transforming the latter. The external power imposition of Western economic, monetary and financial hegemony is indeed a perpetuation through its institutional and political forces as much as through market-driven ones.[12]

It is now seen that the trend for $r*$, as price level changes, is a steady one. This result speaks in favour of the investment accelerator model, wherein the expectation of future profits, even in the face of short-run losses, generates investable resources. In the Islamic political economy, the existence of *Musharakah* and *Mudarabah* (profit- and loss-sharing financial contracts), along with extensive interactions that lead to revised contracts such as debt-rescheduling, would reinforce the expectation of profits. Hence these factors would mobilise investable resources in ways similar to investment accelerator behavioural relations. Conversely, the trend for i/p is random, because interest rate, i, is not a market-determined variable and therefore has no well-defined relationship with p. In the presence of expansionary monetary policy, i declines and p increases or remains constant in the short run, causing i/p to decline. In the presence of tight monetary policy, i increases, but p may increase or decrease. Similar trends exist in the case of fiscal policy. But even in the best case of Keynesian liquidity trap with aggregate demand and supply curves and the corresponding *IS–LM* relationship, price level and interest rate can be held fixed only in the short run in response to the short-run Keynesian production function. Hence in the long run the trend for i/p is again uncertain. In all cases, therefore, the i/p trend remains uncertain, while that for r^* remains steady. Consequently r^* determines a steady and predictable supply of money based on market realities, while i/p determines a speculative supply of money based on speculative demand and random preferences, as shown by the liquidity preference for money.

A RECENT CASE OF ENDOGENOUS MONEY

In 1994 the US Federal Reserve Board took its chairman, Alan Greenspan's, advice to link short-term federal interest rates to what is known as the price rule. According to this rule,

> if prices remained stable, then a stable monetary policy was appropriate because the Fed was creating the right amount of money to keep the economy growing without too much inflation. If the index fell substantially below the lower band, it was time for the Fed to lower the federal-funds rate and loosen. If the index went above the upper band for long, it was time to tighten.[13] The result was an announcement of higher short-term interest rates and lower long-term rates in the US economy.

Although the relationship between interest rate and principal commodity and asset price indices in the price rule makes this rule worrisome to the endogenous theory of money in Islam, there is a mixed sense of endogeneity in it. To the extent that the federal rate is linked to the price index, this is an endogenous phenomenon of money supply. The price-rule premise of money supply thus differs from the theory of targeted money supply for controlling inflation. But to the extent that the price index is a composite of selected real assets that move under the influence of speculative price formation in stock markets, it embodies exogenous factors that can be highly random. This makes the price rule a mix of endogenous and exogenous factors influencing money supply. If the speculative stock market could be replaced by a forward pricing rule, such as *murabaha* in foreign trade financing, and sectoral interlinkages exist in appropriately determined goods markets, then preferences become endogenised by means of market transactions executed according to policy guidance (*Shuratic* guidance on markets). Here the exogeneity factor caused by asset speculation is removed. What results is a price rule that is perfectly endogenous, and as a result money becomes endogenous as well.

CONCLUSION

In this brief chapter we have shown that the concept of money in Islamic economics is essentially an endogenous theory of money. In other systems of economics, money is treated either as an exogenous aggregate, as in Keynesianism and rational expectations theory, or as endogenous, as in the case of the quantity theory of money. Yet the quantity theory is unable to establish causality between quantity of money and price level. Interest as the exchange value of money exists in these latter systems. This randomises the monetary equilibrium. Consequently even the function of money as a store of value and a stable numeraire disappears.

In the Islamic economy, the one-to-one relationship between the monetary and real goods/services sectors replaces the stability and convertibility of money in terms of the rate of profit. But money now ceases to be a function of its own intrinsic exchange value. Instead its circulation is determined by transactions in the real goods/services sector.

The Islamic banks and the Committee on Economic and Commercial Cooperation Among Member States of the Organization of Islamic Conferences cannot bring about structural change in the Muslim countries in the absence of endogenous monetary and financial sectors. Unless a new mode of capital market development is contemplated, it is impossible to see any real Islamic world view of politico-economic change arising as the world economy globalises. The susceptibility of the Muslim countries to uncertain and disempowering external forces will increase if essentially Islamic capital market prescriptions are not realised.

The methodological and functional superiority of the endogenous theory of money over the Keynesian, quantity and rational expectations theories points out that there is a unique way of explaining reality in the Islamic system. This is the epistemological foundation of an Islamic socio-scientific order premised on unification epistemology, which takes up substantive meaning in *Tawhidi* epistemology. In the case of money, banking, political economy and analytical methodology, we have seen in this book that endogenous monetary theory reflects the same epistemology. Thus there are no pluralistic theories in terms of the essence of *Tawhidi* epistemology, only specific problems that present themselves in different ways for treatment by the same methodological approach.

If the Islamic banks are to become a vehicle of Islamic structural transformation and not simply profit-maximisation institutions in spite of the existence of Islamic financial instruments, then not just these instruments but also the Islamic world view will have to be held to the fore. To date money in Islamic economics has been a continuation of the type of money found the works of Fischer, Tobin, Friedman, Keynes and Hume. Consequently the Islamic world has neither engendered a financial force nor a new direction of thinking in money and markets. Consequently, economic stabilisation and growth with distributive equity, both so much desired, have not occurred by any possible realisation of empowerment and entitlement at the grassroots (Principle of Entitlement in Islamic political economy) and ethical market transformation (Principle of Work and Productivity) in any context.

We find that endogenous money is brought together within the framework of the theory and application of Islamic political economy presented here. At the same time, the interactive–integrative *Shuratic* process that underlies Islamic political economy must also be intrinsic to the endogenous theory of money and financial institutions as *Shuratic* forms in the Islamic politico-economic order in particular and the Islamic world view in general.

Notes and References

Foreword

1. For a more detailed answer see M. Umer Chapra, *What is Islamic Economics?* (Jiddah: IDB/IRTI, IDB Prize Winner's Lecture Series, no. 9, 1996).
2. Narrated from Anas ibn Malik by Imam al-Bayhaqi (d. 485/1094) in his *Shu'ab al-Iman* (Beirut: Dar al-Kutub al-'Ilmiyyah, 1990), vol. 2, no. 1779, p. 285.
3. Arnold Toynbee, *A Study of History*, abridged by D. C. Somervelle (London: Oxford University Press, 1958), vol. 2, p. 380, and vol. 1, pp. 495–6.
4. Will and Ariel Durant, *The Lessons of History* (New York: Simon & Schuster, 1968), p. 51.
5. See, for example, M. Umer Chapra, *Towards a Just Monetary System* (Leicester: The Islamic Foundation, 1985) and *Islam and the Economic Challenge* (Leicester: The Islamic Foundation, 1992).

1   Dualism, Perception and World View

1. R. Descartes, 'Discourse on the Method of Rightly Conducting the Reason, and Seeking Truth in the Sciences', in S. Commins and R. N. Linscott (eds), *Man and the Universe: The Philosophers of Science* (New York: Pocket Books, 1954), pp. 163–220.
2. Cultural pluralism for Islam is treated by A. A. Mazrui in 'Islam and the End of History', *The American Journal of Islamic Social Sciences*, vol. 10, no. 4 (Winter 1993), pp. 512–35.
3. D. Howard, *From Marx to Kant* (Albany, NY: State University of New York Press, 1985).
4. F. Fukuyama, *The End of History and the Last Man* (New York: Free Press, 1992).
5. P. Minford and D. Peel, 'The Political Economy of Democracy', in *Rational Expectations and the New Macroeconomics* (Oxford: Martin Robertson, 1983), pp. 144–58.
6. O. Lange and F. M. Taylor, *On the Economic Theory of Socialism* (Minneapolis, MA: University of Minnesota Press, 1938).
7. J. A. Schumpeter, *Capitalism, Socialism, and Democracy* (New York: Harper & Row, 1950).
8. G. L. S. Shackle, *Epistemics and Economics* (Cambridge: Cambridge University Press, 1971).
9. J. M. Henderson and R. E. Quandt, *Microeconomic Theory* (New York: McGraw-Hill, 1980).
10. E. S. Phelps, 'Distributive Justice', in J. Eatwell, M. Milgate and P. Newman (eds), *The New Palgrave: Social Economics* (New York: W. W. Norton, 1989), pp. 31–4.

11. S. Bowles discusses endogenous preferences in his 'What Markets Can – and Cannot – Do', *Challenge*, vol. 34, no. 4 (July/August 1991), pp. 11–16.
12. F. A. Hayek, *Studies in Philosophy, Politics and Economics* (Chicago, Ill: The University of Chicago Press, 1967).
13. L. von Mises, *Epistemological Problems of Economics* (Princeton, NJ: Princeton University Press, 1960).
14. See M. Stanifeld, *What is Political Economy? A Study of Social Theory and Underdevelopment* (New Haven, Conn.: Yale University Press, 1985).
15. R. Nozick, *Anarchy, State and Utopia* (New York: Basic Books, 1974); J. Rawls, *A Theory of Justice* (Cambridge, MA: Harvard University Press, 1971).
16. T. Aquinas, *Summa Theologia, Vol. 1* (New York: Benziger Brothers, 1947).
17. On Bergson see B. Russell, *A History of Western Philosophy* (London: Unwin, reprinted 1990). See also H. Bergson, 'The Evolution of Life', in S. Commons and R. N. Linscott (eds), *The Philosophers of Science* (New York: Pocket Books, 1954), pp. 279–97.
18. The problem of 'one–many' is discussed in R. Rucker, *Infinity and the Mind* (New York: Bantam New Age Books, 1983) pp. 203–37.
19. E. Mandel (trans. B. Pearce), *The Foundation of the Economic Thought of Karl Marx, 1843 to Capital* (New York: Monthly Review Press, 1971).
20. J. A. Schumpeter, *A History of Economic Analysis* (New York: Oxford University Press, 1968).
21. L. Walras, *Elements of Pure Economics* (trans. W. Jaffe) (Richard D. Irwin, 1954).
22. The ethical views of J. M. Keynes are discussed by R. M. O'Donnell in *Keynes: Philosophy, Economics and Politics* (London: Macmillan, 1989).
23. An extensive account of liberal philosophy in economics and politics is given in O. H. Taylor, *Economics and Liberalism* (Cambridge, MA: Harvard University Press, 1967).
24. P. Drucker, *Post-Capitalist Society* (New York: Harper Business, 1993).
25. E. Husserl, *The Crisis of European Sciences and Transcendental Phenomenology* (trans. D. Carr) (Evanston, Ill.: Northwestern University Press, 1970).
26. For the mathematical concept of open cover of sets, see I. J. Maddox, *Elements of Functional Analysis* (Cambridge: Cambridge University Press, 1970).
27. On the inductive nature of econometric methodology, see L. A. Boland, *The Methodology of Economic Model Building, Methodology after Samuelson* (London: Routledge, 1991).
28. On instrumentalism and econometrics, see J. Pheby, *Methodology and Economics, a Critical Introduction* (London: Macmillan, 1988)
29. D. F. Hendry, 'Econometric Modelling with Cointegrated Variables: An Overview', *Oxford Bulletin of Economics and Statistics*, vol. 45, no. 3 (1986), pp. 201–12.
30. H. J. Berman, 'Beyond Marx, Beyond Weber', in *Law and Revolution* (Cambridge, MA: Harvard University Press, 1983).
31. S. Hawking, *A Brief History of Time* (New York: Bantam Books, 1988).
32. For a treatment of Darwinism, see R. Dawkins, *The Selfish Gene* (Oxford: Oxford University Press, 1976). A good discussion of biological

and social Darwinism is provided in C. N. Degler, *In Search of Human Nature* (Oxford: Oxford University Press, 1991).

33. For the developmental application of the concept of world view, see M. A. Choudhury, *Comparative Development Studies: In Search of the World View* (London: Macmillan; New York: St Martin's Press, 1993).

34. M. A. Choudhury, *The Unicity Precept and the Socio-Scientific Order* (Lanham, MA: University Press of America, 1993).

35. On the topic of political cycles, see W. D. Nordhaus, 'The Political Business Cycle', *Review of Economic Studies*, vol. 42 (1975), pp. 169–90.

36. D. Levine, *Needs, Rights, and the Market* (Boulder, CO: Lynne Rienner, 1988).

37. P. J. Hammond, 'On Reconciling Arrow's Theory of Social Choice with Harsanyi's Fundamental Utilitarianism', in G. R. Feiwel (ed.), *Arrow and the Foundations of the Theory of Economic Policy* (London: Macmillan, 1987), pp. 179–221.

38. O. Mehmet, 'Alternative Concept of Development: A Critique of Euro-Centric Theorizing', *Humanomics*, vol. 6, no. 3 (1990), pp. 55–67.

39. J. Buchanan and G. Tullock, *The Calculus of Consent* (Ann Arbor, Mich.: Michigan University Press, 1962).

40. K. Popper, 'Scientific Reduction and the Essential Incompleteness of All Sciences', in *The Open Universe: An Argument for Indeterminisn* (Totowa, NJ: Rowman & Littlefield, 1982), pp. 131–62.

41. A discussion on the thoughts of all these philosophers can be found in B. Russell, *A History of Western Philosophy*, op. cit.

42. C. M. Sherover, *Heidegger, Kant and Time* (Bloomington, IN: Indiana University Press, 1972).

43. For good discussions of some of R. Carnap's views on scientific theory construction, see E. Nagel, 'The Logical Character of Scientific Laws', 'The Cognitive Status of Theories' and 'The Reduction of Theories' in *The Structure of Science, Problems in the Logic of Scientific Explanation* (New York: Harcourt, Brace & World, 1961), pp. 5–38; R. Carnap, 'Causality and Determinism', in M. Gardner (ed.), *Philosophical Foundations of Physics* (New York: Basic Books, 1966). See also A. N. Whitehead, 'Fact and Form', in D. R. Griffin and D. W. Sherburne (eds), *Process and Reality* (New York: The Free Press, 1978), pp. 39–61; K. Godel, 'On Formally Undecidable Propositions of Principia Mathematica and Related Systems', in M. Davies (ed.), *Undecidable* (Hewlett, NY: Raven Press, 1965), pp. 5–38; K. E. Boulding, 'Evolution and Revolution in the Developmental Process', in *Social Change and Economic Growth* (Paris: Development Centre of the Organization for Economic Co-operation and Development, 1967), pp. 19–29.

44. M. A. Choudhury, 'The Epistemic-Ontic Circular Causation and Continuity Model of Socio-Scientific Reality: The Knowledge Premise', *International Journal of Social Economics*, vol. 20, no. 1, 1994, pp. 64–77.

45. J. D. Barrow, *Theories of Everything, the Quest for Ultimate Explanation* (Oxford: Oxford University Press, 1991); S. Weinberg, *Dreams of a Final Theory* (New York: Pantheon, 1992).

46. D. F. Hendry, *PC-Give, An Interactive Econometric Modelling System* (Oxford: Institute of Economics and Statistics and Nuffield College, University of Oxford, 1989). For a treatment of stationary and evolutionary

stochastic processes, see P. J. Dhrymes, 'Spectral Analysis', *Econometrics, Statistical Foundations and Applications* (New York: Harper & Row, 1970), pp. 382–443. For a reduced treatment of non-stationary series in a weakly stationary form, see J. Johnston, 'Lagged Variables', *Econometric Methods* (New York: McGraw-Hill, 1984), pp. 343–83.

47. M. A. Choudhury, *The Epistemological Foundations of Islamic Economic, Social and Scientific Order*, 6 Vols (Ankara, Turkey: Statistical, Economic and Social Research and Training Centre for Islamic Countries, 1995).

2 Post-Marxian, Post-Humean and Post-Kantian Epistemology: Towards the Unification of Knowledge

1. G. W. F. Hegel, *The Philosophy of History* (trans. J. Sibree) (New York: Dover Publications, 1956).

2. H. J. Berman, *Law and Revolution* (see the section on 'Beyond Marx, Beyond Weber') (Cambridge, MA: Harvard University Press, 1983). For a treatise on Marx's approach to scientific inquiry, see S. A. Resnick and R. D. Wolff, *Knowledge and Class, A Marxian Critique of Political Economy* (Chicago, Ill.: University of Chicago Press, 1987).

3. M. A. Choudhury, 'The Muslim Republics of the Commonwealth of Independent States: Their Political Economy under Communism, Capitalism and Islam', in J. C. O'Brien (ed.), *The Evils of Soviet Communism and Other Essays* (West Yorkshire: MCB University Press), pp. 3–32.

4. G. D. H. Cole, *The Meaning of Marxism* (Ann Arbor, Mich.: University of Michigan Press, 1966).

5. M. Blaug, *Economic Theory in Retrospect* (Homewood, Ill.: Richard D. Irwin, 1968).

6. M. Heidegger, *Being and Time* (trans. J. Macquarrie and E. Robinson) (Oxford: Basil Blackwell, 1962).

7. D. Hume, *Treatise on Human Nature* (ed. S. Bigge) (Oxford: Clarendon Press, 1988).

8. J. A. Schumpeter, *History of Economic Analysis* (New York: Oxford University Press, 1954).

9. E. Doak, '100% Money', in M. A. Choudhury (ed.), *Policy-Theoretic Foundations of Ethico-Economics* (Sydney, NS: Centre of Humanomics, University College of Cape Breton, 1988), pp. 97–107.

10. D. Laidler, 'The Quantity Theory is Always and Everywhere Controversial, Why?', *Atlantic Canada Economic Association Papers*, vol. 18 (1989), pp. 98–122.

11. Aristotle (trans. J. E. C. Welldon), *The Nicomachean Ethics* (Buffalo, NY: Prometheus Books, 1987).

12. I. Kant, 'Critique of Pure Reason', in C. Friedrich (ed.), *The Philosophy of Kant* (New York: The Modern Library, 1987), pp. 24–39.

13. I. Kant, 'Metaphysical Foundations of Morals', *The Philosophy of Kant*, op. cit., pp. 140–208.

14. I. Kant, 'Critique of Pure Practical Reason', *The Philosophy of Kant*, op. cit., pp. 209–64.

15. S. Hawking, *Is the End in Sight for Theoretical Physics?* (Cambridge: Cambridge University Press, 1980).

16. I. Kant, 'Metaphysical Foundations of Morals', *Philosophy of Kant*, op. cit.

17. I. Kant, 'Trust in God and the Concept of Faith', in *Immanuel Kant Lectures on Ethics* (ed. L. Infeld) (Indianapolis, IN: Hackett, 1963), pp. 95–8.

18. I. Kant, 'Religion Within the Limits of Reason Alone', *The Philosophy of Kant*, op. cit., pp. 365–411.

19. Ibid.

20. M. Hammond, J. Howarth and R. Keat, *Understanding Phenomenology* (Oxford: Basil Blackwell, 1991). For a discussion of the crisis of Western science, see also E. Husserl, *The Crisis of European Sciences and Transcendental Phenomenology* (trans. D. Carr) (Evanston, Ill.: Northwestern University Press, 1970).

21. H. Reichenbach, *The Philosophy of Space and Time* (trans. M. Reichenbach and J. Freund) (New York: Dover Publications, 1958).

22. K. Hubner, 'The Question of Foundation for the Natural Sciences in Hume's Critical Empiricism, Kant's Transcendentalism, and Reichenbach's Operationalism', in *A Critique of Scientific Reason* (trans. P. R. Dixon, Jr. and H. M. Dixon) (Chicago, Ill.: University of Chicago Press, 1985), pp. 4–12.

23. B. Russell, *The Analysis of Mind* (London and New York: G. Allen & Unwin, 1921).

24. A. N. Whitehead, *Process and Reality* (ed. D. R. Griffin and D. W. Sherburne) (New York: The Free Press, 1978), pp. 61–109.

25. M. A. Choudhury, 'Epistemic–Ontic Circular Causation and Continuity Model of Socio-Scientific Reality: The Knowledge Premise', *International Journal of Social Economics*, vol. 20, no. 1, 1994, pp. 64–77. Another good account of the evolutionary nature of Islamic Law (*Shari'ah*) in the context of *Ijtehad* and *Ijma* is given by M. Asad in *The Principles of State and Government in Islam* (Gibraltar: Dar al-Andalus, 1985).

3 Evolutionary Epistemology and Ethical Social Choice in the Islamic Perspective

1. M. A. Choudhury, *The Epistemological Foundations of Islamic Economic, Social and Scientific Order*, six volumes (Ankara, Turkey: Statistical, Economic and Social Research and Training Centre for Islamic Countries, 1995).

2. I. Kant [1786], *The Foundations of the Metaphysics of Morals* (New York: Bobb-Merrill, 1959). For a critique of Kant's *a priori* philosophy see V. J. Seidler, *Kant, Respect and Injustice, the Limits of Liberal Moral Theory* (London: Routledge & Kegan Paul, 1986); M. A. Choudhury, 'Kantian Perspectives and Ethical Alternative in Social Contract Theory', *Atlantic Canada Economic Association Papers*, vol. XVIII (1989), pp. 164–86.

3. For a treatment of perception with regard to the physical world and sensibility, see M. Sainsbury, *Russell* (London: Routledge & Kegan Paul, 1985), chapter entitled 'Knowledge'. See also Bergson's philosophy on the concept of perception in B. Russell, *A History of Western Philosophy* (London: Unwin, 1990, reprinted).

4. K. R. Popper, *Objective Knowledge* (Oxford: Clarendon Press, 1972).

5. K. R. Popper, 'Natural Selection and the Emergence of Mind', in G. Radnitzky and W. W. Bartley, III (eds), *Evolutionary Epistemology, Rationality, and the Sociology of Knowledge* (La Salle, Ill.: Open Court, 1987), pp. 137–55.

6. D. T. Campbell, 'Evolutionary Epistemology', in *Evolutionary Epistemology, Rationality, and the Sociology of Knowledge*, op. cit., pp. 47–89.

7. W. C. Chittick, *Sufi Path of Knowledge* (Albany, NY: State University of New York, 1989). For a good account of many of the early Muslim philosophers see S. H. Nasr, *Science and Civilization in Islam* (Cambridge, Mass.: Harvard University Press, 1968) and his *Introduction to Islamic Cosmological Doctrines* (Boulder, CO: Shambhala, 1978).

8. These properties may be thought of as essential characteristics of *tawhidi* precept rather than of field. The difference between the concepts of field and precept lies in the primordiality of the latter and the sense perception of the former in the act of creation and knowing. However, this is simply a working concept to help build up an analysis, not a real one in essence, as the unicity precept essentially provides a unified world view.

9. K. E. Boulding, 'Evolution and Revolution in the Development Process', in *Social Change and Economic Growth* (Paris: Organization for Economic Co-operation and Development, 1967), pp. 19–29.

10. K. E. Boulding, 'The Economics of Knowledge and the Knowledge of Economics', in F. R. Glabe (ed.), *Boulding: Collective Papers*, vol. 2 (Boulder, CO: Colorado Association University Press, 1971), pp. 369–79.

11. K. E. Boulding, *The Image: Knowledge in Life and Society* (Ann Arbor, Mich.: University of Michigan Press, 1961).

12. A. Okun, *Equality and Efficiency, the Big Tradeoff* (Washington, DC: Brookings Institute, 1975).

13. For a good account of this neoclassical rationality concept, see R. M. O'Donnell, *Keynes: Philosophy, Economics and Politics* (London: Macmillan, 1989), ch. 12: 'The General Theory II: Behaviour and Rationality'.

14. P. Cagan, 'Monetarism', in J. Eatwell, M. Milgate and P. Newman (eds), *New Palgrave: Money* (New York: W.W. Norton, 1989), pp. 195–205.

15. R. Matthews, *The Creation of Regional Dependency* (Toronto: University of Toronto Press, 1983).

16. I. Wallerstein, *The Modern World System* (New York: Academic Press, 1974).

17. S. A. Resnick and R. D. Wolff, *Knowledge and Class, A Marxian Critique of Political Economy* (Chicago, Ill.: University of Chicago Press, 1987).

18. F. Capra, *The Tao of Physics* (New York: Bantam Books, 1977).

19. I. J. Maddox, *Elements of Functional Analysis* (Cambridge: Cambridge University Press, 1970).

20. M. Blaug, *An Introduction to the Economics of Education* (London: Penguin, 1970).

21. I. J. Maddox, *Elements of Functional Analysis*, op. cit.

22. J. Sheehan, *The Economics of Education* (London: George Allen & Unwin, 1973)

23. M. A. Choudhury, *A Theory of Ethico-Economics* (Hull: Barmarick Publications, 1993).

24. A. Sen, 'The Moral Standing of the Market', in E. F. Paul, J. Paul and F. D. Miller Jr. (eds), *Ethics and Economics* (Oxford: Basil Blackwell, 1985), pp. 1–28.
25. S. Hallaq, 'A Note on the Existence of an Islamic Social Welfare Function', *Humanomics*, vol. 10, no. 2 (1994), pp. 50–7.
26. H. Nikaido, 'Fixed Point Theorems', in J. Eatwell *et al.* (eds), *New Palgrave: General Equilibrium* (New York: W. W. Norton, 1989), pp. 139–44.
27. M. A. Choudhury and U. A. Malik, *The Foundations of Islamic Political Economy* (London: Macmillan; New York: St Martin's Press, 1992).

4   A Theory of Renewal and Continuity in Islamic Science

1. N. Faghih, 'Some Scientific Doctrines in the *Mathnawi* of Mawlana Jalal Al-Din Mawlawi Rumi', *Hamdard Islamicus*, vol. XVI, no. 2 (1993), pp. 79–96.
2. R. A. Nicholson (trans.), *The Mathnawi of Jalaladdin Rumi* (London: Luzac & Co. 1926).
3. For a brief treatment of Laplace transformation see M. Kline, 'Integral Equations', in *Mathematical Thought from Ancient to Modern Times*, vol. 3 (New York: Oxford University Press, 1990), pp. 1052–75.
4. M. Rosenlicht, *Introduction to Analysis* (New York: Dover Publications, 1968).
5. H. Nikaido, 'Fixed Point Theorems', in J. Eatwell, M. Milgate and P. Newman (eds), *General Equilibrium* (New York: W.W. Norton, 1989), pp. 139–44.
6. R. Rucker, 'Infinity', in *Infinity and the Mind, the Science and Philosophy of the Infinite* (New York: Bantam Books, 1983), pp. 1–56.
7. A. W. Moore, 'Reactions', and 'Post-Kantian Metaphysics of the Infinite', in *The Infinite* (London: Routledge, 1991), pp. 131–43, 96–109.
8. G. Cantor, *Contributions to the Foundations of the Theory of Transfinite Numbers* (trans. E. B. Jourdain) (New York: Dover, 1955).
9. I. M. Gel'fand, *Lectures on Linear Algebra* (trans. A. Shenitzer) (New York: Interscience, 1961).
10. A. P. Robertson and W. J. Robertson, *Topological Vector Spaces* (Cambridge: Cambridge University Press, 1966).
11. M. A. Choudhury, *The Epistemological Foundations of Islamic Economic, Social and Scientific Order*, six volumes (Ankara, Turkey: Statistical, Economic and Social Research and Training Centre for Islamic Countries, January 1995).
12. B. Russell, *Introduction to Mathematical Philosophy* (London: George Allen & Unwin, 1970, reprinted).
13. Azm, *Kant's Theory of Time* (New York: The Philosophical Library, 1967).
14. N. Georgescu-Roegen, *The Entropy Law and the Economic Process* (Cambridge, Mass.: Harvard University Press, 1971).
15. M. A. Choudhury, 'The Epistemic–Ontic Circular Causation and Continuity Model of Unified Reality: The Knowledge Premise', paper presented at the Congress of the Society for the Advancement of Socio-Economics, New School of Social Research, March, 1992. Published in *International Journal of Social Economics*, vol. 20, no. 1 (1994), pp. 64–77.

16. For ideas of supersymmetry and renormalisation that look for non-infinite
    solutions of early universe models in the light of quantum chromodynamic
    theory or the solution of Einstein's fundamental equation around black
    holes, see H. Pagel, *Perfect Symmetry, the Search for the Beginning of
    Time* (New York: Bantam Books, 1986).
17. M. A. Choudhury, M. A. and U. A. Malik, *The Foundations of Islamic
    Political Economy* (London: Macmillan; New York: St Martin's Press,
    1992).
18. M. Arif, 'Toward the Shari'ah Paradigm of Islamic Economics: The Be-
    ginning of a Scientific Revolution', *American Journal of Islamic Social
    Sciences*, vol. 2, no. 1 (July, 1985), pp. 79–99.
19. M. A. Choudhury, *The Unicity Precept and the Socio-Scientific Order*
    (Lanham, MA: University Press of America, 1993).
20. Convolution integrals across a nexus of higher topological spaces can also
    be used to explain the process of inter-systemic interaction–integration.
21. A. Einstein, *Relativity, the Special and the General Theory* (trans. R. W.
    Lawson) (London: Methuen, 1960).
22. M. Abu-Saud, 'The Methodology of the Islamic Behavioural Sciences',
    American Journal of Islamic Social Sciences, vol. 10, no. 3 (Fall 1993),
    pp. 382–95; S. Husain, 'Islamic Science: The Making of a Formal Intel-
    lectual Discipline', *American Journal of Islamic Social Sciences*, vol. 10,
    no. 3 (Fall 1993), pp. 305–11; M. A. Choudhury, 'A Critical Examination
    of the Concept of Islamicization of Knowledge in Contemporary Times',
    Muslim Education Quarterly, vol. 10, no. 4 (Jan. 1994), pp. 3–34.

    It is centrally important in the development of an Islamic approach to
    science and the philosophy of science to keep away from metaphysics as
    a substantive ground of knowledge. The roots of scientific *Ahqam* in the
    Qur'an are distinct from and opposed to the perceptual basis of specula-
    tive philosophy. The universe, according to the *Qur'an*, is a purposeful
    and definitive spring of unified knowledge. We discover this spring by
    substantive reference to the *Qur'an*, the authentic *Sunnah* and continuous
    discursion (*Ijtehad*).

    The Islamic philosophers drifted from such epistemic–ontic roots of
    the *Qur'an* when they took to metaphysics as the scientific premise. By
    so doing they were inevitably driven to rely upon and borrow from Greek
    philosophy. The Muslim rationalists thus introduced pantheism into the
    framework of what otherwise could have been a pure Islamic approach to
    scientific reasoning.

    Western philosophy of science is derived from the primordial premise
    of metaphysics. Hence we have the open-ended universes of Popper and
    Kant; the Judaic influences of the Vienna Circle; and the empiricism of
    Descartes and Hume. The debate between science and metaphysics is an
    unresolved one in modern philosophy of science.

    For a discussion of these Western roots of science in metaphysics, see
    D. Gillies, *Philosophy of Science in the Twentieth Century, Four Central
    Themes* (Oxford: Basil Blackwell, 1993). For the unresolved question of
    phenomenology, see M. Hammond, J. Howarth and R. Keat, *Understand-
    ing Phenomenology* (Oxford: Basil Blackwell, 1991). For the role of meta-
    physics in the works of philosophers of *Kalam* (the rationalists), see

S. H. Nasr, *Science and Civilization in Islam* (New York: Barnes & Noble, 1992) and S. M. H. Al-Attas, 'Islam and the Philosophy of Science', *MAAS Journal of Islamic Science*, vol. 6, no. 1 (1990). On the other hand, in recent times there has been renewed interest in deriving scientific roots from the *Qur'an*: M. Bucaille, *The Bible, Qur'an and Science* (Paris: Sejhers, 1987); Keith Moore's work on embryology in the *Qur'an*, and M. A. Choudhury, *The Epistemological Foundations of Islamic Economic, Social and Scientific Order*, six vols (Ankara, Turkey: Statistical, Economic and Social Research and Training Centre for Islamic Countries, 1995); and M. A. Choudhury, *The Unicity Precept and the Socio-Scientific Order* (Lanham, MA: University Press of America, 1993). There is also the interesting work by O. Bakar, *Tawhid and Science, Essays on the History and Philosophy of Islamic Science* (Kuala Lumpur: Secretariat for Islamic Philosophy and Science and Nurin Enterprise, 1991).

5 What is Islamic Political Economy?

1. This is also the view of the following authors: H. Enayat, *Modern Islamic Political Thought* (London: Macmillan, 1982); E. Sivan, *Radical Islam: Medieval Theology and Modern Politics* (New Haven, Conn.: Yale University Press, 1985). K. Ahmad, *Principles of Islamic Economics* (Lahore, Pakistan: Islamic Publications, 1968). K. Ahmad and Z. I. Ansari (eds), *Islamic Perspectives: Studies in Honour of Sayyid Abul A'la Mawdudi* (Leicester: The Islamic Foundation, 1979); M. N. Siddiqi, *Muslim Economic Thinking, A Survey of Contemporary Literature* (Leicester: The Islamic Foundation, 1981); A. A. Maududi, *Mashiyat-e-Islami (Economics of Islam)* (Lahore: Islamic Publications, 1969).
2. *Al-Qur'an*, ch. III, vs. 190.
3. M. Mahdi, *Ibn Khaldun's Philosophy of History* (Chicago, Ill.: University of Chicago Press, 1964).
4. J. Lovelock, 'Ghaia', in *Ghaia, a Way of Knowing* (ed. W. Thompson) (Great Barrington, MA: Lindisfarne Press, 1987).
5. Imam Ghazzali, *Ihya Ulum-id-Din, vol. 1: The Book of Worship* (tr. M. F. Karim) (New Delhi: Kitab Bhavan, 1982).
6. A. Mirakhor, 'Muslim Scholars and the History of Economics', *The American Journal of Islamic Social Sciences*, vol. 4, no. 2 (Dec. 1987), pp. 245–76.
7. Imam Shatibi, *Al-Muwafaqat Fi Usul al-Shariah* (Cairo: Abdallah Draz al-Maktabah al-Tijariyah al-Kubra, undated).
8. A. H. Maslow, *Motivation and Personality* (New York: Harper & Row, 1954).
9. O. Mehmet, *Islamic Identity & Development* (London: Routledge, 1990); V. Nienhaus, 'Epistemology, Methodology and Economic Policy: Some Thoughts on Mainstream, Austrian and Islamic Economics', *Humanomics*, vol. 5, no. 1 (1989), pp. 10–38.
10. M. M. Metwally, 'The Role of the Rate of Interest in Contemporary Islamic Societies', *The Middle East Business and Economic Review*, vol. 1, no. 1 (January 1989), pp. 32–47.
11. H. Zangeneh, 'Islamic Banking: Theory and Practice in Iran', *Comparative Economic Studies*, vol. XXXI, no. 3 (Fall, 1989), pp. 67–84; M. Iqbal and M. F. Khan, *A Survey of Issues and a Program for Research in Monetary*

and Fiscal Economics of Islam (Islamabad: Institute of Policy Analysis, 1981).

12. V. Nienhaus, 'Visions and Realities of Islamic Banking', in *Lectures on Islamic Economics and Banking* (Ruhr-Universitat Bochum Seminar Für Wirtschafts- Und Finanzpolitik, Diskussionsbeitrage, nr. 6, Dec. 1988), pp. 1–66.

13. Z. Ahmed, M. Iqbal and M. F. Khan (eds), *Fiscal Policy and Resource Allocation in Islam* (Islamabad: Institute of Policy Analysis, 1983); A. H. M. Sadeq, *Financing Economic Development, Islamic and Mainstream Approaches* (Petaling Jaya, Malaysia: Longman, 1992); M. S. Khan and A. Mirakhor, *Theoretical Studies in Islamic Banking and Finance* (Houston, Texas: Institute of Research and Islamic Studies, 1987); M. N. Siddiqi, *Banking Without Interest* (Leicester: The Islamic Foundation, 1988); A. A. Islahi, *Economic Views of Ibn Taimiyyah* (Leicester: The Islamic Foundation, 1986); M. A. Choudhury, *Islamic Economic Co-operation* (London: Macmillan; New York: St Martin's Press, 1989); M. A. Choudhury, *Theory and Practice of Islamic Development Co-operation: Recent Experience of Some Asian Countries* (Ankara: Statistical, Economic and Social Research and Training Centre for Islamic Countries, 1993).

14. M. Kahf, *The Islamic Economy: Analytical Study of the Functioning of the Islamic Economic System* (Plainfield, IN: Muslim Students Association of the U.S. and Canada, 1978); M. A. Choudhury, *Contributions to Islamic Economic Theory: A Study in Social Economics* (London: Macmillan Press, 1986); M. A. Choudhury, 'A Theory of Moral Entitlement in Resource Allocation', in Z. Sattar (ed.), *Resource Mobilization and Investment in an Islamic Economic Framework* (Herndon, VA: International Institute of Islamic Thought, 1992), pp. 45–70.

15. M. A. Choudhury, 'A Critique of Developments in Social Economics and the Alternative', *International Journal of Social Economics*, vol. 18. nos 11, 12 (1991), pp. 36–61; M. A. Choudhury, *A Theory of Ethico-Economics* (Hull: Barmarick Publications, 1993); R. Kurtner, 'Economists Really Should Get Out More Often', *Business Week*, 24 April 1989; M. Prowse, 'The Birth of a Broader Economic Discipline', *London Financial Times*, 2 April 1991; P. M. Boarman, 'Beyond Supply and Demand: The Framework of the Market Economy', *Challenge*, March/April 1994, pp. 31–8.

16. A. Shariati, *On the Sociology of Islam* (trans. H. Algar) (Berkeley, CA: Mizan Press, 1979); M. Yadegari, 'Shariati and the Reconstruction of Social Sciences', *American Journal of Islamic Studies*, vol. 1, no. 1 (Spring 1984), pp. 53–9.

17. A. M. Baqir as-Sadr, *Our Philosophy* (tr. S. C. Inati) (London: Muhammadi Trust & KPI Ltd. 1987); A. M. Baqir, *Iqtisaduna* (Beirut: Dar al-Fikr, 1968).

18. Z. Sardar, *Islamic Futures, the Shape of Ideas to Come* (Petaling Jaya, Malaysia: Pelanduk Publications, 1988).

19. M. A. Choudhury and U. A. Malik, *The Foundations of Islamic Political Economy* (London: Macmillan, 1992).

20. M. A. Choudhury, 'Syllogistic Deductionism in Islamic Social Choice Theory', *International Journal of Social Economics*, vol. 17, no. 11 (1990), pp. 4–20.

21. M. Staniland, *What is Political Economy? A Study of Social Theory and*

Underdevelopment (New Haven, Conn.: Yale University Press, 1985).

22. J. M. Buchanan, *What Should Economists Do?* (Indianapolis, Ind.: Liberty Press, 1979).

23. A. Quinton, *Utilitarian Ethics* (La Salle, Ill.: Open Court, 1989).

24. D. R. Fusfeld, *The Age of the Economist* (Scott, Foresman & Co., 1986).

25. K. J. Arrow, *The Limits of Organization* (New York: W. W. Norton, 1974).

26. M. A. Choudhury, 'Micro–Macro Interface in Islamic Economic Theory', *The Middle East Business and Economic Review*, vol. 3, no. 1 (1991), pp. 29–38. For a coverage of Keynesian political economy, see K. K. Kurihara, *The Keynesian Theory of Economic Development* (New York: Columbia University Press, 1959).

27. W. C. Mitchell, 'The Shape of Political Theory to Come: From Political Sociology to Political Economy', *The American Behavioural Scientist*, vol. II, no. 2 (1967), pp. 8–21.

28. D. C. Mueller, *Public Choice* (Cambridge: Cambridge University Press, 1979).

29. G. W. F. Hegel, *The Philosophy of History* (New York: Dover Publications, 1956); M. Cornforth, *Dialectical Materialism, Vol. Three: The Theory of Knowledge* (London: Lawrence & Wishart: 1954).

30. G. D. H. Cole, *The Meaning of Marxism* (Ann Arbor, Mich.: The University of Michigan Press, 1966).

31. F. A. Hayek (ed.) *Collectivist Economic Planning* (London: Routledge & Kegan Paul, 1935).

32. F. A. Hayek, *The Constitution of Liberty* (Chicago, Ill.: The University of Chicago Press, 1960); L. von Mises, *The Ultimate Foundation of Economic Science* (Kansas City: Sheed Andrews & McMeel, 1976).

33. A. Sen, 'Freedom and Consequences', in *On Ethics and Economics* (Oxford: Basil Blackwell, 1990), pp. 58–89.

34. R. Nozick, *Anarchy, State and Utopia* (New York: Basic Books, 1974).

35. von Mises, *The Ultimate Foundation*, op. cit.

36. M. A. Choudhury, 'The Tawhidi Precept in the Sciences', *MAAS Journal of Islamic Science*, vol. 7, no. 1 (Jan.–June 1991), pp. 29–44.

37. M. A. Choudhury, 'The Ethical Numeraire', *International Journal of Social Economics*, vol. 19, no. 1 (1992), pp. 60–72.

38. Such a concept of unfolding knowledge is recognised by Al-Arabi. See W. C. Chittick, *Sufi Path of Knowledge* (Albany, NY: State University of New York, 1989).

39. M. A. Choudhury, 'Social Choice in an Islamic Economic Framework', *The American Journal of Islamic Social Sciences*, vol. 8, no. 2 (Sept. 1991), pp. 259–74; 'The Humanomic Structure of Islamic Economic Theory', *Journal of King Abdulaziz University: Islamic Economics*, vol. 2 (1990), pp. 47–64.

40. Ibn Taimiyyah, *Al-Hisbah fil Islam* (*Public Duties in Islam: The Institution of the Hisbah*) (trans. M. Holland) (Leicester: The Islamic Foundation, 1983).

41. F. I. Abdallah, 'Notes on Ibn Hazm's Rejection of Analogy (Qiyas) in Matters of Religious Law', *The American Journal of Islamic Social Sciences*, vol. 2, no. 2 (Dec. 1985), pp. 207–24.

42. Imam Ghazzali, *Ihya Ulum id-Din*, op. cit.

43. Al-Qur'an, chapter XXIX, verses 19–20.
44. G. L. S. Shackle, *Epistemics and Economics* (Cambridge: Cambridge University Press, 1972).
45. For the concept of bounded uncertainty, see G. L. S. Shackle, *Decision, Order and Time in Human Affairs* (Cambridge: Cambridge University Press, 1969).
46. M. A. Choudhury, *The Principles of Islamic Political Economy: A Methodological Inquiry* (London: Macmillan, 1992).
47. M. A. Choudhury, 'Islamic Economics as a Social Science', *International Journal of Social Economics*, vol. 17, no. 6 (1990), pp. 35–59.
48. A. Kaufmann, *Introduction to the Theory of Fuzzy Subsets*, vol. I (Academic Press, 1975).
49. J.-M. Grandmont, 'Temporary Equilibrium', in John Eatwell, M. Milgate and P. Newman (eds), *The New Palgrave: General Equilibrium* (New York: W. W. Norton, 1989), pp. 297–304.
50. This is also in the nature of sustainable development. See G. H. Brundtland, *Our Common Future* (New York: Oxford University Press, 1987).
51. This is a type of Herbert Simon's 'satisfycing' model. See H. A. Simon, *The New Science of Management Decision* (New York: Harper & Row, 1960).
52. For an explanation of this, see B. Kanitscheider, 'Einstein's Treatment of Theoretical Concepts', in P. C. Aichelburg and R. U. Sexl (eds), *Albert Einstein, His Influence on Physics, Philosophy and Politics* (Germany: Friedr. Vieweg & Sohn, 1979), pp. 137–58. See also G. Maxwell, 'The Ontological Status of Theoretical Entities', in H. Feigl and G. Maxwell (eds), *Minnesota Studies in the Philosophy of Science, Vol. III, Scientific Explanation, Space and Time* (Minneapolis, Minn.: University of Minnesota Press, 1962), pp. 3–27.
53. The idea of Islamicisation of knowledge has found new favour among contemporary Muslim writers. See I. al-Faruqi, *Islamization of Knowledge: General Principles and Work Plan* (Herndon, VA: International Institute of Islamic Thought, 1989).
54. I. J. Maddox, *Elements of Functional Analysis* (Cambridge: Cambridge University Press, 1970).
55. G. Becker, *The Economic Approach to Human Behavior* (Chicago, Ill.: The University of Chicago Press, 1976).
56. M. A. Choudhury, 'Contemporary Islamic Economic Thought', *Muslim Education Quarterly*, vol. 8, no. 1 (1990), pp. 40–9.
57. *Al-Qur'an*, chapter II.
58. *Al-Qur'an*, chapter XLV, verse 22.
59. M. A. Choudhury, 'A Theory of Moral Entitlement Applied to Resource Allocation', in Z. Sattar (ed.), *Resource Mobilization and Investment in an Islamic Economic Framework* (Herndon, VA: International Institute of Islamic Thought, 1992), pp. 45–70.
60. This is one of the fundamental concerns of the last sermon of Prophet Muhammad. See also *Al-Qur'an*, chapter II, verse 188. The entire Chapter II of Qur'an is implicative of establishing entitlement through the act of spending in the good cause as God has ordained it.
61. See for example Z. Ahmad, *Islam, Poverty and Income Distribution* (Leicester: The Islamic Foundation, 1991); S. N. H. Naqvi, *Ethics and Economics:*

An Islamic Synthesis (Leicester: The Islamic Foundation, 1981); A. Ghazali, *Development, An Islamic Perspective* (Petaling Jaya, Malaysia: Pelanduk Publications, 1990).

62. *Al-Qur'an*, chapter II, verses 274–80. The abolition of *Riba* is a central point of the last sermon of Prophet Muhammad.

63. M. A. Saud, 'Money, Interest and Qirad', in K. Ahmed (ed.), *Studies in Islamic Economics* (Leicester: The Islamic Foundation, 1980), pp. 59–84; M. A. Mannan, *Islamic Economics: Theory and Practice* (Lahore, Pakistan: Shah Muhammad Ashraf Press, 1975); M. A. Choudhury, 'The Doctrine of Riba', *(Peshawar) Journal of Development Studies*, vol. II, no. 1 (1979), pp. 47–68.

64. S. M. Ismail, 'Musharekat and Muzarebat', in *Capitalism, Socialism and Islamic Economic Order* (Lahore, Pakistan: Oriental Publications, 1989), pp. 440–75; M. N. Siddiqi, 'Some Economic Aspects of Mudarabah', *Review of Islamic Economics*, vol. 1, no. 2 (1991), pp. 21–33.

65. For the grants economy, see K. E. Boulding and T. F. Wilson, *Redistribution Through the Financial System, The Grants Economy of Money and Credit* (New York: Praeger, 1978).

66. *Al-Qur'an*, chapter VII, verse 31.

67. For a list of the various types of instrument used in Islamic financial institutions, see *Annual Reports of the Islamic Development Bank* (Jeddah, Saudi Arabia, various issues).

6 Why Cannot Neoclassicism Explain Resource Allocation and Development in the Islamic Political Economy?

1. M. A. Choudhury, *Comparative Development Studies: In Search of the World View* (London: Macmillan; New York: St Martin's Press, 1993); 'A Mathematical Formulation of a Knowledge-Based World View of Development Theorizing', in E. Ahmed (ed.), *Economic Growth and Human Resource Development in Islamic Perspective* (Herndon, VA: The International Institute of Islamic Thought, 1993), pp. 17–29; 'A Critique of Developments in Social Economics and Alternative', *International Journal of Social Economics*, vol. 17, nos 11/12 (1991), pp. 36–61; 'Islamic Economics as a Social Science', *International Journal of Social Economics*, vol. 17, no. 6 (1990), pp. 35–59; and Chapter 5 of this book.

2. O. H. Taylor, *Economics and Liberalism* (Cambridge, MA: Harvard University Press, 1967); O. Lange and F. M. Taylor, *On the Economic Theory of Socialism* (ed. B. E. Lippincott) (Minneapolis, Minnesota: University of Minnesota Press, 1938); O. Lange, 'The Foundations of Welfare Economics', *Econometrica*, vol. 10 (1942), pp. 215–28.

3. E. S. Phelps, 'Distributive Justice', in J. Eatwell, M. Milgate and P. Newman (eds), *New Palgrave: Social Economics* (New York: W.W. Norton, 1989), pp. 31–4.

4. J. Quirk and R. Saposnik, *Introduction to General Equilibrium Theory and Welfare Economics* (New York: McGraw-Hill, 1968).

5. A. Sen, 'The Moral Standing of the Market', in E. F. Paul, J. Paul and F. D. Miller Jr. (eds), *Ethics and Economics* (Oxford: Basil Blackwell, 1985), pp. 1–28.

6. L. Robbins, *An Essay on the Nature and Significance of Economic Science* (London: Macmillan, 1935).
7. G. Debreu, *Theory of Value, An Axiomatic Analysis of Economic Theory* (New York: John Wiley & Sons, 1959).
8. J. M. Henderson and R. E. Quandt, *Microeconomic Theory, A Mathematical Approach* (New York: McGraw-Hill, 1971).
9. S. Martin, *Industrial Economics, Economic Analysis and Public Policy* (New York: Macmillan, 1988).
10. M. Parkin and R. Bade, 'Talking with Assar Lindbeck', in *Economics, Canada in the Global Environment* (Don Mills, Ont.: Addison-Wesley, 1991), pp. 1–4.
11. J. M. Buchanan, *The Limits of Liberty, Between Anarchy and Leviathan* (Chicago, Ill.: The University of Chicago Press, 1975).
12. P. Minford and D. Peel, 'The Political Economy of Democracy', in *Rational Expectations and the New Macroeconomics* (Oxford: Martin Robertson, 1983), pp. 144–58.
13. K. J. Arrow, *The Limits of Organization* (New York: W. W. Norton, 1974); J. K. Whitaker, '*The Limits of Organization* Revisited', in G.R. Feiwel (ed.), *Arrow and the Foundations of the Theory of Economic Policy* (London: Macmillan, 1987), pp. 565–83; O. E. Williamson, 'Kenneth Arrow and the New Institutional Economics', in G. R. Feiwel, *Arrow and the Foundations*, op. cit., pp. 584–99.
14. A. Bergson, 'A Reformulation of Certain Aspects of Welfare Economics', *Quarterly Journal of Economics*, vol. 52 (Feb. 1938), pp. 310–34.
15. W. F. Sharpe, *Portfolio Theory and Capital Markets* (New York: McGraw-Hill, 1970).
16. G. L. S. Shackle, *Epistemics and Economics* (Cambridge: Cambridge University Press, 1972).
17. E. Barker, *The Political Thought of Plato and Aristotle* (New York: Dover Publications, 1959).
18. B. Russell, *A History of Western Philosophy* (London: Unwin Hyman, 1990, reprinted); C-Yao Hsieh and M-Hua Ye, *Economics, Philosophy, and Physics* (Armonk, NY: M. E. Sharpe, 1991).
19. M. A. Choudhury, 'Kantian Perspectives and Ethical Alternatives in Social Contract Theory', *Atlantic Canada Economic Association Papers*, vol. 18 (1989), pp. 164–86.
20. The following sections are extracts from the author's conference paper, 'Epistemic–Ontic Circular Causation and Continuity Model of Socio-Scientific Reality: The Knowledge Premise', paper presented at the Congress of the Society for the Advancement of Socio-Economics, New School of Social Research, New York, March 1992. The paper appeared in *The International Journal of Social Economics*, vol. 21, no. 1 (1994), pp. 64–77.
21. J. M. Henderson and R. E. Quandt, *Microeconomic Theory, A Methematical Approach* (New York: McGraw-Hill, 1958).
22. J. Quirk and R. Saposnik, *Introduction to General Equilibrium Theory and Welfare Economics* (New York: McGraw-Hill, 1968).
23. G. L. S. Shackle, *Epistemics and Economics, A Critique of Economic Doctrines* (Cambridge: Cambridge University Press, 1972); T. Parsons,

The Structure of Social Actions (New York: The Free Press of Glencoe, 1964).

24. Henderson and Quandt, *Microeconomic Theory*, op. cit.
25. Y. P. Venieris and F. D. Sebold, *Macroeconomic Models and Policy* (New York: John Wiley & Sons, 1977). The quantity theory equation has a *post hoc* error in terms of the indeterminacy of the causal relation between prices and money supply. See D. Laidler, 'The Quantity Theory is Always and Everywhere Controversial – Why?', *Atlantic Canada Economic Association Papers*, vol. 18 (1989), pp. 98–122; M. Desai, 'Endogenous and Exogenous Money', in J. Eatwell, M. Milgate and P. Newman (eds), *The New Palgrave: Money* (New York: W. W. Norton, 1989), pp. 146–50; M. A. Choudhury, 'The Endogenous Theory of Money and Islamic Capital Markets', *Journal of Economic Cooperation Among Islamic Countries*, vol. 12, nos 3 and 4 (1991), pp. 75–96.
26. Various kinds of rationalism are discussed by A. Etzioni in *The Moral Dimension, Toward a New Economics* (New York: The Free Press, 1988).
27. S. Bowles, 'What Markets Can – and Cannot – Do', *Challenge*, vol. 34, no. 4 (July–August 1991), pp. 11–16.
28. The following sections are summarised from the author's paper, 'The Muslim Republics of the Commonwealth of Independent States: Their Political Economy under Communism, Capitalism and Islam', presented at the Sixty-Eighth Western Economic Association Conference, Lake Tahoe, Nevada, July 1993. Published in J. C. O'Brien (ed.), *The Evils of Soviet Communism and Other Essays* (Bradford, West Yorkshire: MCB University Press, 1994), pp. 3–32.
29. I. Kant, *Groundwork of the Metaphysic of Morals* (trans. H. J. Paton) (New York: Harper Torchbooks, 1964); C. M. Sherover, *Heidegger, Kant and Time* (Bloomington, IN: Indiana University Press, 1972); M. A. Choudhury, *The Unicity Precept and the Socio-Scientific Order* (Lanham: University Press of America, 1993).
30. M. A. Choudhury, *The Epistemological Foundations of the Islamic Economic, Social and Scientific Order*, 6 vols (Ankara, Turkey: Statistical, Economic and Social Research and Training Centre for Islamic Countries, January 1995).
31. M. A. Choudhury, 'Islamic Economics as a Social Science', *International Journal of Social Economics*, vol. 17, no. 6 (1990), pp. 35–59.
32. M. A. Choudhury, 'Conflict Resolution and Social Consensus Formation in Islamic Social Choice and Welfare Menu', *International Journal of Social Economics*, vol. 20. no. 1 (1993), pp. 64–77.
33. E. Borensztein, 'The Strategy of Reform in the Centrally Planned Economies of Eastern Europe: Lessons and Challenges', *Papers on Policy Analysis and Assessment* (Washington, DC: International Monetary Fund Paper Series, 1993).
34. *IMF Survey*, 9 August 1993, 'Reforming Centrally Planned Economies: What Have We Learned?'.
35. R. A. Gordon, *Goal of Full Employment* (New York: John Wiley, 1967). Note that the social welfare function, $W = W(x,p,u)$ satisfies all the conditions required for welfare maximisation, namely, $\partial W/\partial x > 0$, x being the rate of change of output; and $\partial W/\partial p > 0$, p being the rate of change

in CPI; $\partial W/\partial u > 0$, u being the rate of change of employment (also the unemployment rate). The constraint of the optimisation problem, namely that domestic prices should be competitive with the world prices of goods, is also satisfied. Yet social welfare maximisation takes place along a welfare surface that is rapidly collapsing inwards towards the origin, that is, $W \rightarrow 0$, with adverse changes among x, p and u. We thus have a perverse case of welfare equilibrium and optimality, although all the neoclassical conditions of welfare maximisation are satisfied. Such is the methodology of neoclassicism that remains incapable of addressing *process* realities.

36. M. Morishima, *Walras' Economics* (Cambridge: Cambridge University Press, 1977); *Equilibrium, Stability and Growth, A Multisectoral Analysis* (Oxford: Clarendon Press, 1964. For a mathematical version of decomposable techniques see Henderson and Quandt, *Microeconomic Theory*, op. cit., ch. 9.

37. M. S. Salleh, *An Islamic Approach to Rural Development – the Arqam Way* (London: ASOIB International, 1992).

38. M. A. Choudhury and U. A. Malik, *The Foundations of Islamic Political Economy* (London: Macmillan; New York: St Martin's Press, 1992).

39. A. Mirakhor and I. Zaidi, *Islamic Banking*, IMF Occasional Paper no. 49, 1989; M. S. Khan and A. Mirakhor, *Theoretical Studies in Islamic Banking and Finance* (Houston, TX: The Institute for Research and Islamic Studies, 1987).

40. Market consequentialism is discussed by A. Sen, 'The Moral Standing of the Market', in E. F. Paul, F. D. Miller, Jr. and J. Paul (eds), *Ethics & Economics* (Oxford: Basil Blackwell, 1985), pp. 1–28. The ethicised market is formalised in M. A. Choudhury, 'A Theory of Moral Entitlement', in Z. Sattar (ed.), *Resource Mobilization and Investment in an Islamic Economic Framework* (Herndon, VA: International Institute of Islamic Thought, 1992), pp. 45–70.

41. Another concept of the share economy during times of stagflation is given by M. L. Weitzman, *The Share Economy* (Cambridge, Mass.: Harvard University Press, 1984).

42. M. Desai, 'Endogenous and Exogenous Money', in J. Eatwell, M. Milgate and P. Newman (eds), *The New Palgrave: Money* (New York: W.W. Norton, 1989), pp. 146–50.

43. D. Laidler, 'The Quantity Theory is Always and Everywhere Controversial – Why?', *ACEA Papers*, vol. 18 (1989), pp. 98–122.

44. For the concept of embedded economy, see R. J. Holton, *Economy and Society* (London: Routledge, 1992). See also M. Gottlieb, *A Theory of Economic Systems* (New York: Academic Press, 1984). For the concept of total social system see K. E. Boulding, 'Economics as a Moral Science', in F. F. Glass and J. R. Staude (eds), *Humanistic Society* (Pacific Palisades, CA: Goodyear, 1972), pp. 151–64.

45. The neoclassical idea of *praxis* is given by Ludwig von Mises, *Epistemological Problems of Economics* (Princeton, NJ: Princeton University Press, 1960).

46. The author does not exonerate himself on this account in reference to his earlier works. See, for example, M. A. Choudhury, *Contributions to Islamic Economic Theory: A Study in Social Economics* (London: Macmillan;

New York: St Martin's Press, 1986). This was a learning process for the author in this pioneering venture. Over the years the learning experience led to his *magnum opus, The Epistemological Foundations of Islamic Economic, Social and Scientific Order*, 6 vols (Ankara, Turkey: Statistical, Economic and Social Research and Training Centre for Islamic Countries, 1995). For a critique of scientific theories see K. Hubner, *Critique of Scientific Reason* (trans. P. R. Dixon, Jr. and H. M. Dixon) (Chicago, Ill.: Chicago University Press, 1985).

7 Integrating the Grassroots with Paradigms of Trade and Development: The Case of Malaysia

1. M. S. Salleh, *An Islamic Approach to Rural Development – the Arqam Way* (London: ASOIB International, 1992).
2. M. A. Choudhury and M. S. Salleh, 'The Grassroots Approach to Sustainable Development: The Dar al-Arqam Way in Malaysia', paper presented at the Canadian Economic Association Meeting, the Learned Societies Conference, Carleton University, Ottawa, June 1993. See also M. S. Salleh, 'An Ethical Approach to Development: The Arqam Philosophy and Achievement', *Humanomics*, vol. 10, no. 1 (1994), pp. 25–60.
3. For many such agricultural and villagisation projects see Salleh, 'An Ethical Approach', op. cit.
4. For a study of various kinds of grassgroots organization, see P. Ekins (ed.), *A New World Order, Grassroots Movements for Global Change* (London: Routledge, 1992).
5. M. S. Omar, *Merdeka Kedua* (Tinta Merah, Kuala Lumpur, 1990). Quoted in Salleh, 'An Ethical Approach', op. cit.
6. Editorial, 'Darul Arqam Generasi Yang Perlu Diperhitungkan', *ERA*, Tahun, no. 3 (1987). Quoted in Salleh, 'An Ethical Approach', op cit.
7. Quoted in Salleh, ibid.
8. All the statistical information below is taken from *The Second Outline Perspective Plan, 1991–2000* (Kuala Lumpur: Government of Malaysia, 1991). For an examination of the Islamic approach to development in Malaysia's development plans, particularly NEP, see A. Ghazali, *Development: an Islamic Perspective* (Kuala Lumpur: Pelanduk Publications, 1990).
9. *Fortune*, 'Snapshot of the PAC Rim', 7 October 1991.
10. *Business Week*, 'Asia: The Next Era of Growth', 11 November 1991. On the idea of 'animal spirit' in the US economy, see J. Schlefer, 'Making Sense of the Productivity Debate: A Reflection on the MIT Report', *Technology Review*, Aug.–Sept. 1989, pp. 28–40.
11. J. O. Moller, 'The Competitiveness of U.S. Industry: A View From the Outside', *Business Horizon*, Nov.–Dec., 1991, pp. 27–34.
12 On the deindustrialization of the United States, see H. S. Gardner, *Comparative Economic Systems* (Chicago, Ill.: Dryden Press, 1988), chapter 4.
13. R. T. Naylor, 'Impressions of an IMF/World Bank Meeting', in J. Torrie (ed.), *Banking on Poverty, the Global Impact of the IMF & World Bank* (Toronto: Between the Lines, 1983), pp. 35–40.
14. *IMF Survey*, 'IMF Addresses Poverty in Structural Adjustment Programs', 10 January 1994. See also B. Bernstein and J. M. Boughton, *Adjusting to*

Development: The IMF and the Poor (Washington, DC: IMF Papers on Policy Analysis and Assessment, Series no. 93/4).

15. Some issues of the *IMF Survey* have voiced this concern.

16. C. Tisdell, 'Imperialism, Economic Dependence and Development: A Brief Review of Aspects of Economic Thought and Theory', *Humanomics*, vol. 5, no. 2 (1989), pp. 3–20.

17. For the emergence of the idea of Eurocentricity from world systems theory, see I. Wallerstein, *The Modern World System* (New York: Academic Press, 1974).

18. J. J. Polak, 'Economic Policy Objectives and Policymaking in the Major Industrial Countries', in M. Guth (moderator) *Economic Policy Coordination* (Hamburg: International Monetary Fund and HWWA-Institut für Wirtschaftsforschung, 1988). See also a critique of the industrialised countries' approach to macroeconomic coordination in M. A. Choudhury, 'Book Review: *Financing the World Economy in the Nineties* (ed. J. J. Sijben) (Kluwer Academic Publishers, 1989), *Weltwirtschaftliches Archiv*, vol. 126, no. 3 (1990), pp. 608–10.

19. M. G. deVries, *Balance of Payments Adjustment, 1945–1986, the IMF Experience* (Washington, DC: IMF, 1987).

20. On the methodological impossibility of full employment, see G. D. N. Worswick, 'Full Employment', in J. Eatwell, M. Milgate and P. Newman (eds), *The New Palgrave: Social Economics* (New York: W. W. Norton, 1989), pp. 90–4.

21. For a critique of economic theory and policy, see C. Gonick, *The Great Economic Debate, Failed Economics and a Future for Canada* (Toronto: James Lorimer, 1987).

22. On the theory of stagnation in economic growth, see J. Schlefer, 'Making Sense of the Productivity Debate', op. cit., pp. 28–40.

23. The ineffectiveness of the Baker–Brady Plan is discussed in N. Raymond, 'The "Lost Decade" of Development: The Role of Debt, Trade and Structural Adjustment', *The U.S. National Committee for World Food Day*, October 1991, pp. 1–14.

24. That the service section of the MFN clause in the Uruguay Round will particularly help the US is evidenced by the emphasis placed on this item in the GATT Agreement. See *IMF Survey*, 'Trade Agreement Mandates Broad Changes', 10 January 1994.

25. The modern defeat of Muslims is seen as commencing with Iraq's defeat in the Gulf War (1991). See M. A. Choudhury, 'Islamic Futures After the Desert Storm', *Hamdard Islamicus*, vol. 14, no. 4 (1991), pp. 5–21. See also M. A. Choudhury, 'Muslims, Islam and the West Today', *Hamdard Islamicus*, vol. 17, no. 1 (Jan. 1994), pp. 19–34.

26. When writing about Germanic supremacy, Hegel claimed that 'The German Spirit is the Spirit of the new World. Its aim is the realization of absolute Truth as the unlimited self-determination of Freedom – *that* Freedom which has its own absolute form itself as its purpose.' See G. W. F. Hegel, *The Philosophy of History* (trans. J. Sibree) (New York: Dover Books, 1956), part IV, pp. 341. See also F. Fukuyama, *The End of History and the Last Man* (New York & Toronto: Free Press & Maxwell Macmillan Canada, 1992).

27. Cultural pluralism is another misleading idea in explaining movements and modernisation in Islam. See A. Mazrui, 'Islam and the End of History', *American Journal of Islamic Social Sciences*, vol. 10, no. 4 (Winter 1993), pp. 512–35. Islam remains opposed to cultural pluralism as a basis of development. Rather it presents a unified way of life, thought and knowledge across cultures and peoples. See also M. A. Choudhury, 'A Critique of Modernist Synthesis in Islamic Thought: Special Reference to Political Economy', *American Journal of Islamic Social Sciences*, vol. 14, no. 4 (1994), pp. 475–503.

28. J. L. Esposito, *The Islamic Threat: Myth or Reality?* (Oxford: Oxford University Press, 1993).

29. The impossibility of distributive justice in neoclassical economics is shown by E. S. Phelps in 'Distributive Justice', *New Palgrave: Social Economics*, op. cit., pp. 31–4.

30. On the topic of micro–macro interface in Islamic political economy, see M. A. Choudhury, 'Micro–Macro Interface in Islamic Economic Theory', *Middle East Business and Economic Review*, vol. 3, no. 1 (1991), pp. 29–38. See also M. A. Choudhury and U. A. Malik, *The Foundations of Islamic Political Economy* (London: Macmillan; New York: St Martin's Press, 1992), chapter 7.

31. On the role of the United States in APEC, see M. A. Choudhury, 'Institution – Economy Interface of Canadian Debt and Deficits', *Economic Theory and Social Institutions: A Critique with Special Reference to Canada* (Lanham: The University Press of America, 1994), pp. 377–89.

32. For an example of a proposal on future OIC reconstruction, see A. A. AbuSulayman, *The Islamic Theory of International Relations* (Herndon, VA: International Institute of Islamic Thought, 1991). See also M. A. Choudhury, 'Social Choice in an Islamic Economic Framework', *The American Journal of Islamic Science*, vol. 7, no. 2 (1991), pp. 259–74.

33. See also M. A. Choudhury, 'Intergrating the Grassroots with World Development', *Bangladesh Observer*, 30 Dec. 1994. For other coverage on grassroots development, see P. Ekins, *A New World Order, Grassroots Movements for Global Change* (London: Routledge, 1992).

34. *IMF Survey*, op. cit.

35. F. Stewart, 'Proposals for a Review of GATT Article XVIII: An Assessment', in *Uruguay Round Papers on Selected Issues* (New York: United Nations, 1989), pp. 1–43.

36. M. A. Choudhury, *Comparative Development Studies: In Search of the World View* (London: Macmillan; New York: St Martin's Press, 1993).

37. See, for example, J. Quirk and R. Saposnik, *Introduction to General Equilibrium Theory and Welfare Economics* (New York: McGraw-Hill, 1968).

38. On endogenous preference theory, see S. Bowles, 'What Markets Can – and Cannot – Do', *Challenge*, vol. 34, no. 4 (July–Aug. 1991), pp. 11–16. Endogenous preference theory in what is termed the principle of ethical endogeneity is the keynote of the paradigm of ethico-economics presented in the journal *Humanomics*, edited by this author (Hull: Barmarick Publications). See also M. A. Choudhury, 'A Mathematical Formulation of the Knowledge-Based Worldview of Development', in E. Ahmad (ed.), *Economic Growth and Human Resource Development in an Islamic Perspective*

(Herndon, VA: International Institute of Islamic Thought, 1993), pp. 17–29.

39. M. A. Choudhury, *The Unicity Precept and the Socio-Scientific Order* (Lanham: The University Press of America, 1993).

40. The knowledge-centred precept of epistemic–ontic circular causation and continuity is developed in detail by the author through derivation from the *Qur'an*. For a brief but mathematical treatment see his 'Epistemic–Ontic Circular Causation and Continuity Model of Socio-Scientific Reality: The Knowledge Premise', *International Journal of Social Economics*, vol. 20, no. 1 (1994), pp. 64–77. A knowledge-centred post-capitalist society is also conceptualised by Peter Drucker. However, Drucker does not abandon the capitalist order in post-capitalist society. Hence knowledge as innovation and a source of generating factor productivity alone, is seen to enchance the ever intensifying post-capitalist society yet within the capitalist order. See P. F. Drucker, *Post-Capitalist Society* (New York: Harper Business, 1993).

41. For an elementary concept of the basic needs approach to development, see International Labour Organization, *The Basic Needs Approach to Development* (Geneva: ILO, 1976). On the moral values embedded in the basic needs precept, see D. Levine, *Needs Rights, and the Market* (Boulder, CO: Lynne Rienner, 1988).

42. The two-sector model of economic growth provides regimes of specialisation in the neoclassical framework. See H. Uzawa, 'Optimal Growth in a Two-Sector Model of Capital Accumulation', *Review of Economic Studies*, vol. 31 (1964), pp. 1–24.

43. On the theme of transfer dependency and economic underdevelopment, see R. Matthews, *The Creation of Regional Dependency* (Toronto: University of Toronto Press, 1983).

44. On the principles of *Shari'ah*, see [Imam] Shatibi, *Al-Muwafaqat fi Usul al-Shariah* (Cairo: Abdallah Draz al-Maktabah al-Tijatiyah al-Qubra, undated).

45. M. Asad, *The Principles of State and Government in Islam* (Gibraltar: Dar al-Andalus, 1985); *This Law of Ours* (Gibraltar: Dar al-Andalus, 1987).

46. For an introduction to the Markovian Process, see M. D. Intrilligator, *Econometric Models, Techniques, & Applications* (Englewood Cliffs, NJ: Prentice-Hall, 1978).

47. For a brief history of *Ijma* and *Qiyas*, see A. Hasan, *The Doctrine of 'Ijma' in Islam* (Islamabad: Islamic Research Institute, 1984).

48. For dynamic input-output coefficiencts, see O. Lange, *Introduction to Econometrics* (Oxford: Pergamon Press, 1966).

49. M. A. Choudhury, *Theory and Practice of Islamic Development Co-operation in Contemporary Times: Experience of Some Asian Countries* (Ankara, Turkey: Statistical, Economic, Social Research and Training Centre for Islamic Countries, 1993).

50. See various IDB Annual Reports for financing instruments with special reference to foreign trade financing. For an economic theory of foreign trade financing, see M. A. Choudhury, 'The Idea of Islamic Economic Co-operation in Contemporary Perspectives', *Journal of Economic Development*, vol. 14, no. 2 (1989), pp. 77–97, and 'A Generalized Theory of Islamic Development Financing', *Managerial Finance*, vol. 19, no. 7 (1993),

pp. 47–69. See also M. Ariff and M. A. Mannan (eds), *Developing a System of Financial Instruments* (Jeddah, Saudi Arabia: Islamic Research and Training Institute, Islamic Development Bank, 1990).

51. On the debate on population increase and development, see C. Skinner, 'Population Myth and the Third World', *Social Policy*, Summer 1988, pp. 57–62.

52. The concept of 'measure' used here corresponds to mathematical measure. See A. Friedman, *Foundations of Modern Analysis* (New York: Dover Publications, 1982).

53. A. Quinton, *Utilitarian Ethics* (La Salle, Ill: Open Court, 1989). See also J. H. Mittelman, *Out From Underdevelopment, Prospects for the Third World* (London: Macmillan, 1988) for a critique of the neoclassical theory of development and bondage in the Third World.

54. W. D. Nordhaus, 'The Political Business Cycle', *Review of Economic Studies*, vol. 42 (1975), pp. 169–90. See also P. Minford and D. Peel, 'The Political Economy of Democracy', in *Rational Expectations and the New Macroeconomics* (Oxford: Martin Robertson, 1983), pp. 144–58.

8 The Concept of Money in Islam

1. M. A. Choudhury, 'Money and Islamic Financial Institutions', *Middle East Business and Economic Review*, vol. 6, no. 2 (1994), pp. 57–75. The endogenous theory of money in Islamic political economy seems to have totally escaped the attention of contemporary Islamic economists. Even recent works on money and banking in the Islamic framework do not refer to this principal concept. See for example V. Nienhaus, *Lectures on Islamic Economics and Banking* (mimeo., University of Bochum, Dec. 1988), pp. 1–66; M. U. Chapra, *Towards a Just Monetary System* (Leicester: The Islamic Foundation, 1985); M. U. Chapra, 'The Endogenous Theory of Money and Islamic Capital Markets', *Journal of Economic Cooperation Among Islamic Countries*, vol. 12, no. 2 (1992), pp. 75–96.

2. Consider the following formalisation: $dM/dt = (1/m)(dD/dt)$, or $dM/dD = (1/m)$, where m denotes the money multiplier. Compare this multiplier relation with the quantity-of-money equation $M = PT/V = Y/V$, where national income, Y, is given by $Y = PT$. If we further assume that $y = aD$, D, being deposits in banks, creating money supply, then $M = (a/V) D$. We thereby have by comparison of equations, the resulting equations $M = V/a$. This shows the relationship between the money multiplier and the velocity of money supply.

3. The volatility of the monetary *numeraire* increases in paper issues and reduces in the gold standard. Thus, present days volatility of paper-based monetary *numeraire* increases the methodological problem of defining stable money in the received economic system.

4. M. Friedman, 'Quantity Theory of Money', in J. Eatwell, M. Milgate and P. Newman (eds), *New Palgrave: Money* (New York: W. W. Norton, 1989), pp. 40.

5. M. A. Zarqa, 'An Islamic Perspective on the Economics of Discounting in Project Evaluation', in Z. Ahmad, M. Iqbal and M. F. Khan (eds), *Fiscal Policy and Resource Allocation in Islam* (Jeddah, Saudi Arabia:

International Centre for Research in Islamic Economics, King Abdulaziz University; Islamabad, Pakistan: Institute of Policy Analysis, 1983), pp. 203–34.

6. M. N. Siddiqi, 'Economics of Profit-Sharing', in *Fiscal Policy and Resource Allocation in Islam*, pp. 163–85.

7. R. Wilson, *Banking and Finance in the Arab Middle East* (London: Macmillan, 1983). See also T. Wohlers Scharf, *Arab and Islamic Banks* (Paris: Organization for Economic Co-operation and Development, 1983).

8. M. A. Choudhury and U. A. Malik, *The Foundations of Islamic Political Economy* (London: Macmillan; New York: St Martin's Press, 1992).

9. International Association of Islamic Banks, *The Aggregate Balance Sheet of the International Association of Islamic Banks* (Cairo, 1988).

10. A. Ahmad, *Development and Problems of Islamic Banks* (Jeddah, Saudi Arabia: Islamic Research and Training Institute, Islamic Development Bank, 1987).

11. COMCEC Coordinating Office, Standing Committee for Economic and Commercial Cooperation of the Organization of the Islamic Countries, *Report: Ninth Session of the COMCEC, Istanbul, 1–4 September 1993* (Ankara, Turkey, September 1993).

12. O. Mehmet, *Westernizing the Third World* (London: Routledge, 1995).

13. T. E. Nugent, 'Greenspan Hews to Price Rule', *The Wall Street Journal Europe*, 25–6 February 1994.

Index